When a word has two main meanings but is the same part of speech, the most usual meaning is given first. In the same way, where alternative spellings are given, the most widely used is given first.

If the form of a word changes in an unusual way (as in an adjective – **good**, **better**, **best**; or in a verb – **lead**, **led**), this information is given after the part of speech. Where a letter should be doubled when changing the form, for example, **beg**, **begging**, this is also given. Unusual forms of verbs have their own separate entry as well – **said** and **am** for example.

One of the main uses of a dictionary is to check and learn the spelling of a word. English spelling is famous for its oddities so after certain words in this dictionary you will find the symbol ▪ to warn you that you may be confusing the word with another.

Reading, writing, talking, thinking –
everyone needs words, all the time.
Sometimes, however, you may not be quite sure
of the meaning of a particular word, or how to spell it.
And that's when you need a dictionary.
In this Ladybird dictionary you will find
nearly four thousand words,
some familiar and some not so familiar,
with their meanings and spellings.

Acknowledgments:
The Ladybird Dictionary is based on definitions from the Longman Dictionaries and Reference Division database, and is published by arrangement with Longman Group UK Ltd. The publishers wish to thank Heather Gay BSc, PhD, Senior Lexicographer, Longman Group UK Ltd, for her considerable help in its preparation. Co-ordinating editor Audrey Daly.

Ladybird books are widely available, but in case of
difficulty may be ordered by post or telephone from:

Ladybird Books – Cash Sales Department
Littlegate Road Paignton Devon TQ3 3BE
Telephone 0803 554761

A catalogue record for this book is available
from the British Library

Published by Ladybird Books Ltd Loughborough Leicestershire UK
Ladybird Books Inc Auburn Maine 04210 USA

Printed in EC

Dictionary

illustrations by
MIKE NICHOLLS and JUDITH WOOD
of Hurlston Design

a (also **an** *before a vowel sound*)
1 one; **2** each; every:
*6 times **a** day*

abbreviation *noun*
a shortened form of a word

ability *noun* power and skill

able *adjective* having the
power, skill, knowledge,
time, etc, needed to do
something

about *adverb, preposition* **1** here
and/or there; **2** a little more
or less; almost, nearly;
3 concerning, of

above *adverb, preposition* **1** in or
to a higher place; higher
than; **2** greater or more than

abroad *adverb* to or in another
country: *living **abroad***

absent *adjective* not present;
away; **absence** *noun*

accept *verb* **1** to take or
receive something; **2** to
agree to

accident *noun* something,
especially something
unpleasant or damaging, that
happens by chance;
accidentally *adverb*

ache (*say* **ayk**) *verb* to have a
continuous pain; **ache** *noun*

¹acid also **acidic** *adjective*
having a bitter or sour taste
like that of lemons

²acid *noun* a chemical
substance that burns

acorn *noun* the nut of the oak
tree

acquaintance *noun* a person
you have met but do not
know well

acre *noun* a measure of land
equal to 4,840 square yards
or about 0.4047 hectares
(see last page)

acrobat *noun* a person skilled
in walking on ropes or wires,
balancing, walking on hands,
etc, especially at a circus;
acrobatic *adjective;*
acrobatically *adverb*

*circus acrobat swinging from the
high bar*

across *adverb, preposition*
1 from one side to the other;
2 to, at, or on the opposite side

¹act *verb* **1** to play the part of
somebody in a play or film;
2 to behave as if playing a
part; to pretend; **3** to behave
in a certain way: *to **act** bravely*

²act *noun* **1** something done:
*an **act** of cruelty;* **2** a law;
3 one of the main parts into
which a play is divided

action *noun* **1** movement using
force or power for some
purpose; **2** something done;
3 out of action not working
properly

active *adjective* always doing
things; **actively** *adverb*

activity *noun* **1** the condition
of being active; **2** something
that is done, especially for
interest

actor feminine **actress** *noun* a person who acts a part in a play or film

actual *adjective* real and clear; **actually** *adverb*

add *verb* **1** to put together with something else; **2** to say something extra; **addition** *noun*; **additional** *adjective*

address *noun* the number of the building, name of the street and town, etc, where a person lives or works

adjective *noun* a word that describes something

admire *verb* to think of with pleasure and respect; to have a good opinion of something or somebody; **admiration** *noun*

admit *verb* (**admitted**) **1** to allow somebody to enter; to let in; **2** to confess; **admission** *noun*

adult *noun* **1** a fully grown person, especially a person over 18; **2** a fully grown animal or bird; **adult** *adjective*

advantage *noun* something that may help you to be successful or to get something you want; **advantageous** *adjective*

adventure *noun* an exciting and often dangerous journey, activity, etc; **adventurous** *adjective*

adverb *noun* a word which tells you how, when, or where something is done

advertise *verb* to make something known to a lot of people; **advertisement** *noun*

advice *noun* a suggestion from one person to another on how that other should act

advise *verb* to tell somebody what you think he or she should do

¹aerial *adjective* from or in the air: *an **aerial** view*

²aerial *noun* a wire, rod, etc, that receives or sends out radio waves

Starship 1, *United States Air Force aeroplane*

aeroplane *noun* a flying vehicle that has wings and at least one engine

afford *verb* to have enough money to be able to buy or pay for something

afraid *adjective* **1** full of fear; **2** sorry for something that has happened or is likely to happen: *I'm **afraid** I've broken your pen*

after *preposition* following in time, place, or order; behind; later than

afternoon *noun* the part of the day between midday and evening

afterwards *adverb* later; after that

again *adverb* **1** once more: *Please say that **again**; **2** now and again** sometimes, but not very often

against *preposition* **1** on an opposite side to; **2** next to; touching

age *noun* **1** the period of time a person has lived or a thing has existed; **2** a period of time in history: *the Middle Ages;* **3 ages** a long time; **aged** *adjective*

ago *adjective* back in time from now; in the past

agree *verb* **1** to accept an idea, opinion, etc; **2** to have the same thoughts, opinions, or feelings as somebody else; **agreement** *noun*

ahead *adverb, adjective* **1** in front; into a forward position; **2** in or into the future

aim *verb* **1** to point or direct something at an object, especially with the intention of hitting it; **2** to intend to do something; **aim** *noun*

¹air *noun* **1** the mixture of gases which surrounds the Earth and which we breathe; **2** an appearance or feeling: *an air of excitement;* **3** a tune; ▓ **heir**

²air *verb* **1** to make clothes, sheets, beds, etc, warm or dry; **2** to make a room fresh by letting in air; ▓ **heir**

aircraft *noun* a flying vehicle, such as a helicopter, aeroplane, or glider

air force *noun* a group of people who use aircraft for fighting or defence

air hostess *noun* (feminine) a stewardess on an aeroplane

airport *noun* a place where aircraft can land and take off and which is regularly used by passengers

alarm *noun* **1** something such as a bell or flashing light by which a warning of danger is given; **2** a sudden feeling of fear; **alarm** *verb*

alarm clock *noun* a clock that can be set to make a noise at the time that you want to wake up

an alarm clock

album *noun* **1** a book which is used for collecting photographs, stamps, etc; **2** an LP

alcohol *noun* a substance present in wine, beer, etc, that can make people feel drunk if they have too much of it; drinks containing this liquid; **alcoholic** *adjective*

¹alert *adjective* ready to act suddenly

²alert *noun* a warning to be ready for danger; **alert** *verb*

alike *adjective, adverb* the same or nearly the same

alive *adjective* having life; living

all *adjective, adverb, pronoun* **1** the complete amount, quantity, or number of; the whole of; **2** completely; **3** everybody or everything

alligator

alligator *noun* a large dangerous reptile that is related to and looks like a crocodile

allow *verb* to let somebody do or have something

all right *adverb, adjective* **1** safe or healthy; **2** good enough; **3** Yes, I/we agree

ally *noun* a person or country that helps or supports you

almost *adverb* very nearly

alone *adjective, adverb* **1** without others; **2** only: *He alone knows the secret*

along *preposition, adverb* **1** in the direction of the length of; following the course of; **2** forward; on

aloud *adverb* **1** in a voice that may be heard; **2** in a loud voice

alphabet *noun* the set of letters used in a language, especially when arranged in order; **alphabetical** *adjective*

already *adverb* by or before a particular time

also *adverb* as well; too

although *conjunction* in spite of the fact that

altogether *adverb* completely; considering all things

always *adverb* at all times; for ever

am *see* BE

a.m. in the morning (short for *ante meridiem*)

A

amateur *noun* **1** a person who does something, such as acting, painting pictures, or taking part in a sport, for enjoyment and without being paid for doing it; **2** a person who has no experience or skill in doing something; **amateur** *adjective*

amber *noun* **1** a hard yellowish substance used for making ornaments and jewellery; **2** a yellowish colour

ambulance *noun* a motor vehicle for carrying sick or injured people, especially to hospital

among also **amongst** *preposition* in the middle of; surrounded by; between

amount *noun* a quantity or sum

amp also **ampere** *noun* a measure of electric current

amplifier *noun* an electronic instrument used in a radio, record player, etc, to increase the sound; **amplify** *verb*

amuse *verb* to make somebody laugh or feel cheerful; **amusement** *noun*

an *see* A

analyse *verb* to examine something carefully in order to find out what it is made of or how it is put together; **analysis** *noun*

anchor *noun* a heavy metal weight attached to a ship and lowered into the water to keep the ship from moving

ancient (*say* **aynshunt**) *adjective* in, of, or having existed since times long ago

and *conjunction* as well as; too

angel *noun* a messenger from God, who is usually thought of as a person with large wings dressed in white; **angelic** *adjective*

anger *noun* a fierce feeling that makes you want to hurt or fight somebody; **angrily** *adverb*; **angry** *adjective*

angle *noun* the shape made by two straight lines that meet at a point; the space between these lines

angling *noun* the sport of catching fish with a hook and line

animal *noun* a living creature that can move itself when it wants to move; any living thing that is not a plant

ankle *noun* the thin part of the leg just above the foot

announce *verb* to make something known; to say in public; **announcement** *noun*

annoy *verb* to make somebody a little angry; **annoyance** *noun*

anorak *noun* a waterproof jacket with a hood

another *pronoun, adjective* 1 one more of the same sort; 2 a different one

answer *noun* 1 the information that tells you what you want to know when you ask a question; 2 a reply to a greeting, letter, etc; 3 something which is discovered as a result of thinking, using numbers, etc; **answer** *verb*

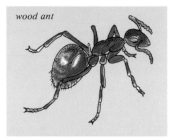

wood ant

ant *noun* a small insect that usually lives on the ground in large groups

antelope *noun* an animal that looks like a deer and runs fast

antenna *noun (plural* **antennae** *or* **antennas***)* 1 either of two long thin parts on the head of an insect, shrimp, etc, that are used for feeling; 2 an aerial

anticlockwise *adjective, adverb* in the opposite direction to the movement of the hands of a clock; circular movement to the left

anxious (*say* **angshus**) *adjective* 1 worried or fearful; 2 having a strong wish to do something; **anxiety** *noun*; **anxiously** *adverb*

any *adjective, pronoun* 1 one, some, or all; a number or amount; 2 no matter which, what, where, how, etc; 3 in **any case** also **at any rate** whatever may happen

anybody also **anyone** *pronoun* any person

anything *pronoun* 1 any one thing; something; 2 no matter what

anyway *adverb* whatever else is done; no matter what happens

anywhere *adverb* in, at, or to any place

apart *adverb* **1** separate; away from another or others; **2** to pieces

apartment *noun* a flat

ape *noun* a large monkey without a tail or with a very short tail

apologise *verb* to say that you are sorry; **apology** *noun*

apparatus *noun* machines, tools, etc, that work together or are used together for a particular purpose

appear *verb* **1** to come into sight; **2** to seem; **appearance** *noun*

appetite *noun* a wish for food

applaud *verb* to praise or show that you like something by clapping or cheering; **applause** *noun*

apple *noun* a hard round fruit with a red, green, or yellow skin

appreciate *verb* to be grateful for something; **appreciation** *noun*

approve *verb* to agree to; to say that something is good; **approval** *noun*; **approvingly** *adverb*

apricot *noun* a soft juicy yellowish orange fruit

April *noun* the fourth month of the year

apron *noun* a piece of clothing worn over your other clothes to keep them clean

aquarium *noun* a glass or plastic container for fish, or a building containing many of these

arch *noun* a curved top part of a door, bridge, etc, that rests on two supports

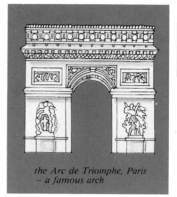

the Arc de Triomphe, Paris – a famous arch

A

archaeology *noun* the study of the buried remains of ancient times, such as houses, pots, tools, and weapons; **archaeological** *adjective*; **archaeologist** *noun*

are *see* BE

area *noun* **1** a particular space, surface, or part of the world; **2** the measure of a surface: *the area of a rectangle*

aren't *see* BE

argue *verb* to disagree in words; to quarrel; **argument** *noun*

arithmetic *noun* the adding, subtracting, multiplying, dividing, etc, of numbers

arm *noun* the part of the body between the shoulder and the hand

armchair *noun* a chair with supporting parts on which you can rest your arms

16th century German armour

armour *noun* a covering of metal worn by fighting men in old times to protect them

arms *noun* weapons; **armed** *adjective*

army *noun* a large number of people trained for fighting

around *adverb, preposition* **1** on all sides; surrounding; **2** in various directions or places

arrange *verb* **1** to put in order; **2** to make plans or prepare for something; **arrangement** *noun*

arrest *verb* to take somebody prisoner; **arrest** *noun*

arrive *verb* **1** to reach a place, especially after a journey; **2** to happen; come; **arrival** *noun*

arrow *noun* **1** a thin straight pointed stick that is shot from a bow; **2** a mark shaped like an arrow which shows you the way

art *noun* the making of beautiful things by drawing, painting, etc; **artist** *noun*

article *noun* **1** a particular or separate thing or object; **2** a piece of writing in a newspaper, magazine, etc

as *conjunction, preposition* **1** used to compare people or things: *He can run as fast as I can;* **2** for the reason that; because; **3** while, when; **4** like; similar to; in the same way

¹ash *noun* a tall tree with hard wood

²ash *noun* the grey powder left after something has burnt

ashamed *adjective* feeling shame or guilt

ask *verb* **1** to put a question; **2** to make a request for or to; **3** to invite

asleep *adjective* sleeping

asteroid *noun* any of the small bodies that move round the sun in the area between Mars and Jupiter

astrology *noun* the skill of understanding the effects that the stars, planets, etc, are supposed to have on our lives; **astrologer** *noun*

astronaut *noun* a person who travels in space

astronomy *noun* the scientific study of the sun, moon, stars, etc; **astronomer** *noun*

at *preposition* **1** used to show where or when; **2** **at all** in any way

ate *see* EAT

athletics *noun* a branch of sport that includes running, jumping, and throwing

atlas *noun* a book of maps

A

atmosphere *noun* **1** the mixture of gases surrounding any large body in space, especially the Earth; **2** the air; **atmospheric** *adjective*

atom *noun* a very small part of a substance; **atomic** *adjective*

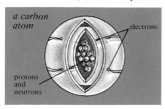

a carbon atom
electrons
protons and neutrons

attach *verb* to fix; to fasten; to join; **attachment** *noun*

attack *verb* **1** to be violent towards somebody; to fight, speak, or write against; **2** to harm; **attack** *noun;* **attacker** *noun*

attempt *verb* to make an effort to do something; to try; **attempt** *noun*

attend *verb* **1** to be present at; **2** to listen to or watch carefully; **attendance** *noun;* **attendant** *noun*

attention *noun* the act of fixing the mind on something, especially by watching or listening carefully; **attentive** *adjective*

attic *noun* room at the top of a house, just under the roof

attract *verb* **1** to cause to like, admire, or notice; **2** to draw towards one: *magnets* ***attract*** *iron;* **attractive** *adjective*

audience *noun* the people listening to or watching a play, speech, show, etc

audio *adjective* concerned with sound

August *noun* the eighth month of the year

aunt also **auntie, aunty** *noun* the sister of your father or mother; the wife of your uncle

aurora *noun (plural* **auroras** *or* **aurorae***)* coloured lights in the sky that can be seen at night in the most northern and southern parts of the world

automatic *adjective* able to work without human help

automobile *noun* a car

autumn *noun* the season between summer and winter; **autumnal** *adjective*

avenue *noun* **1** a road between two rows of trees; **2** a wide street in a town

average *adjective* **1** being the amount found by adding together several quantities and then dividing by the number of quantities; **2** usual or ordinary; **average** *noun*

avoid *verb* to keep away from somebody or something; **avoidable** *adjective*

awake *adjective* having woken up; not asleep

away *adverb* from this or that place; to, at, or in another place

awful *adjective* very bad; terrible; shocking; **awfulness** *noun*

awkward *adjective* **1** clumsy; **2** not well made for use; difficult to use; **awkwardly** *adverb;* **awkwardness** *noun*

axe *noun* a tool with a heavy metal blade on the end of a long handle, used to cut wood

A

baboon *noun* a large monkey

baby *noun* **1** a very young child, especially one who has not learnt to speak; **2** a very young animal or bird

¹back *noun* **1** the part of the body of a human or animal down the middle of which runs the spine; **2** the part that is furthest from the front: **background; 3 at the back (of)** behind; **back** *adjective;* **backless** *adjective*

²back *adverb* **1** towards or at the back; **2** to or at a place or time where something or somebody was before

³back *verb* **1** to go or cause to go backwards; **2** to be or make the back of; **3** to bet money on

backward *adjective* **1** directed towards the back, the beginning, or the past; **2** behind in development; **backwardly** *adverb;* **backwardness** *noun*

backwards *adverb* **1** away from your front; towards the back; **2** with the back first; **3** with the back where the front should be; back to front

bacon *noun* salted or smoked meat from the back or sides of a pig, often sold in thin slices

bacteria *noun* – *plural (singular* **bacterium***)* very small living things, some of which cause disease; **bacterial** *adjective*

bad *adjective* **(worse, worst) 1** not good; **2** serious; severe; **badly** *adverb;* **badness** *noun*

badge *noun* a small sign worn to show what you are, do, or have done

badger *noun* a grey animal that has a white face with two black stripes and lives underground

badminton *noun* a game like tennis played with a shuttlecock instead of a ball

badminton racket and shuttlecock

bag *noun* a container made of soft material, opening at the top

baggage *noun* the bags, cases, etc, you take with you when you travel

bagpipes *noun (always plural)* a musical instrument which is played by blowing air into a bag and through pipes

bake *verb* to cook in an oven **baker** *noun*

¹balance *noun* steadiness

²balance *verb* to keep yourself or something else steady, especially in a difficult position

bald *adjective* with little or no hair; **baldness** *noun*

ball *noun* 1 a round object used in games; anything of a round shape; 2 a large party for dancing

ballet (*say* balay) *noun* a form of dancing performed by specially trained dancers whose movements to music tell a story

hot air balloon

balloon *noun* 1 a large bag of light material filled with hot air or a light gas to make it rise up in the air; 2 a small rubber bag that can be blown up, used as a toy

ban *verb* (**banned**) to forbid, especially by law; **ban** *noun*

banana *noun* a long curved fruit with yellow skin

band *noun* 1 a group of musicians; 2 a group of people; 3 a thin flat narrow piece of material for fastening things together: **rubber band**; 4 an area into which something can be divided, such as a band of radio waves or a range of frequencies; ■ **banned**

bandage *noun* a strip of material for covering a wound

bang *noun* 1 a sharp blow; 2 a sudden loud noise; **bang** *verb*

¹bank *noun* 1 land along the side of a river, lake, etc; 2 a heap of earth, sand, snow, etc

²bank *noun* a place in which money is kept and paid out when you want it: **banker, bank manager, bank note**

¹bar *noun* 1 a long piece of wood or metal; 2 a piece of solid material; 3 a group of notes in music, marked off by lines; 4 a place where drinks are sold

²bar *verb* (**barred**) 1 to close with a bar; 2 to block

barber *noun* a person who cuts men's hair and shaves them

bare *adjective* 1 naked; not covered; 2 empty; **bare** *verb*; ■ **bear**

barely *adverb* only just; hardly

¹bark *noun* the sound made by a dog; **bark** *verb*

²bark *noun* the strong outer covering of a tree

barley *noun* a plant grown for food and making drinks, such as beer

barn *noun* a farm building for storing crops

barrel *noun* 1 a round wooden container with curved sides and a flat top and bottom; 2 the part of a gun that is shaped like a tube

base *noun* the bottom of anything

B

baseball *noun* a game played with a bat and ball between two teams of nine players each

basement *noun* the rooms in a house below street level

basin *noun* 1 a shallow container for water; 2 a round container for food

basket *noun* a container made of woven sticks or other such material

basketball *noun* a game in which each team of five players tries to throw a large ball through the other team's basket

bass (*say* base) *noun* the lowest part sung or played in music; **bass** *adjective*

bassoon *noun* a musical instrument with a low sound, that is played by blowing

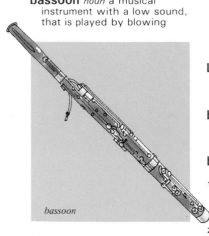
bassoon

¹bat *noun* a wooden stick used for hitting a ball in various games; **bat** *verb;* **batsman** *noun;* **batter** *noun*

²bat *noun* a flying mammal like a mouse, that is active at night

bath *noun* a large water container in which your whole body can be washed; **bath** *verb*

bathe *verb* 1 to go swimming; 2 to pour water or other liquid over; **bathe** *noun;* **bather** *noun*

bathroom *noun* a room where people wash or have a bath

battery *noun* a box that produces or stores electricity

battle *noun* a fight between enemies; a struggle; **battle** *verb*

bay *noun* a part of the shore which curves inwards

be *verb* (**am, are, is, being, was, were, been, aren't, isn't, wasn't, weren't**) 1 to exist; to live; 2 to become; 3 to belong to the group of; 4 to take place; to occur; 5 to have a particular quality, job, purpose, position, cost, etc; ▪ **bee**

beach *noun* a shore covered in sand or stones and used for swimming and sunbathing; ▪ **beech**

bead *noun* a small ball of glass or other material which can be threaded on to a string or wire

beak *noun* the hard horny mouth of a bird

¹beam *noun* a large long heavy piece of wood, steel, or concrete, used to support a building

²beam *noun* 1 a line of light shining from something bright; 2 a bright look or smile

³beam *verb* 1 to send out light; to shine; 2 to smile brightly and happily

14

bean *noun* **1** the seed of a climbing plant, often used as food; **2** a seed of some other plants, from which food or drink can be made: **coffee bean;** been

polar bear

¹**bear** *noun* a large and heavy animal with thick rough fur; bare

²**bear** *verb* (**bears, bearing, bore, borne**) **1** to carry; to support; **2** to give birth; **3** to suffer; bare

beard *noun* hair on the face mostly below the mouth; **beardless** *adjective*

¹**beat** *verb* (**beats, beating, beat, beaten** *or* **beat**) **1** to hit many times; **2** to move regularly; **3** to do better than

²**beat** *noun* **1** a repeated hit, stroke, or blow; **2** time in music or poetry

beautiful *adjective* very goodlooking; very pleasing; **beautifully** *adverb;* **beauty** *noun*

beaver *noun* a fur covered animal with a broad flat tail, that builds dams across streams

because *conjunction* for the reason that

become *verb* (**becomes, becoming, became, become**) to come to be

bed *noun* **1** an article of furniture to sleep on: **bedroom, bedclothes; 2** a piece of ground prepared for plants; **3** the bottom of a river, lake, or sea

bee *noun* an insect that makes honey, often lives in groups, and can sting painfully; be

beech *noun* a tree with a smooth grey trunk, spreading branches, and dark green or copper coloured leaves; beach

beef *noun* the meat of farm cattle

beehive *noun see* HIVE

been *see* BE; bean

beer *noun* a drink made from grain

beetle *noun* an insect with hard wing coverings

beetroot *noun* a plant with a large round red root, cooked and eaten as a vegetable

before *preposition, adverb* **1** in front of; ahead; **2** at an earlier time than

beg *verb* (**begged**) to ask for food, money, etc; **beggar** *noun*

begin *verb* (**begins, beginning, began, begun**) to start

behave *verb* to act in a good or bad way; **behaviour** *noun*

behind *preposition, adverb* **1** to or at the back of; where something or somebody was earlier; **2** late

being *noun* a living thing, especially a person

B

belief *noun* the feeling that something is true or real; trust; **believable** *adjective;* **believably** *adverb;* **believe** *verb*

bell *noun* a round hollow metal object, that makes a ringing sound when struck

belong *verb* **1** to be your own; **2** to be a part or member of

below *preposition, adverb* in or at a lower place than; underneath

belt *noun* a piece of cloth or leather worn round the waist

bench *noun* a long seat for two or more people

bend *verb* (**bends, bending, bent**) to force something into or out of a curve or angle; **bend** *noun*

beneath *preposition* in or at a lower position than; below

²best *noun* **1** something that is the most good; **2** your greatest, highest, or finest effort, state, or performance

bet *verb* (**bets, betting, bet** *or* **betted**) to risk money on the result of a future event; **bet** *noun*

better *see* GOOD, WELL

between *preposition* **1** in the space or at the time separating; **2** as a connection of; **3** with a part for each of

beyond *preposition, adverb* **1** on or to the further side of; **2** later than; **3** out of reach of; much more than

Bible *noun* the holy book of the Christians, consisting of the *Old Testament* and the *New Testament;* **biblical** *adjective;* **biblically** *adverb*

tandem –
a bicycle made
for two people

beret (*say* beray) *noun* a round soft flat hat

berry *noun* a small soft fruit; ▪bury

berth *noun* **1** a place where a ship can be tied up, as in a harbour; **2** a sleeping place in a ship or a train; ▪birth

beside *preposition* at or close to the side of

besides *adverb, preposition* as well; also

¹best *see* GOOD, WELL

bicycle *also* **cycle** *or* **bike** *noun* a two-wheeled vehicle which you pedal with your feet; **bicyclist** *noun*

big *adjective* (**bigger**) large in size, weight, importance, etc

big bang theory *noun* the idea that everything in the universe began with the explosion of a single piece of material so that the pieces of it are still flying apart

B

bill *noun* 1 a list of things bought and their price; 2 a plan for a new law

billiards *noun* a game played on a cloth-covered table with balls knocked against each other using cues

billion *adjective, noun* the number 1,000,000,000 (a thousand million); **billionth** *adjective, noun* (a billion once meant a million million, but this is no longer in current use)

bin *noun* a large wide-mouthed container with a lid for bread, flour, etc, or for waste

binary (*say* bye-nary) *adjective* using the numbers 0 and 1 only, as computers do

bingo *noun* a game played by covering numbered squares on a card

binoculars *noun (plural)* a pair of special glasses used for looking at objects in the distance

biology *noun* the scientific study of living things; **biological** *adjective;* **biologically** *adverb;* **biologist** *noun*

birch *noun* a tree with smooth wood and thin branches

bird *noun* a creature with wings and feathers that lays eggs

birth *noun* the act or time of being born; ◼ **berth**

birthday *noun* the date on which you were born

biscuit *noun* any of many types of flat thin dry cake

bishop *noun* a priest in charge of other priests

¹**bit** *noun* 1 a small piece, quantity, or amount; 2 the smallest piece of information which can be held on a computer

²**bit** *noun* 1 a metal bar put in the mouth of a horse as part of a bridle and used for controlling its movements; 2 a part of a tool for making holes

bitch *noun* a female dog

¹**bite** *verb* (**bites, biting, bit, bitten**) to cut or wound with the teeth; ◼ **byte**

²**bite** *noun* 1 an act of biting 2 a piece bitten off; 3 a wound made by biting; ◼ **byte**

an archbishop (above) is in charge of other bishops

B

17

bitter *adjective* **1** having a sharp, sour taste; **2** very cold; **3** causing anger, pain, or sadness; **bitterly** *adverb*; **bitterness** *noun*

black *noun* **1** the colour of coal; the darkest colour; **2** a person with dark-coloured skin; **black** *adjective*; **blackness** *noun*

blackboard *noun* a dark smooth surface for writing or drawing on with chalk

black hole *noun* a part of outer space containing a star whose gravity is so strong that not even light can escape from it

blade *noun* **1** the flat cutting part of a knife, sword, razor, or other cutting tool; **2** a long flat leaf of grass

blame *verb* to say that somebody is the cause of something bad; **blame** *noun*

blanket *noun* a thick warm cloth made of wool, used as a cover on a bed

blazer *noun* a jacket, sometimes with the badge of a school, club, etc, on it

bleach *verb* to make something white; **bleach** *noun*

bleed *verb* (**bleeds, bleeding, bled**) to lose blood

bless *verb* **1** to ask God's favour for something; **2** to make holy; **blessing** *noun*

blew *see* BLOW; ■ **blue**

¹**blind** *adjective* unable to see; **blind** *verb*; **blindly** *adverb*; **blindness** *noun*

²**blind** *noun* a covering for a window, made of cloth or other material

blink *verb* to shut and open the eyes quickly

¹**block** *noun* **1** a large piece of wood, stone, etc; **2** a large building divided into separate flats or offices; **3** a building or group of buildings between two streets; **4** something that gets in the way

²**block** *verb* to prevent movement

blond *feminine* **blonde** *adjective* with fair skin and light-coloured hair

blood *noun* red liquid which carries oxygen to all parts of the body and is pumped round by the heart; **bloody** *adjective*

apple blossom

blossom *noun* the flowers of a flowering tree or bush

¹**blot** *noun* a mark that spoils something or makes it dirty

²**blot** *verb* (**blotted**) **1** to make blots; **2** to dry or remove with blotting paper

blouse *noun* a loose piece of clothing for women, reaching from the neck to the waist

¹**blow** *verb* (**blows, blowing, blew, blown**) **1** to move by a current of air; **2** to send air out quickly from your mouth or nose; **3** to force air into or through something; **4 blow up** to break by exploding; **blower** *noun*; **blowy** *adjective*

²blow *noun* **1** a hard stroke with the hand, a weapon, etc; **2** a shock

blue *noun* the colour of the clear sky on a fine day; **blue** *adjective*; **blueness** *noun*; **bluish** *adjective*; ■ **blew**

blunt *adjective* **1** not sharp; **2** rough and plain, without trying to be polite or kind; **bluntness** *noun*; **bluntly** *adverb*

blush *verb* to become red in the face

¹board *noun* **1** a thin flat piece of cut wood; **2** a stiff flat surface used for a special purpose: **chessboard, dartboard, noticeboard**; **3** the cost of meals; **4** a group of people with a special job, like running a company; **5 on board** or **aboard** in or on a ship or public vehicle

²board *verb* **1** to cover with wooden boards; **2** to go on board a ship or public vehicle; **3** to get or supply meals and somewhere to live for payment; **boarder** *noun*

boast *verb* to praise yourself; **boaster** *noun*; **boastful** *adjective*

boat *noun* a small open ship

body *noun* **1** the whole of a person or animal, but not the mind; **2** this without the head or limbs; **3** a dead person or animal; **4** a number of people who do something together; **5** a person: **anybody, nobody, somebody**

bog *noun* an area of soft wet ground

¹boil *noun* a painful swelling under the skin

²boil *verb* **1** to make liquid so hot that it gives off steam; **2** to cook food in boiling water

bold *adjective* daring; brave; without fear; **boldly** *adverb*; **boldness** *noun*

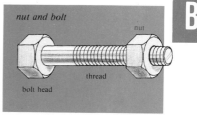

nut and bolt

¹bolt *noun* **1** a metal bar that slides across to fasten a door or window; **2** a screw with no point

²bolt *verb* **1** to run away suddenly, as if frightened; **2** to swallow quickly; **3** to fasten with a bolt

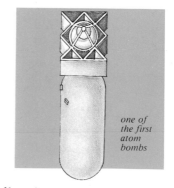

one of the first atom bombs

¹bomb *noun* a hollow container filled with materials that will explode

²bomb *verb* to attack with bombs, especially by dropping them from aircraft

bone *noun* one of the hard white parts of the body, round which are the flesh and skin; **boneless** *adjective;* **bony** *adjective*

bonfire *noun* a large fire built in the open air

bonnet *noun* **1** a round hat tied under the chin; **2** a metal lid over the front of a car

¹book *noun* a collection of sheets of paper fastened together as a thing to be read, or to be written in: **bookcase, bookmark, book token**

²book *verb* to arrange to have or do something later; **bookable** *adjective;* **booking** *noun*

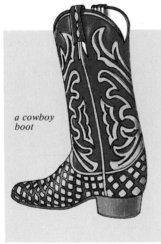

a cowboy boot

boot *noun* **1** a shoe of leather, rubber, etc, with a part that covers the ankle; **2** a space at the back of a car for luggage

border *noun* **1** an edge; **2** the dividing line between two countries; ■**boarder**

¹bore *verb* to make somebody tired or not interested, by something dull; **boredom** *noun;* **boring** *adjective*

²bore *noun* a person or thing that is dull or uninteresting

³bore *verb* to make a round hole or passage in or through something; **borer** *noun*

⁴bore *see* BEAR

born *adjective* **1** given life; **2** at birth; originally; ■**borne**

borne *see* BEAR; ■**born**

borrow *verb* to get the use of something which you are going to give back later; **borrower** *noun;* **borrowing** *noun*

botany *noun* the scientific study of plants; **botanist** *noun*

both *pronoun, adjective* the two; this one and the other

bottle *noun* a tall round container, usually of glass or plastic, with a narrow neck

bottom *noun* **1** the base on which something stands; the lowest part; **2** the part of the body on which you sit

bough *noun* a branch of a tree; ■**bow**

bought *see* BUY

bounce *verb* **1** to spring back or up again from the ground or something hard; to make something do this; **2** to jump or spring up and down; **bounce** *noun;* **bouncily** *adverb;* **bounciness** *noun;* **bouncy** *adjective*

¹bound *adjective* **1** fastened; **2** certain to; sure to; **3** going towards

²bound *verb* to jump or bounce

¹bow *(say like how)* *verb* to bend forward the head or upper part of the body to show respect; **bow** *noun;* **bowed** *adjective;* 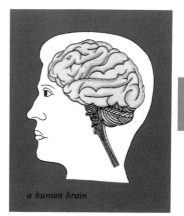 **bough**

²bow *(say like low)* *noun* **1** a piece of wood held in a curve by a tight string and used for shooting arrows; **2** a long thin piece of wood with stretched horsehairs fastened along it, used for playing stringed instruments; **3** a knot with loops

¹bowl *noun* a deep round container for holding liquids, flowers, sugar, etc; **bowlful** *noun*

²bowl *verb* **1** to throw the ball towards the batsman in cricket or rounders; **2** to play the games of **bowls** or **bowling**

¹box *noun* a container made from wood, cardboard, plastic, or metal, with stiff sides and a lid

²box *verb* to fight somebody or hit with the fists; **boxer** *noun;* **boxing** *noun*

boy *noun* a young male person; ■ **buoy**

bra also **brassière** *noun* a piece of women's underwear worn to support the breasts

bracelet *noun* a band or ring worn round the wrist or arm as an ornament

bracket *noun* **1** a piece of metal or wood put on a wall to support something; **2** a pair of signs (−) or [−] used round a piece of information

¹brain *noun* the organ inside the head with which you think and feel

a human brain

²brain *verb* (slang) to hit hard on the head

¹brake *noun* something for slowing down or stopping a car, bicycle, train, etc; ■ **break**

²brake *verb* to use brakes; ■ **break**

¹branch *noun* **1** a stem growing from the trunk of a tree or from another stem; **2** a part of a company, shop, etc

²branch *verb* to become divided into two parts

brass *noun* **1** a very hard bright yellow metal; **2** musical instruments made of this metal

brave *adjective* having courage and ready to suffer danger or pain; **bravely** *adverb;* **bravery** *noun*

bread *noun* a common food made of baked flour

breadth *noun* the distance from side to side; width

21

¹break *verb* **(breaks, breaking broke, broken)** **1** to cause to fall to pieces; **2** to fall to pieces; ■ **brake**

²break *noun* **1** an opening made by breaking or being broken; **2** a pause for rest; ■ **brake**

breakfast *noun* the first meal of the day

breast *noun* **1** either of the two parts of a woman's body that produce milk; **2** the upper front part of the body between the neck and the stomach

breath *noun* air taken into and let out of the body; **breathless** *adjective;* **breathy** *adjective*

breathe *verb* to take air into the body and let it out; **breathing** *noun*

¹breed *verb* **(breeds, breeding, bred)** **1** to produce young; **2** to keep animals so that they will produce young ones

²breed *noun* a type of animal

brick *noun* a hard piece of baked clay used for building

bridge *noun* something that carries a road over a valley, river, etc, and is usually built of wood, stone, iron, etc

bridle *noun* leather bands on a horse's head for controlling it

brief *adjective* lasting a short time

bright *adjective* **1** giving out or throwing back light very strongly; **2** having a strong clear colour; **3** clever; quick at learning; **brightly** *adverb;* **brightness** *noun*

bring *verb* **(brings, bringing, brought)** **1** to fetch, carry, or take with you; **2** to cause or lead to

broad *adjective* wide **broadly** *adverb;* **broadness** *noun*

broadcast *verb* to send out by radio or television; **broadcast** *noun;* **broadcaster** *noun*

broke *see* BREAK

broken *adjective* **1** in pieces; **2** not working

brooch *noun* an ornament worn on women's clothes, fastened by a pin

broom *noun* a brush with a long handle

brother *noun* a boy or man with the same parents as another person

brought *see* BRING

brown *noun, adjective* the colour of earth; **brownish** *adjective*

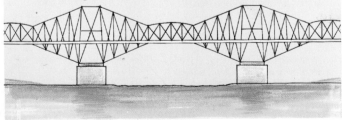

a cantilever bridge: like the Forth Railway Bridge in Scotland

bruise *noun* a mark left on the skin where it has been hit; **bruise** *verb*

¹**brush** *noun* an instrument for cleaning, smoothing, or painting, made of sticks, stiff hair, nylon, etc

²**brush** *verb* to clean or smooth with a brush

¹**bubble** *noun* a hollow ball of liquid containing air or gas; **bubbly** *adjective*

²**bubble** *verb* to make bubbles

buck *noun* the male of certain animals, such as the deer and the rabbit

bucket *noun* a round open metal or plastic container with a handle, for holding or carrying water, coal, etc

buckle *noun* a fastener for joining the ends of two straps

bud *noun* a flower or leaf before it opens

budgerigar

budgerigar also **budgie** *noun* a small brightly coloured bird often kept in a cage

buffalo *noun* a large wild ox that is black and has long curved horns

bug *noun* **1** a small insect; **2** a mistake or fault in a computer program

build *verb* (**builds, building, built**) to make by putting pieces together; **builder** *noun;* **building** *noun*

bulb *noun* **1** a round root of certain plants; **2** the glass part of an electric lamp that gives out light

bull *noun* the male form of cattle and some other animals

bulldozer *noun* a powerful machine used for pushing heavy objects, earth, etc, out of the way

bullet *noun* a type of shot fired from a gun

bully *noun* somebody who likes to hurt or frighten weaker people; **bully** *verb*

¹**bump** *verb* to strike or knock against something

²**bump** *noun* **1** a sudden blow or shock; **2** a raised round swelling; **bumpy** *adjective*

bun *noun* a small round sweet cake

bunch *noun* a number of things fastened, held, or growing together

bundle *noun* a number of things tied, fastened, or held together

bungalow *noun* a house all on one level

bunk also **bunk bed** *noun* a bed fixed to the wall (as on a ship); **bunk beds** *noun* two beds one above the other

B

buoy *noun* a floating object fastened to the bed of the sea to show ships where there are rocks;  **boy**

burglar *noun* a thief who breaks into houses, shops, etc; **burglary** *noun*

¹**burn** *verb* (**burns, burning, burnt** *or* **burned**) **1** to be on fire; **2** to hurt, damage, or destroy by fire

²**burn** *noun* a hurt place produced by burning

burrow *noun* a hole in the ground made by an animal, in which it lives or hides

burst *verb* (**bursts, bursting, burst**) **1** to break suddenly because of the pressure inside; **2** to do something suddenly

bury *verb* **1** to put a dead person into the ground; **2** to hide away; **berry**

bus *noun* a large motor vehicle for carrying passengers

bush *noun* a small low tree; **bushy** *adjective*

business *noun* **1** a person's work; **2** trade and the getting of money: **businessman, businesswoman**; **3** an activity, such as a shop, that earns money; **4** a personal or private thing that concerns you; **businesslike** *adjective*

busy *adjective* working; not free; having a lot to do; **busily** *adverb*

but *conjunction* only; except that

butcher *noun* a person who sells meat

butter *noun* **1** yellow fat made from milk; **2** a substance like butter: **peanut butter; buttery** *adjective*

buttercup *noun* a yellow wild flower

butterfly *noun* an insect with four often beautifully coloured wings

butterflies

small copper

brown argus

button *noun* **1** a small usually round or flat thing fixed to a piece of clothing and passed through a **buttonhole** to act as a fastener; **2** a knob or object like a button, for starting, stopping, or controlling a machine

buy *verb* (**buys, buying, bought**) to get something by giving money; **buyer** *noun;* **by**

buzz *verb* to make a low steady noise, as bees do; **buzz** *noun;* **buzzer** *noun*

by *preposition* **1** near; beside; **2** by way of; through; **buy**

byte *noun* an amount of information stored in a computer, equal to eight bits; **bite**

cabbage *noun* a large round vegetable with thick green leaves used as food

cabin *noun* **1** a small room on a ship; **2** a small wooden house

cable *noun* **1** a thick, heavy strong rope, wire, or chain; **2** a set of wires laid underground and used for carrying electricity, telephone calls, and television programmes: **cable TV**

cactus *noun (plural* **cacti** *or* **cactuses)** a prickly plant with thick leaves and stems, that grows in hot dry places

café **(say caffay)** *noun* a small restaurant where you can buy drinks and light meals

cage *noun* a box made of wires or bars in which animals or birds may be kept

cake *noun* a food made by mixing flour, eggs, sugar, etc, and usually baked

calculate *verb* to work out by using numbers; **calculation** *noun;* **calculator** *noun*

the famous cannon "Mons Meg" built in 1449

calendar *noun* a set of tables or sheets of paper showing the days, weeks, and months of the year

calf *noun (plural* **calves)** the young of the cow or some other large animals

¹**call** *verb* **1** to shout; to cry out; **2** to make a short visit; **3** to telephone somebody; **4** to name

²**call** *noun* **1** a shout; **2** a short visit; **3** a telephone conversation

calm *adjective* peaceful; quiet; **calmly** *adverb;* **calmness** *noun*

came *see* COME

camel *noun* a large long-necked animal used for riding or carrying goods in desert countries. The *dromedary* has one hump and the *Bactrian camel* has two humps

camera *noun* an instrument for taking photographs or filming

¹**camp** *noun* a place with tents or huts where people live for a short time or spend their holidays

²**camp** *verb* **1** to make a camp; **2** to sleep in a tent; **camper** *noun;* **camping** *noun*

¹**can** *verb* **(could, cannot, can't)** to know how to; to be able to

²**can** *noun* a tin in which foods are stored

canal *noun* a man-made river

canary *noun* a small yellow bird often kept as a pet

candle *noun* a wax stick with a string in the middle which gives light when it burns

cannon *noun* a large and powerful gun

25

cannot can not

canoe *noun* a long light narrow boat, pointed at both ends, and moved by a paddle; **canoeist** *noun*

can't *see* CAN

cap *noun* **1** a soft flat hat; **2** a covering for the end of a bottle or tube

capital *noun* **1** the chief city of a country, where the government is; **2** a large letter, such as A, B, or C

captain *noun* **1** the leader of a team or group; **2** the person in command of a ship or aircraft; **3** an officer in the army or navy

car also **motor car** *noun* a vehicle on wheels, driven by an engine, for carrying people

caravan *noun* **1** a small house on wheels which can be pulled by a car or horse; **2** a group of people travelling together through desert areas

card *noun* **1** also **playing card** one of a pack of 52 small sheets of stiffened paper marked to show number and suit and used for various games; **2** a piece of stiffened paper, usually with a picture on the front and a message inside, sent to a person on a birthday, at Christmas, etc; a **postcard**

cardboard *noun* a stiff material like thick paper, used for making boxes, book covers, etc

cardigan *noun* a knitted woollen jacket with sleeves

¹care *noun* **1** looking after somebody or something; protection; **2** thought; serious attention; **3** something that makes you worried or sad; **careful** *adjective;* **carefully** *adverb;* **careless** *adjective;* **carelessly** *adverb*

²care *verb* **1** to be worried or concerned about something; to look after somebody; **2** to like; to want

carol *noun* a religious song sung especially at Christmas

carpenter *noun* a person who makes and repairs wooden objects; **carpentry** *noun*

carpet *noun* a piece of heavy woven material for covering the floor of a room

carriage *noun* **1** a vehicle with wheels that is pulled by horses; **2** a part of a train in which you sit

carriage used by HM The Queen – 1902 State Landau

26

carrot *noun* a vegetable with a long orange-red root

carry *verb* to take up somebody or something in your arms, on your back, etc, and move them from one place to another; **carrier** *noun*

cart *noun* a wooden vehicle pulled by an animal and used for carrying goods

cartoon *noun* **1** a funny drawing; **2** a film made by photographing a set of drawings

cartridge *noun* **1** a metal or paper tube containing explosive for use in a gun; **2** a small plastic container that holds ink for use in a *cartridge pen*

carve *verb* **1** to cut wood or stone in order to make a special shape; **2** to cut meat into pieces or slices; **carver** *noun*

¹**case** *noun* **1** an example of something; a particular occasion; a state or condition; **2** a question to be decided in a court of law; the facts and arguments used on each side

²**case** *noun* a container in which goods can be stored or moved; a *suitcase*

cassette *noun* a small flat plastic case containing tape for use in a tape recorder or *cassette recorder*

¹**cast** *verb* **1** to throw or drop; to throw off; **2** to make an object by pouring hot metal or plastic into a special shape *(mould)*; **3** to make a spell and put it into effect

²**cast** *noun* **1** an act of throwing; **2** all the actors and actresses in a play, film, etc

castle *noun* a large strong building with thick walls and towers

casual *adjective* **1** not planned or arranged; **2** not for special use; **casually** *adverb*

cat *noun (young* **kitten***)* a small animal with soft fur and sharp teeth and claws, often kept as a pet or in buildings to catch mice and rats

¹**catch** *verb* **(catches, catching, caught) 1** to get in your hand and hold; **2** to run after and take hold of an animal, person, or thing; **3** to get an illness; **catcher** *noun*

²**catch** *noun* **1** something that is caught; **2** a hook or fastener for a door, window, etc

a caterpillar of the fritillary butterfly feeding on a violet leaf

caterpillar *noun* an early stage in the life of a butterfly or moth which is like a small worm with short legs

cathedral *noun* the chief church of a city

cattle *noun* large four-legged animals, especially cows

caught *see* CATCH; ▇ **court**

cauliflower *noun* a vegetable with green leaves around a large white head of flowers

cause *noun* a person, thing, or event that makes something happen; a reason; **cause** *verb*

C

27

cave *noun* a deep hollow place underground or in the side of a cliff or hill

ceiling *noun* the inside of the top of a room

celery *noun* a vegetable with greenish white stems used as food

cellar *noun* an underground room used for storing goods; ■ **seller**

cello

cello (*say* chello) *noun* a large violin with a deep sound, that is played held between the knees

Celsius also **centigrade** *adjective* the scale of temperature in which water freezes at 0° and boils at 100°; compare FAHRENHEIT

cement *noun* a grey powder that becomes like stone when mixed with water and allowed to dry

cent *noun* a coin worth 0.01 of a dollar; ■ **scent, sent**

centigrade *see* CELSIUS

centimetre *noun* a measure of length equal to 0.01 metres or 0.4 inches (*see last page*)

centipede *noun* a creature like an insect, with a long body and many pairs of legs

central heating *noun* a way of heating a building in which heat is produced in one place and carried by pipes to other parts of the building

central processor also **central processing unit** or **CPU** *noun* the main part of a computer, which deals with the data and controls other parts

centre *noun* 1 the middle; 2 a place where a lot of people come for a special purpose: **Health Centre, shopping centre; central** *adjective*

century *noun* a period of 100 years

cereal *noun* 1 any kind of grain, such as wheat, oats, and rice; 2 food made from grain, usually eaten at breakfast; ■ **serial**

ceremony *noun* a special set of actions used for making an important event, occasion, or happening

¹**certain** *adjective* sure; **certainly** *adverb*

²**certain** *adjective* some

chain *noun* a length of metal rings joined to one another

chair *noun* a piece of furniture to sit on, which usually has a back, seat, four legs, and sometimes arms: **rocking chair**

chalk *noun* **1** a soft white material formed from the shells of very small sea animals; **2** a piece of this material, white or coloured, used for writing or drawing; **chalky** *adjective*

challenge *verb* **1** to offer to fight or play a game against; **2** to test or question; **challenge** *noun*

chance *noun* **1** something which happens without cause; luck; **2** something which may or may not happen; **3** an opportunity; a time when something may be done; **4** a risk

¹**change** *verb* **1** to make or become different; **2** to give, take, or put something in place of something else; **3** to put on different clothes

²**change** *noun* **1** something that has become different; **2** the money returned when you give too much for something

channel *noun* **1** a narrow piece of water joining two seas; **2** a way along which water can flow; **3** a band of television or radio waves

chapel *noun* a small church, or part of a church

character *noun* **1** the qualities and nature of somebody or something; **2** a person in a book, play, etc

¹**charge** *verb* **1** to ask money for; **2** to say that a person has done something wrong; **3** to run or hurry

²**charge** *noun* **1** a price asked for something; **2** a statement that a person has done wrong; **3** a hurried attack; **4** *in charge of* responsible for; caring for or looking after

chase *verb* to run after; **chase** *noun*

cheap *adjective* costing only little money; **cheaply** *adverb*

¹**cheat** *noun* **1** a dishonest person; **2** a trick

²**cheat** *verb* to trick somebody; to do something which is dishonest

¹**check** *verb* to make sure that something is right; ■ **cheque**

²**check** *noun* **1** an act of checking; **2** a pattern of squares; ■ **cheque**

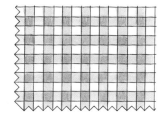

checked material

cheek *noun* **1** a fleshy part on either side of the face under the eyes; **2** rudeness

cheer *verb* **1** to make happy; **2** to shout because you are pleased; **cheer** *noun*

cheerful *adjective* happy; **cheerfully** *adverb*; **cheerfulness** *noun*

cheese *noun* food made from milk

cheetah *noun* a spotted wild animal of the cat family, that can run very fast

chef (*say* shef) *noun* a head cook in a hotel or restaurant

chemist (*say* kemist) *noun* a person who owns or runs a shop where medicines are sold

C

29

chemistry *noun* a science which studies substances like gases, liquids, metals, etc; **chemical** *adjective, noun*

cheque *noun* a specially printed order form to a bank to pay money; ■ **check**

cherry *noun* a small red round fruit with a seed like a stone; the tree on which this grows

chess *noun* a game for two players, with 16 pieces, or **chessmen** each, which are moved across a square **chessboard** with 64 black and white squares

chest *noun* **1** the upper front part of the body; **2** a large strong box

chestnut *noun* **1** a reddish brown nut; the tree on which this grows; **2** a reddish brown colour

chest of drawers *noun* a piece of furniture with drawers

chew *verb* to crush food with the teeth

chick *noun* the young of a bird, especially a chicken

chicken *noun* a bird kept by people for its eggs and meat

chicken pox *noun* a disease, caught especially by children, causing fever and spots

¹chief *noun* a leader; a ruler; the head of a party, group, etc

²chief *adjective* the most important; **chiefly** *adverb*

child *noun* (*plural* **children**) a boy or girl; a son or daughter; **childhood** *noun*; **childish, childlike** *adjective*

chimney *noun* a hollow passage for taking away smoke from a fireplace

chimpanzee

chimpanzee *noun* a large ape

chin *noun* the front part of the face below the mouth

china *noun* **1** a hard white substance made by baking fine clay at high temperatures; **2** plates, cups, etc, made from this

chip *noun* **1** a small piece of brick, wood, paint, etc, broken off; **2** a long thin piece of potato cooked in deep fat; **3** a tiny piece of metal or plastic used in computers to store information or make the computer work; **chip** *verb*

a silicon chip, used in computers

chocolate *noun* a sweet or food made from cocoa

choice *noun* the act of choosing; somebody or something chosen

choir (*say* **kwire**) *noun* a group of people who sing together

choke *verb* to stop breathing because of something blocking your throat

choose *verb* (**chooses, choosing, chose, chosen**) to pick out from a number of things or people the one you want

¹chop *verb* (**chopping**) to cut with an axe or sharp knife

²chop *noun* a slice of meat containing a bone

chose *see* CHOOSE

chosen *see* CHOOSE

Christian *noun* a person who believes in Jesus Christ; **Christianity** *noun*

Christmas also **Christmas Day** *noun* 25th December; the day on which Jesus Christ is said to have been born

church *noun* a building in which Christians meet to pray to God

cider (*say* **syder**) *noun* a drink made from apple juice

cigarette *noun* a narrow tube of thin paper filled with finely cut tobacco for smoking

cinema *noun* a building in which films are shown

circle *noun* 1 a perfectly round, closed, curved line; a ring; 2 a group of people; **circle** *verb*; **circular** *adjective*

circuit (*say* **sir-kit**) *noun* the path of an electric current

circus *noun* a show given by performers and trained animals, often in a large tent

city *noun* a large and important town, often having a cathedral

claim *verb* 1 to ask for something that you say belongs to you; 2 to say that something is true; **claim** *noun*

¹clap *verb* (**clapping**) to hit the palms of your hands together loudly to show that you are pleased with something

²clap *noun* 1 the sound of clapping; 2 a loud noise: *a clap of thunder*

clarinet

clarinet *noun* a musical instrument that you blow

class *noun* 1 a group of people or things of the same kind; 2 a group of people who are taught together or the time during which they are taught: **classroom**

claw *noun* a sharp curved nail on the toe of an animal or bird; **claw** *verb*

clay *noun* heavy earth, used for making bricks, pots, etc, when baked

¹clean *adjective* not dirty; **cleanness** *noun;* **cleanly** *adverb*

²clean *verb* to make or become clean; **cleaner** *noun*

¹clear *adjective* easy to see through: **clear glass; 2** easily heard, seen, read, or understood; **3** open; not having anything in the way; **4** bright; sunny and not cloudy; **clearly** *adverb;* **clearness** *noun*

²clear *verb* **1** to make or become clear; **2** to take away

clever *adjective* quick at learning and understanding; **cleverly** *adverb;* **cleverness** *noun*

cliff *noun* a high very steep piece of land, usually close to the sea

climb (*say* **clime**) *verb* to go up, over, or through using the hands and feet; **climb** *noun;* **climber** *noun*

cling *verb* (**clings, clinging, clung**) to hold on tightly

¹clip *noun* a small plastic or metal object for holding things together

²clip *verb* **1** to hold with a clip; **2** to cut with scissors or another sharp instrument

clock *noun* an instrument for measuring and showing time

clockwise *adjective, adverb* in the same direction as the movement of the hands of a clock

¹close (*say like* **doze**) *verb* to shut

²close (*say like* **dose**) *adjective* near; not far away; **closely** *adverb;* **closeness** *noun*

cloth *noun* **1** material made from wool, hair, cotton, etc, by weaving, and used for making clothes, covers, etc; **2** a piece of this used for a special purpose: **tablecloth, dishcloth**

clothes *noun* the things you wear

clothing *noun* clothes worn together on different parts of the body

a type of cloud formation called cirrocumulus

cloud *noun* **1** a mass of very small drops of water floating high in the sky; **2** a mass of dust, smoke, etc, which floats in the air; **cloudy** *adjective*

clown *noun* a person, especially in the circus, who makes people laugh

club *noun* **1** a group of people who join together for sport, amusement, etc; **2** a heavy wooden stick; **3** a playing card with one or more three-leafed figures printed on it in black

clue *noun* something that helps to find an answer to a question, difficulty, etc

clumsy *adjective* awkward or careless; **clumsily** *adverb;* **clumsiness** *noun*

clung *see* CLING

¹**coach** *noun* 1 a bus used for long-distance travel; 2 a railway carriage; 3 a large four-wheeled vehicle pulled by horses; 4 somebody who trains sportsmen, students, etc

²**coach** *verb* to train or teach a person or group

coal *noun* a black or dark brown material dug out of the earth, that can be burned to give heat

coarse *adjective* not fine or smooth; rough; **coarsely** *adverb;* **coarseness** *noun;* ■course

coast *noun* the land next to the sea

coat *noun* 1 a piece of clothing with long sleeves, worn for warmth; 2 an animal's fur, wool, hair, etc

cobweb *noun* a very fine net of sticky threads made by a spider to catch insects

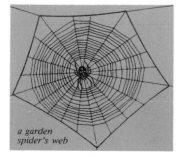
a garden spider's web

cock *noun* a fully grown male bird, especially a chicken

cocoa *noun* 1 a dark brown powder made by crushing the cooked seeds of the *cacao tree,* used for giving foods and drinks a chocolate flavour; 2 a drink made from hot milk or water mixed with this powder

coconut *noun* a large brown nut with a thick hard shell, white flesh, and a hollow centre filled with a milky juice

cod also **codfish** *noun* a type of large sea fish used for food

code *noun* a way of using words, letters, numbers, etc, to keep messages secret

coffee *noun* 1 a brown powder made by crushing the beans of the coffee tree, used for making drinks or flavouring food; 2 a drink made by adding hot water and/or milk to this powder

coffin *noun* a box in which a dead person is buried

¹**coil** *verb* to wind into a set of rings one above the other

²**coil** *noun* 1 a connected set of rings into which a rope, wire, etc, can be wound; 2 a single one of these rings

coin *noun* a flat round piece of metal, made by a government for use as money

¹**cold** *adjective* having very little heat; not warm; **coldly** *adverb;* **coldness** *noun*

²**cold** *noun* 1 the absence of heat; cold weather; 2 an illness of the nose and/or throat

collar *noun* **1** the part of a shirt, dress, or coat that stands up or folds down round the neck; **2** a leather or metal band round an animal's neck

collect *verb* to gather together; **collection** *noun;* **collector** *noun*

college *noun* a place where people study after they have left school

come *verb* **(comes, coming, came, come) 1** to move towards the person speaking, or a particular place; **2** to arrive; **3** to happen; **4** to become; **5 come to** to reach; to add up to something; **6 come from** to be made by; to be born or live in

comedian feminine **comedienne** *noun* a person who tells jokes, does amusing things, or acts in funny plays and films

Halley's comet, which can be seen from Earth about every 76 years

¹**colour** *noun* **1** the quality which allows the eyes to see the difference between (for example) a red and a blue flower of the same size and shape; **2** red, blue, green, black, yellow, white, etc; **colourful** *adjective;* **colouring** *noun;* **colourless** *adjective*

²**colour** *verb* to cause something to have colour or a different colour, especially with a crayon or pencil

comb **(***say like*** home)** *noun* a piece of bone, metal, plastic, etc, with teeth, used for cleaning, tidying, and straightening the hair; **comb** *verb*

comet *noun* a body in space, with a bright head and a long tail, that moves round the sun

¹**comfort** *noun* **1** freedom from pain, trouble, etc; **2** help, kindness, etc, given to somebody who is sad, ill, in pain, etc; **comfortable** *adjective;* **comfortably** *adverb*

²**comfort** *verb* to give comfort to; to cheer up; **comforter** *noun*

comic *noun* **1** a person who is amusing; a comedian; **2** a magazine for children containing stories told in drawings

comma *noun* the mark (,) used in writing and printing for showing a short pause

¹command *verb* **1** to order; **2** to be in charge of; **commander** *noun*

²command *noun* **1** an order; **2** power; control

common *adjective* **1** belonging to or shared by two or more people; **2** found or happening often and in many places; **3** ordinary; usual

communicate *verb* to make known; to pass on or send information

communication *noun* **1** a piece of information, news, etc, that is communicated; **2** communications roads, railways, radio, telephone, television, or other ways of sending information, moving goods, or travelling between two places

community *noun* a group of people who live together and/or who share the same interests or beliefs

compact disc *noun* a thin plastic disc used for storing information such as sound recordings that is smaller and stronger than an LP and is played on a special machine using lasers

company *noun* **1** people to be with; **2** a group of people doing business; a firm

compare *verb* to see if things are alike or different; **comparison** *noun;* ▣ **compere**

compass *noun* an instrument for showing direction, usually with a needle which always points to the north

compere *noun* a person who introduces the acts in a show; **compere** *verb;* ▣ **compare**

competition *noun* a test of strength, skill, etc, to show who is best at something; **compete** *verb;* **competitor** *noun*

complain *verb* to say that you are angry, unhappy, or sad about something; to say that something is not good; **complaint** *noun*

¹complete *adjective* whole; with nothing left out; **completeness** *noun*

²complete *verb* to make whole or perfect; to finish; **completely** *adverb;* **completion** *noun*

complicated *adjective* difficult to understand or deal with

compliment *noun* something nice said about somebody

computer *noun* an electronic machine that can store information and make calculations at very high speeds

concentrate *verb* to keep all your thoughts, attention, etc, on one thing; **concentration** *noun*

concern *verb* **1** to be worried about; **2** to make unhappy or troubled; to worry; **concern** *noun*

a bearing compass, used by hikers and mountaineers

concert *noun* music played by a number of singers and/or musicians

concrete *noun* a building material made by mixing sand, small stones, cement, and water

condition *noun* **1** the state that somebody or something is in; **2** something that is said to be necessary or that must happen before something else happens

conductor *noun* **1** a person who controls a group of people playing music; **2** a person who collects fares on a bus or train

cone *noun* a shape or object with a round base and a point at the top: **ice cream cone, fir cone**

confess *verb* to admit a fault or something you have done wrong; **confession** *noun*

conscience *noun* part of your mind that judges what you do, and makes you feel guilty, good, evil, etc

conscious *adjective* awake, able to understand what is happening; **consciously** *adverb*; **consciousness** *noun*

conservation *noun* saving and protecting

consider *verb* to think about

considerable *adjective* fairly large

consist *verb* to be made up of

consonant *noun* any of the letters of the English alphabet, or their sounds, except a, e, i, o, or u; compare VOWEL

constant *adjective* happening all the time; **constantly** *adverb*

constellation *noun* a large group of stars

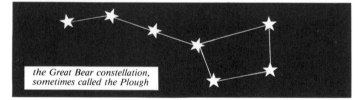

the Great Bear constellation, sometimes called the Plough

confuse *verb* to mix up in your mind; **confusion** *noun*

conjunction *noun* a word that joins two parts of a sentence

conjure *verb* to do clever tricks which seem magical, usually by very quick movement of the hands; **conjuror** or **conjurer** *noun*

connect *verb* to join; **connected** *adjective*; **connection** *noun*

contain *verb* to have inside; to hold; **container** *noun*

content *adjective* satisfied; happy; **contented** *adjective*

contents *noun* what is contained in an object or a book

continent *noun* any of the seven main masses of land on the Earth; **continental** *adjective*

continual *adjective* happening often; repeated; **continually** *adverb*

continue *verb* to go on

continuous *adjective* never stopping; **continuously** *adverb*

¹**control** *verb* **(controlled)** **1** to have power over somebody or something; **2** to direct; to guide

²**control** *noun* **1** the ability to control; power; **2** an instrument, knob, switch, etc, for controlling a machine: **volume control**

convenient *adjective* suitable; **conveniently** *adverb*

conversation *noun* a talk

cook *verb* to prepare food for eating by using heat; **cook** *noun*; **cooker** *noun*

cool *adjective* **1** neither warm nor cold; **2** calm; not excited; **cool** *verb*; **coolly** *adverb*; **coolness** *noun*

copper *noun* a soft reddish metal that is easily shaped and allows heat and electricity to pass through it readily

¹**copy** *noun* **1** a thing made to be exactly like another; **2** a single example of a magazine, book, etc

²**copy** *verb* to make or do something exactly the same as something else

cord *noun* a thick string or thin rope

cork *noun* **1** a soft light material that comes from the bark of a tree; **2** a round piece of this used to seal a bottle

corn *noun* the seed of grain plants, such as wheat

corner *noun* **1** the point at which two lines, surfaces, or edges meet; **2** the place where two roads or paths meet

¹**correct** *verb* to make right; to mark the mistakes in; **correction** *noun*

²**correct** *adjective* right; **correctly** *adverb*; **correctness** *noun*

corridor *noun* a long narrow part of a building; a passage off which rooms open

¹**cost** *noun* the price you pay when you buy something

²**cost** *verb* **(costs, costing, cost)** to have as a price

costume *noun* the clothes typical of a certain time in history, country, etc; the clothes worn by an actor or actress

cot *noun* a small bed for a young child

cottage *noun* a small house in the country

cotton *noun* **1** a tall plant grown in warm areas for the soft white hair that surrounds its seeds; **2** this soft white hair used to make thread, cloth, cotton wool, etc

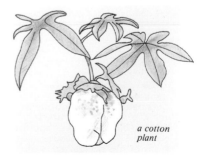

a cotton plant

couch *noun* a long piece of furniture on which you can lie or sit

¹**cough** (*say* coff) *verb* to push air out from the throat suddenly, with a rough sharp noise

²**cough** *noun* an act or sound of coughing

could (**couldn't**) *see* CAN

council *noun* a group of people who are chosen to make laws, rules, or decisions or to give advice; **councillor** *noun*; ■ **counsel, counsellor**

counsel *noun* advice; **counsel** *verb*; **counsellor** *noun*; ■ **council, councillor**

count *verb* 1 to say the numbers in order; 2 to find out how many there are; 3 to add up; **count** *noun*

counter *noun* 1 a narrow table or flat surface on which goods are shown or at which people in a shop, bank, etc, are served; 2 a small flat object used in playing games

country *noun* 1 an area of land that has its own government; 2 the land outside cities or towns: **countryside**

couple *noun* 1 two things of the same kind; 2 a man and a woman together, especially a husband and wife

courage *noun* the feeling of not being afraid; bravery; **courageous** *adjective*

course *noun* 1 the direction taken by somebody or something; 2 an area of land or water on which a race is held or certain types of sport played; 3 a set of lessons; 4 any of the several parts of a meal; 5 **of course** *adverb* certainly; as everyone knows or must agree; ■ **coarse**

court *noun* 1 a place where somebody is questioned about a crime, and where people decide whether or not he or she is guilty; 2 the officials, servants, etc, who attend a king and queen; 3 an open space where games are played: **tennis court**; ■ **caught**

cousin *noun* the child of your uncle or aunt

¹**cover** *verb* to place or spread something upon, over, or in front of something else

²**cover** *noun* 1 anything that protects by covering: **bed cover, book cover**; 2 a lid; a top

covering *noun* something that covers or hides

cow *noun* (*male* **bull**, *young* **calf**) the fully grown female form of cattle, elephants, and certain other large animals

coward *noun* a person who avoids danger or pain because he or she has no courage; **cowardly** *adjective*; **cowardice** *noun*; **cowardliness** *noun*

cowboy *noun* a man who rides a horse and looks after cattle in America

crab *noun* a sea animal with five pairs of legs and a hard shell

a type of crab

38

¹**crack** *verb* 1 to break without dividing into separate parts; 2 to make a sudden sharp sound

²**crack** *noun* 1 a thin line or split where something is broken; 2 a loud sharp sound

cracker *noun* 1 a small thin biscuit; 2 a paper toy which bangs when its ends are pulled, used especially at Christmas

cradle *noun* a small rocking bed for a baby

cream *noun* the thick fatty part of milk which rises to the top; **creaminess** *noun;* **creamy** *adjective*

creature *noun* an animal of any kind

creep *verb* (**creeps, creeping, crept**) to move slowly and quietly

crew *noun* the people working on a ship, plane, etc

¹**cricket** *noun* an outdoor game played with a ball and bat, by two teams of eleven players each; **cricketer** *noun*

²**cricket** *noun* a type of small brown insect

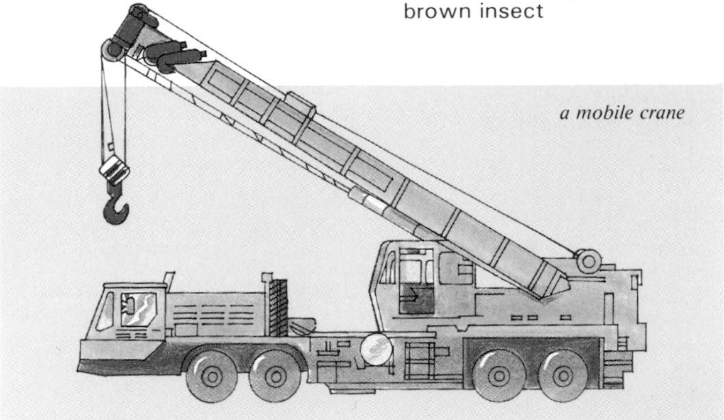

a mobile crane

crane *noun* a machine for lifting and moving heavy objects

crash *noun* 1 a sudden loud noise; 2 a violent vehicle accident; 3 a sudden failure of a computer or a computer program; **crash** *verb*

crawl *verb* to move slowly with your body close to the ground, or on your hands and knees

cried *see* CRY

crime *noun* something that is wrong and can be punished by law; **criminal** *noun*

¹**crisp** *adjective* 1 hard and dry; easily broken; 2 firm; fresh; **crispy** *adjective*

²**crisp** also **potato crisp** *noun* a thin piece of potato cooked in very hot fat, dried, and sold in packets

a crocodile looks very like an alligator, except that the big teeth in its lower jaw can be seen even when its mouth is closed

C

crocodile *noun* **1** a large reptile that lives on land and in lakes and rivers in the hot wet parts of the world; **2** a line of people walking in pairs

crooked *adjective* not straight; bent; **crookedly** *adverb;* **crookedness** *noun*

crop *noun* **1** a plant or part of a plant such as grain, fruit, or vegetables grown by a farmer; **2** the amount of grain, vegetables, etc, cut and gathered at one time

¹cross *noun* **1** a figure or mark formed by one straight line crossing another; anything shaped like × or +; **2** an animal or plant that is a mixture of breeds

²cross *verb* **1** to go, pass, or reach over or across; **2** to cause an animal or plant to breed with one of another kind; **crossing** *noun*

³cross *adjective* angry; bad-tempered; **crossly** *adverb*

crow *noun* a large shiny black bird with a loud rough cry

crowd *noun* a large number of people gathered together; **crowded** *adjective*

crown *noun* a circle of gold with jewels in it, worn on the head by a king or queen at special times

cruel *adjective* liking to hurt other people or animals; unkind; **cruelly** *adverb;* **cruelty** *noun*

crumb *noun* a very small piece of dry food, such as bread or cake

crush *verb* to hurt or damage by pressing heavily

crust *noun* the hard part on the outside of bread or some other things; **crusty** *adjective*

¹cry *verb* **(cries, crying, cried)** **1** to produce tears from your eyes; **2** to make loud sounds because of fear, sadness, etc

²cry *noun* a loud call; a shout

cub *noun* the young of various types of meat-eating wild animals, such as the lion, bear, etc

cube *noun* a solid object that has six equal square sides

cuckoo *noun* **1** a grey bird that lays its eggs in other birds' nests; **2** the call of this bird

cucumber *noun* a long green vegetable which is usually eaten raw with cold food

cue *noun* a long straight wooden stick, slightly thicker at one end than the other, used for hitting the ball in snooker, billiards, etc; ■ queue

cup *noun* 1 a small round container, usually with a handle, from which liquids are drunk: **cupful**; 2 a specially shaped bowl, usually made of gold or silver, given as a prize in a competition

cupboard *noun* a piece of furniture with space inside where things may be stored

¹cure *verb* to make somebody better when they have been ill; to make a disease, illness, etc, go away

²cure *noun* a way of making somebody or something better; a drug or medicine that cures an illness, disease, etc

curious *adjective* 1 wanting to know or learn about things or people; 2 odd; strange; peculiar; **curiosity** *noun*

¹curl *verb* to twist into or form a round or curved shape

²curl *noun* 1 a roll or round shape; 2 a small piece of twisted hair; **curliness** *noun;* **curly** *adjective*

currant *noun* 1 small dried seedless grape; 2 a small bush or the small fruits in bunches on them; ■ current

current *noun* a flow of water, gas, electricity, etc; ■ currant

curtain *noun* a piece of hanging cloth that can be drawn to cover a window or door or to divide a room

curve *verb* to bend into a smooth round shape; **curve** *noun*

cushion *noun* a bag filled with a soft substance on which you can lie, sit, etc

custard *noun* a thick sweet yellow sauce

customer *noun* a person who buys something

cut *verb* (**cuts, cutting, cut**) to make an opening in, separate, or remove something with a knife, scissors, etc; **cut** *noun*

¹cycle *noun* a bicycle or motorcycle

²cycle *verb* to bicycle; **cyclist** *noun*

cygnet (*say* signet) *noun* a young swan

cymbals *noun* a musical instrument consisting of a pair of round thin metal plates struck together to make a loud ringing noise; ■ symbols

cymbals – a percussion instrument (that is, one that is played by being struck)

C

41

dad, daddy *noun* father

daddylonglegs *noun* a large fly with very long legs

daffodil *noun* a yellow flower that grows in the spring

dagger *noun* a short pointed knife used as a weapon

daily *adjective, adverb* happening or done once every day

dairy *noun* a place where milk, butter, and cheese are made or a shop where they are sold

daisy *noun* a small wild or garden flower, yellow in the centre and white round the edge

daisies

dam *noun* a wall or bank built to keep back water

¹**damage** *noun* harm, especially to things

²**damage** *verb* to cause damage to; to hurt

damp *adjective, noun* slightly wet; not properly dry; **dampness** *noun*

¹**dance** *verb* to move to music; **dancer** *noun*

²**dance** *noun* **1** a set of movements performed to music; **2** a party for dancing; **3** a piece of music for dancing

dandelion *noun* a small yellow wild flower

dangerous *adjective* not safe; likely to cause harm or damage; **danger** *noun;* **dangerously** *adverb*

dare *verb* **1** to be brave or rude enough to do or say something; **2** to challenge; **dare** *noun*

dark *adjective* without light; nearly black; **dark** *noun;* **darkness** *noun*

dart *noun* a small pointed arrow thrown at a round board in the game of **darts**

dash *noun* **1** a sudden quick run; **2** a mark (–) used in writing or printing; **dash** *verb*

data *noun* measurements, facts, and information that can be put into a computer to run a program

¹**date** *noun* **1** time shown by the number of the day, the month, and the year; **2** an arrangement to meet at a particular time and place

²**date** *noun* a small brown sweet fruit with a long stone

daughter *noun* a person's female child

dawn *noun* the time of day when light first appears and the sun rises

day *noun* **1** the time when it is light: **daytime, daylight; 2** twenty four hours

dead *adjective* **1** no longer alive; **2** unable to feel

deaf *adjective* unable to hear or hear well; **deafness** *noun*

deal *verb* (**deals, dealing, dealt**) **1** to give out a share of something; **2 deal with** to do what is necessary with something or somebody; **deal** *noun;* **dealer** *noun*

dear *adjective* **1** much loved; **2** a term used to begin a letter; **3** costing a lot of money;  **deer**

death *noun* the end of life

decay *verb* to go bad; **decay** *noun*

deceive *verb* to cause somebody to accept as true or good what is false or bad

December *noun* the twelfth and last month of the year

decide *verb* to arrive at an answer or make a choice about something; **decision** *noun*

¹decimal *adjective* having to do with the number ten

²decimal *noun* a number like .5, .375, .06, etc

deck *noun* **1** a floor of a ship or bus; **2** a machine for playing records or tapes: **record deck, tape deck**

deckchairs

deckchair *noun* a folding chair that you use outdoors

decorate *verb* to make something more beautiful or colourful; **decoration** *noun*

deep *adjective* **1** going far down; **2** going a long way in; **3** going a certain amount or distance in one direction; **4** strong and dark; **5** low; **deeply** *adverb*; **deepness** *noun*; **depth** *noun*

deer *noun* (*plural* **deer**) (*male*

D

buck, *female* **doe** *or* **hind,** *young* **fawn***)* a large wild animal that eats grass and can run very fast;  **dear**

degree *noun* a unit for measuring the temperature of something or the size of an angle

delay *verb* **1** to put off until later; **2** to make late; **3** to act slowly; **delay** *noun*

delicacy *noun* something that is good to eat but is rare or costs a lot of money

delicate *adjective* **1** easily harmed or broken; **2** beautiful and pleasing but small and not strong; **delicately** *adverb*

delicious *adjective* nice to smell or taste

delight *verb* to give great pleasure; **delight** *noun*; **delightful** *adjective*

deliver *verb* **1** to send or take something to a particular place; **2** to help somebody to have a baby; **3** to say; to read aloud; **delivery** *noun*

den *noun* **1** the home of a wild animal; **2** a secret or private place

dentist also **dental surgeon** *noun* a person who looks after your teeth

dependant *noun* a person who depends on another; **dependent** *adjective*

Canadian fawns

43

depend on *verb* **1** to rely on someone or something; to need; **2** to be influenced by; to be a result of

depth *see* DEEP

describe *verb* to give a picture of something in words; **description** *noun*

¹desert (*say* dez-ert) *noun* a large sandy piece of land where there is hardly any rain and very few plants or animals; ■ **dessert**

²desert (*say* de-zert) *verb* to leave completely; ■ **dessert**

deserve *verb* to be worthy of something good, or bad, by doing something good or bad

desk *noun* a table, often with drawers, at which you read, write, etc

dessert (*say* de-zert) *noun* a (usually) sweet dish you eat at the end of a meal; ■ **desert**

destroy *verb* to ruin or wreck; **destruction** *noun*

detect *verb* to find out or discover; **detection** *noun;* **detector** *noun*

detective *noun* a policeman who finds out about crimes

determined *adjective* having made up your mind to do something; **determination** *noun*

develop *verb* to make or become larger, more active, more complete, etc; to grow; **developer** *noun;* **development** *noun*

devil *noun* **1** an evil spirit or person; **2 Devil** the most evil spirit; the enemy of God

dew *noun* small drops of water which form on the ground during the night; ■ **due**; **dewy** *adjective*

diagram *noun* a drawing that explains something or shows how its parts are arranged

diamond *noun* **1** a very hard valuable jewel; **2** a shape with four equal sides that stands on one of its points; **3** a playing card which has these shapes in red

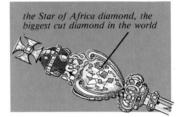

the Star of Africa diamond, the biggest cut diamond in the world

diary *noun* a book with separate spaces for each day of the year, in which you write down things you have done or will do

dice *see* DIE

dictionary *noun* a book that gives the meaning of words

did *see* DO

didn't *see* DO

¹die *verb* (**dies, dying, died**) to stop living

²die *noun* (*plural* **dice**) a small cube, with a different number of spots from one to six on each side, that is used in many games

different *adjective* not of the same kind; **difference** *noun;* **differently** *adverb*

difficult *adjective* not easy; hard to do, understand, etc; **difficulty** *noun*

dig *verb* (**digs, digging, dug**) **1** to break up and move earth; **2** to make a hole by taking away earth or soil

digger *noun* **1** somebody or something that digs; **2** a tool or machine for digging the earth

digit *noun* **1** any number from nought to nine; **2** a finger or toe; **digital** *adjective*

dining room *noun* a room in which you eat meals

dinner *noun* a main meal, eaten either at midday or in the evening

dinosaur *noun* any of several types of reptiles, some very large, that lived millions of years ago

disappear *verb* to go out of sight; **disappearance** *noun*

disappoint *verb* to become sad or make somebody sad because what was expected or hoped for did not happen; **disappointed** *adjective;* **disappointing** *adjective;* **disappointment** *noun*

disapprove *verb* to have a bad opinion of somebody or something; **disapproval** *noun*

disc *noun* **1** any round flat thing; **2** a gramophone record: **disc jockey**

disciple *noun* somebody who is faithful to or follows a leader

D

diplodocus –
a plant-eating dinosaur

direct *verb* **1** to tell somebody the way; **2** to control or manage; **director** *noun*

direction *noun* **1** the course or way in which a person or thing moves; **2 directions** information that tells you what to do, how to do something, or where to go

directly *adverb* **1** in a direct manner; straight; **2** at once

dirt *noun* soil, mud, dust, or anything that is not clean

dirty *adjective* **1** covered with dirt; **2** making you, your clothes, or your things unclean; **dirtily** *adverb*

disagree *verb* not to agree; **disagreement** *noun*

discipline *noun* good behaviour and the obeying of rules; the training of somebody to behave in this way

disco *noun* a place where people dance to pop records

discover *verb* to find out or find something, especially for the first time; **discoverer** *noun;* **discovery** *noun*

disease *noun* an illness; **diseased** *adjective*

dish *noun* **1** a large, flat, and often round plate on which your food is served; **2** prepared food of one kind

dishonest *adjective* not honest; **dishonestly** *adverb;* **dishonesty** *noun*

face mask — snorkel

air cylinder

life jacket

wet suit

flippers

a scuba diver (scuba stands for self contained underwater breathing apparatus)

disk *noun* a round flat plate covered with a magnetic material on which data for use in a computer is stored

dislike *verb* not to like; **dislike** *noun*

distance *noun* 1 the amount of space between two places; 2 **in the distance** far away; **distant** *adjective*

ditch *noun* a long narrow not very deep channel dug in the ground for water to drain into

dive *verb* 1 to jump head first into water; 2 to move quickly or suddenly; **dive** *noun*

diver *noun* a person who works under water and wears a special **diving suit** to help him or her to breathe

divide *verb* 1 to separate into smaller parts or groups; to share; 2 to find out how many times one number will go into another number

division *noun* 1 one of the parts or groups into which something is divided; 2 dividing sums

do *verb* (**does, doing, did, done, doesn't, don't, didn't**) 1 to carry out; to act; 2 to deal with something; 3 to be suitable for something; to be enough; 4 **That will do!** That's enough!; 5 **How do you do?** a form of words used when introduced to somebody; 6 **make do with something** also **make something do** to use something even though it may not be perfect or enough; 7 **What do you do?** What is your work?

dock *noun* a place where ships are loaded or repaired

doctor *noun* a person whose job is to look after sick people

doe *noun* the female of any animal of which the male is called a buck, such as the deer or the rabbit ■**dough**

does *see* DO

doesn't *see* DO

dog *noun* (female **bitch**, young **puppy**) a common four-legged animal, kept as a pet or for hunting, working, etc

doing *see* DO

doll *noun* a toy made to look like a person

dollar *noun* the money used in America, Australia, and some other countries. There are one hundred cents to one dollar and its sign is $.

dolphin *noun* a sea animal which swims in groups and is very intelligent

done *adjective* 1 finished; 2 *see* DO

donkey *noun* an animal like a horse but smaller and with longer ears

don't *see* DO

door *noun* 1 a flat surface that opens and closes the entrance to a building, room, or piece of furniture; 2 the opening for a door: **doorway**; 3 **answer the door** to go and open the door to see who is there

dot *noun* a small round spot; **dot** *verb*

¹**double** *adjective* 1 having two parts; 2 made for two; **double** *adverb*

²**double** *noun* 1 something that is twice as much as another; 2 a person who looks like another; 3 **doubles** a game of tennis, badminton, etc, for two pairs of players

³**double** *verb* 1 to multiply a number or amount by two; 2 to fold or bend sharply or tightly over

double bass *noun* a musical instrument with a deep sound, like a very big violin

double-decker *adjective* having two layers or two floors

doubt *verb* not to be sure about something; **doubt** *noun*

dough (*say* doe) *noun* a thick mixture of flour and water used for making bread, cakes, etc; ■ **doe**

¹**down** *adverb, preposition adjective* 1 to or in a lower place or position; 2 along

²**down** *noun* small soft feathers on a bird

downhill *adjective, adverb* towards the bottom of a hill

downstairs *adverb, adjective* on or to a lower floor of a building; **downstairs** *noun*

downwards *adverb* 1 from a higher to a lower place; 2 towards the ground or floor

dozen *noun (plural* **dozen** *or* **dozens)** 1 a group of twelve; 2 **dozens of** lots of; **dozen** *adjective*

drag *verb* (**dragged**) 1 to pull a heavy thing along; 2 to move along slowly; 3 to look for something by pulling a heavy net along the bottom of a lake or river

the Welsh Dragon used in heraldry

dragon *noun* an imaginary animal in stories that is said to breathe fire

47

¹drain *verb* **1** to make a liquid, usually water, flow away; **2** to make or become gradually dry or empty

²drain *noun* a pipe, tube, etc, that drains something away

drake *noun* a male duck

a blue-winged teal drake

drank *see* DRINK

draught *noun* air blowing into a room

draughts *noun* a game for two, each with twelve round pieces, on a board of sixty four squares

¹draw *verb* (**draws, drawing, drew, drawn**) **1** to make pictures with a pencil, pen, etc; **2** to pull; to pull up or out; **3** to move; **4** to attract; **5** to end a game, battle, etc, without either side winning; **6 draw the curtain** to close or open the curtain

²draw *noun* a game, battle, etc, which neither side wins

drawer *noun* a sliding container, like a box without a top, that fits into a piece of furniture

drawing *noun* **1** making pictures; **2** a picture done by pencil, pen, etc

drawn *see* DRAW

¹dream *noun* **1** thoughts that you have or pictures that you see when you are asleep; **2** something not real you hope for or imagine

²dream *verb* (**dreams, dreaming, dreamed** *or* **dreamt**) to have a dream

¹dress *verb* **1** to put clothes on; **2 dress up** to put on special clothes; **3** to clean and cover up a wound

²dress *noun* a piece of clothing for a woman or girl that has a top and skirt

dressing table *noun* a piece of bedroom furniture with drawers and a mirror

drew *see* DRAW

drink *verb* (**drinks, drinking, drank, drunk**) to take liquid into the mouth and swallow it; **drink** *noun*

drip *verb* (**dripped**) to fall or let fall in drops; **drip** *noun*

¹drive *verb* (**drives, driving, drove, driven**) to make an animal or a vehicle move in the direction you want; **driver** *noun*

²drive *noun* **1** a journey in a vehicle; **2** a road to a house: a **driveway**

¹drop *noun* **1** a small amount of liquid; **2** a small round sweet; **3** a fall

²drop *verb* (**dropped**) **1** to fall suddenly or in drops; **2** to let fall or lower; **3 drop in** to visit

drove *see* DRIVE

drown *verb* **1** to die by being under water so that you are unable to breathe; **2** to kill by holding under water too long; **3** to make such a loud noise that another sound can no longer be heard

drowsy *adjective* sleepy

drug *noun* a medicine

drum kit as used by a group

¹drum *noun* **1** a round musical instrument which you play by beating with your hand or a stick; **2** a large container shaped like a drum

²drum *verb* **(drummed) 1** to beat or play a drum; **2** to make noises like those from a drum; **drummer** *noun*

¹drunk *adjective* having had too much alcohol

²drunk *see* DRINK

¹dry *adjective* **1** not wet; not containing water; **2** thirsty; **3** dull and not interesting; **dryly, drily** *adverb;* **dryness** *noun*

²dry *verb* **1** to make or become dry; **2** to preserve food by removing liquid

¹duck *noun (male* **drake,** *young* **duckling)** a common water bird with short legs and a short neck

²duck *verb* **1** to lower your head or body quickly, so as to avoid being hit; **2** to push under water

duckling *noun* a young duck

due *adjective* **1** owing; to be paid; **2** expected; ▪ **dew**

due to *preposition* because of; caused by

dug *see* DIG

dull *adjective* **1** not bright, strong, or sharp; **2** cloudy; grey; **3** not interesting or exciting

dumb *(say* dum*) adjective* unable to speak

dumpling *noun* a ball of dough cooked with meat in a stew or filled with jam or fruit

during *preposition* all through, or at some point in the course of

dusk *noun* the time when daylight is fading

¹dust *noun* powder made up of very small pieces; **dusty** *adjective*

²dust *verb* **1** to clean the dust from something; **2** to cover with dust or fine powder

dustbin *noun* a container with a lid, for holding rubbish

duty *noun* **1** what you must do either because of your job or because you think it right; **2** a tax; **dutiful** *adjective*

duvet *(say* du-vay*) noun* a large bag filled with soft warm material, such as feathers, used on a bed to take the place of all other coverings

dwarf *noun* **1** a person, animal, or plant of much less than the usual size; **2** a small imaginary manlike creature in fairy stories

each *adjective, pronoun, adverb* every one separately; for or to every one

eager *adjective* wanting to do something very much; keen; **eagerly** *adverb;* **eagerness** *noun*

eagle *noun* a very large strong bird that hunts other birds and animals

¹ear *noun* **1** the part of the body with which you hear: **earache, earlobe; 2 all ears** listening eagerly

²ear *noun* the seeds at the top of a stalk of corn, wheat, etc

early *adverb, adjective* **1** before the usual or right time; **2** near the beginning of the day or another period of time

earn *verb* **1** to get money by working; **2** to get something that you deserve; ■**urn**

earring *noun* a piece of jewellery worn on the ear

earth *noun* **1 Earth** the planet on which we live; **2** soil; **3** the wire which connects a piece of electrical equipment to the ground; **4** the hole where certain wild animals live, such as foxes

earthquake *noun* a sudden shaking of the Earth's surface, that may cause great damage

earwig *noun* a thin brown insect

easel *noun* a stand for a blackboard or a painting

east *noun* one of the four main points of the compass; the direction in which the sun rises; **east** *adjective, adverb;* **easterly** *adjective;* **eastern** *adjective*

Easter *noun* the time when Christians remember the death of Jesus Christ and his rising from the grave

easy *adjective* able to be done without much trouble; not difficult; **easily** *adverb*

eat *verb* **(eats, eating, ate, eaten)** to take food into the mouth and swallow it

in this solar eclipse, the moon is passing between the Earth and the sun

eclipse *noun* the blocking off of the sun's light when the moon passes between it and the Earth, or of the moon's light when the Earth passes between it and the sun

edge *noun* **1** the thin sharp cutting part of a knife, saw, etc; **2** the place or line where something begins or ends

educate *verb* to teach; to train the character or mind of something; **education** *noun*

eel *noun* a long slippery fish that looks like a snake

effect *noun* **1** a result; **2** a result produced on the mind or feelings; **effective** *adjective*

effort *noun* **1** a show of strength; **2** trying hard with body or mind

e.g. for example

egg *noun* **1** a round or oval object which comes out of the body of a female bird, fish, or reptile and contains new life; **2** the seed of life in a woman or female animal, which joins with the male seed to make a baby

eight *adjective, noun* the number 8; **eighth** *adjective, adverb (see last page)*

eighteen *adjective, noun* **1** the number 18; **2** '18' certificate a film that can only be watched by people eighteen and over; **eighteenth** *adjective, adverb (see last page)*

eighty *adjective, noun* the number 80; **eightieth** *adjective, adverb (see last page)*

either *adjective, pronoun* **1** one or the other of two; **2** one and the other of two; each

elastic *noun* a stretchy material which springs back into its original shape after being pulled; **elastic** *adjective*

elbow *noun* the joint where the arm bends

elder *adjective, noun* the older of two

eldest *adjective, noun* the oldest of three or more

electricity *noun* the power produced by a battery or sent along wires which gives us heat and light and makes machines work; **electric** or **electrical** *adjective*; **electrically** *adverb*; **electrician** *noun*

electronic *adjective* connected with any apparatus that works by electronics

electronics *noun* the science concerned with radio, television, and other similar apparatus

elephant *noun* a very large animal that has two long curved tusks and a long trunk with which it can pick things up

an African elephant

eleven *adjective, noun* the number 11; **eleventh** *adjective, adverb (see last page)*

else *adverb* **1** besides; as well; **2** different; other; **3 or else** or otherwise

embarrass *verb* to make somebody feel awkward or silly; **embarrassment** *noun*

embroidery *noun* patterns or pictures sewn on material to make it look pretty; **embroider** *verb*

emerald *noun* **1** a bright green jewel; **2** bright green; **emerald** *adjective*

emergency *noun* something that happens very suddenly and must be dealt with immediately

employ *verb* to give work to; **employee** *noun*; **employer** *noun*; **employment** *noun*

empty *adjective* containing nothing or nobody; **emptiness** *noun*; **empty** *verb*

E

encourage *verb* to give courage, praise, or hope to somebody so that he or she will do something; **encouragement** *noun*; **encouragingly** *adverb*

¹end *noun* **1** the furthest part of anything; the point where something stops; **2** the latest point; the time when something stops

²end *verb* to come to an end; to finish

enemy *noun* **1** a person who does not like another person and is not friendly to him or her; **2** a country that fights against us in a war

energy *noun* **1** the power to do things; being full of life and strength; **2** the power which does work and drives machines: **atomic/electrical energy**

engine *noun* **1** a machine that uses fuel, such as petrol or electricity, to make something move; **2** the front part of a train that pulls the carriages: **engine driver**

engineer *noun* a person who plans, makes, or looks after machines, roads, bridges, etc; **engineering** *noun*

enjoy *verb* to get happiness from; **enjoyable** *adjective*; **enjoyment** *noun*

enough *adjective, adverb* as much or as many as may be needed

enter *verb* to come or go in or into; **entry** *noun*

entertain *verb* **1** to have people as guests or give a party; **2** to make somebody amused or interested; **entertainment** *noun*

entire *adjective* whole, complete; **entirely** *adverb*

entrance *noun* a way into a place

envelope *noun* a paper cover for a letter

equal *adjective* the same in number, size, etc; as good, big, many as; **equal** *noun* **equal** *verb*; **equally** *adverb*

Equator *noun* an imaginary line drawn round the world halfway between its North and South Poles

George Stephenson's Rocket, *an early steam engine*

equip *verb* (equipped) to give the things that are necessary for doing something; **equipment** *noun*

escape *verb* to get free from something or somebody; **escape** *noun*

especially *adverb* 1 more than usual; particularly; 2 specially

etc also **et cetera** and the rest; and so on

¹**even** *adjective* 1 smooth, flat, level; 2 equal; 3 **even number** a number that can be divided exactly by two; **evenly** *adverb*; **evenness** *noun*

²**even** *adverb* 1 a word to show that something is more than you expect; 2 still; yet: *It's even colder than yesterday*

evening *noun* the end of the day and early part of the night

event *noun* 1 a happening; 2 a race, competition, etc, arranged as part of a day's sports

ever *adverb* 1 at any time; 2 always; 3 **ever so/such** very

every *adjective* each one; all

everybody also **everyone** *pronoun* every person

everything *pronoun* all; the whole, made up of a number of things

everywhere *adverb* in or to all places

evil *adjective* very bad; wicked; **evil** *noun*

exact *adjective* completely correct; **exactly** *adverb*

exaggerate (*say* egzajerate) *verb* to say that something is bigger, better, worse, etc, than it really is; **exaggeration** *noun*

examine *verb* 1 to look at closely, in order to find out something; 2 to ask somebody questions or to do something, in order to test knowledge or skill; **exam, examination** *noun*; **examiner** *noun*

example *noun* 1 something taken from a number of things of the same kind, which shows a general rule or what the other things are like; 2 a person or action that you should try to copy

excellent *adjective* very good; **excellence** *noun*; **excellently** *adverb*

except *conjunction, preposition* apart from; leaving out

exciting *adjective* making you feel very lively and active and have strong pleasant feelings; **excite** *verb*; **excitement** *noun*

the exclamation mark on this road sign is a warning

exclamation mark *noun* a sign (!) used in writing to show surprise, shock, etc

E

53

¹**excuse** (*say* excuze) *verb* **1** to forgive somebody for a small fault; to say that somebody is not to blame; **2** to free somebody from something he or she should do

²**excuse** (*say* excuse) *noun* the reason given when asking to be forgiven or not to be blamed

exercise *noun* **1** the use of your body so as to strengthen it and keep fit; **2** something, such as a piece of schoolwork, that is done for practice: **exercise book; exercise** *verb*

exist *verb* to live or to be real

exit *noun* a way out of a place

expand *verb* to get or make larger; **expansion** *noun*

experience *verb;* **experienced** *adjective*

explain *verb* **1** to say what something means; **2** to be the reason for something; **explanation** *noun*

explode *verb* to blow up or burst with a loud noise; **explosion** *noun*

¹**express** *noun* **1** also **express train** a fast train that does not stop at many stations; **2** a service given by the post office, railways, etc, for carrying things faster

²**express** *verb* to show a feeling, opinion, or fact in words or in some other way

expression *noun* **1** a word or phrase that is spoken; **2** the look on somebody's face

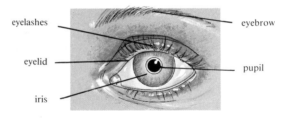

eyelashes

eyelid

iris

eyebrow

pupil

human eye

expect *verb* **1** to think or believe that something will happen; to suppose; **2** to wait for

expensive *adjective* costing a lot of money

experience *noun* **1** knowledge or skill which comes from practice rather than from books; **2** something that happens to you and has an effect on your mind;

extend *verb* to make longer; **extension** *noun*

eye *noun* **1** the part of the body with which you see: **eyebrow, eyelash, eyelid, eyesight; 2** the hole in a needle through which the thread passes; **3** the dark spot on a potato, from which a new plant can grow; **4** the small loop of metal or thread into which a hook fits for fastening a piece of clothing

¹face *noun* **1** the front part of the head from the chin to the hair; **2** a look or expression; **3** the front part of something

²face *verb* **1** to turn the face towards something; **2** to look at and not try to avoid

fact *noun* something that is known to be true; something that has actually happened

factory *noun* a building where things are made in large quantities, usually by machines

fade *verb* to lose strength, colour, freshness, etc

Fahrenheit *noun* a scale of temperature in which water freezes at 32° and boils at 212°; compare CELSIUS, CENTIGRADE

fail *verb* **1** not to succeed, or not to do what you wanted; **2** not to pass an examination; **failure** *noun*

¹faint *adjective* **1** weak and about to lose your senses; **2** not clear, strong, or bright; **faintly** *adverb*

²faint *verb* to feel weak and lose your senses; **faint** *noun*

¹fair *adjective* **1** honest; keeping to the rules; **2** good, but not very good; average; **3** light in colour; not dark; **fairly** *adverb*; ■ **fare**

²fair *noun* an outdoor show with rides, games, and other things to amuse you: **fairground**; ■ **fare**

fairy *noun* a small imaginary person with wings and magical powers

faith *noun* belief in something; **faithful** *adjective*; **faithfully** *adverb*

fall *verb* (**falls, falling, fell, fallen**) **1** to drop to a lower place; **2** to come down; **3** to become lower; **fall** *noun*

falling star *noun* a shooting star

false *adjective* **1** not true or correct; **2** not faithful or loyal; **3** not real; **falsely** *adverb*

family *noun* a group made up of a parent or parents and their children; a group of people related by blood or marriage

famous *adjective* being well known and talked about; **fame** *noun*; **famed** *adjective*

¹fan *noun* an instrument used to make air move

lady's dress fan

²fan *verb* (**fanned**) to cause air to blow on something or somebody

³fan *noun* a very keen follower or supporter

¹fancy *verb* **1** to form a picture of; to imagine; **2** to believe without being certain; **3** to have a liking for or wish for; **fancy** *noun*

²fancy *adjective* more decorated, brightly coloured, or expensive than ordinary things; **fancily** *adverb*

F

far *adverb* (**farther** *or* **further**, **farthest** *or* **furthest**) **1** at or to a great distance; **2** very much

fare *noun* the price charged to carry a person on a bus, train, or taxi; ■ **fair**

farewell goodbye

farm *noun* land and buildings used for growing crops and/or keeping animals; **farm** *verb*; **farmer** *noun*

farther *see* FAR

fashion *noun* the way of dressing or behaving that is considered the best at a certain time; **fashionable** *adjective*

fast *adjective* **1** moving quickly; **2** firmly fixed; **3** showing a time that is later than the true time; **fast** *adverb*

fasten *verb* to make or become firmly fixed or closed; **fastener** *noun*

¹fat *adjective* (**fatter**) **1** having too much or a lot of fat; **2** thick and round; **fatness** *noun*

²fat *noun* **1** the material under the skin of people and animals which helps to keep them warm; **2** the white part of meat that can be used for cooking; **fatty** *adjective*

fate *noun* the power which seems to cause everything to happen; **fateful** *adjective*; ■ **fête**

father *noun* a man who has children

fault *noun* **1** a mistake; **2** a bad or weak point in your character; **faulty** *adjective*

favour *noun* **1** something kind done for somebody; **2** **in favour of** believing in or choosing; on the side of

favourite *noun* something that is liked more than others; **favourite** *adjective*

fear *noun* the feeling that you have when danger is near or when you are afraid; **fear** *verb*; **fearful** *adjective*; **fearless** *adjective*

feast *noun* **1** a specially good or grand meal; **2** a day kept in memory of some happy religious event

feat *noun* a clever action, showing strength, skill, or courage; ■ **feet**

feather *noun* one part of the soft, light covering of a bird's body; **feathery** *adjective*

February *noun* the second month of the year

feed *verb* (**feeds, feeding, fed**) to give food to

feel *verb* (**feels, feeling, felt**) **1** to touch; **2** to know through your senses; **3** to think; **feel** *noun*; **feeling** *noun*

feet *see* FOOT; ■ **feat**

fell *see* FALL

¹felt *noun* thick firm cloth made of wool

²felt *see* FEEL

felt-tip pen *noun* a pen with a soft tip made of felt

female *noun* a girl or a woman; any person or animal that gives birth to young

feminine *adjective* concerning girls or women

¹fence *noun* a wall made of wood or wire, round a garden, field, etc

²fence *verb* **1** to fight with a sword as a sport; **2** to put a fence round something

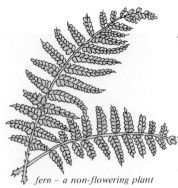
fern – a non-flowering plant

fern *noun* a plant with feathery leaves and no flowers

ferret *noun* a small animal used for catching rats and rabbits

ferry *noun* a boat for carrying people and things across a narrow stretch of water

fetch *verb* to go and get and bring back

fête (*say* fate) *noun* a large outdoor entertainment usually held to collect money for a special purpose; ■ **fate**

fever *noun* an illness in which you develop a very high temperature

few *adjective, pronoun, noun* **1** not many; not enough; **2** a small number

¹**field** *noun* **1** a piece of land on a farm usually surrounded by a fence or wall, and used for animals or crops; **2** any open area where games or sports are played, something is mined, or a certain activity is practised: **airfield, oilfield**

²**field** *verb* to catch or stop the ball in games like cricket

fierce *adjective* angry, wild, and cruel; **fiercely** *adverb;* **fierceness** *noun*

fifteen *adjective, noun* **1** the number 15; **2** a complete team of fifteen players in **rugby union** football; **3** '15' **certificate** a film that can only be watched by people aged fifteen or over; **fifteenth** *adjective, adverb (see last page)*

fifty *adjective, noun* the number 50; **fiftieth** *adjective, adverb (see last page)*

¹**fight** *verb* (**fights, fighting, fought**) **1** to use your body or weapons against somebody or something; **2** to use argument against somebody, or each other

²**fight** *noun* an act of fighting; a battle or struggle

figure *noun* **1** the shape of a person's body; **2** any of the number signs from 0 to 9; **3** a drawing or diagram

¹**file** *noun* **1** an arrangement of drawers, shelves, boxes, or cases for storing papers in an office; **2** a collection of information used or stored in a computer; **3** a metal instrument with a rough edge for making things smooth: **nail file; 4** a line of people one behind the other

²**file** *verb* **1** to put papers into a file; **2** to make something smooth with a file; **3** to walk in a line

fill *verb* **1** to make something full; to become full; **2** to block up a gap or a hole

¹**film** *noun* **1** a story shown in a cinema or on television; **2** the material in a camera on which you take photographs; **3** a thin layer of any material

²**film** *verb* to make a cinema picture

F

filthy *adjective* very dirty

fin *noun* a part of a fish that helps it to swim

final *adjective* last; coming at the end; **finally** *adverb*

find *verb* (**finds, finding, found**) **1** to discover something after you have been looking for it; **2 find out** to learn; **3** to discover somebody or something by chance

¹fine *noun* money paid as a punishment; **fine** *verb*

²fine *adjective* **1** beautiful and good; **2** very thin; **3** in very small bits; **4** bright and sunny; not wet; **finely** *adverb*

finger *noun* **1** one of the five movable parts at the end of your hand: **fingernail**; **2** *keep your **fingers** crossed* to hope for the best

¹finish *verb* to bring something to an end; to stop

²finish *noun* the end or last part

fir also **firtree** *noun* a straight tree that has leaves shaped like needles, and cones; ■ **fur**

¹fire *noun* **1** the heat and light given off by things that are burning: **fire engine, fire escape, fire alarm, firework**; **2** a heap of burning wood or coal for cooking, heating, etc: **fireplace, firelight, fire lighter, fireguard**; **3** a small gas or electric heater; **4** shooting by guns; **5 catch fire** to begin to burn; **6 set on fire** also **set fire to** to light something not really meant to burn

²fire *verb* to shoot a gun

¹firm *adjective* **1** strong; solid; hard; **2** steady and not easily moved; **firmly** *adverb*; **firmness** *noun*

²firm *noun* a business

first *adjective, noun, adverb* **1** before any others; **2** the person, thing, or group to do or be something first; **3** for the first time; **4 at first** at the beginning *(see last page)*

¹fish *noun (plural* **fish** *or* **fishes***)* a creature which lives in water and uses its fins and tail to swim

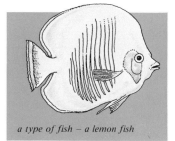

a type of fish – a lemon fish

²fish *verb* to try to catch fish; to look for something; **fisherman** *noun*

fist *noun* the hand with the fingers closed in tightly

¹fit *noun* **1** a sudden short attack of an illness; **2** a strong feeling

²fit *adjective* (**fitter**) **1** right and good enough; **2** in good health; **fitness** *noun*

³fit *verb* (**fitted**) to be the right kind, size, or shape

five *adjective, noun* the number 5; **fifth** *adjective, adverb (see last page)*

fix *verb* **1** to fasten firmly; **2** to arrange; **3** to cook or prepare; **4** to put in order or mend

Union Jack
(United Kingdom)

Stars and Stripes
(United States of America)

Hammer and Sickle
(USSR)

flag *noun* a piece of cloth with a pattern or picture on it, used as the sign of a country, club, etc

flake *noun* a small thin piece

flame *noun* a bright red or yellow piece of burning gas

flan *noun* a round flat open pie

¹flap *noun* a wide flat thin part of anything that folds or hangs down over an opening

²flap *verb* (flapped) 1 to wave slowly up and down or to and fro, making a noise

¹flash *verb* 1 to shine for a moment; 2 to move very fast

²flash *noun* a sudden quick bright light

¹flat *adjective* (flatter) 1 smooth and level with no pieces sticking out; 2 below the true note; 3 not having enough air in it; **flatten** *verb;* **flatness** *noun*

²flat also **apartment** *noun* a set of rooms on one floor of a building

flavour *noun* a taste; **flavour** *verb;* **flavouring** *noun;* **flavourless** *adjective*

flaw *noun* a small sign of damage, such as a mark or crack, that makes something not perfect; **flaw** *verb;* **flawless** *adjective;* **floor**

flea *noun* a small jumping insect that feeds on blood; **flee**

flee *verb* (fleeing, fled) to escape by hurrying; **flea**

flesh *noun* 1 the soft substance, including fat and muscle, that covers the bones and lies under the skin; 2 the meat of animals used as food; 3 the soft part of a fruit or vegetable that can be eaten; **fleshy** *adjective*

flew *see* FLY; **flue**

flex *noun* a length of wire for carrying electricity

flight *noun* 1 the act of flying; 2 a trip by plane; 3 a group of birds or aircraft flying together; 4 a set of stairs

float *verb* to stay at the top of liquid or to be held up in air without sinking

floe *noun* a large piece of ice floating in the sea; **flow**

¹flood *noun* the covering with water of a place that is usually dry

²flood *verb* to fill or become covered with water

floor *noun* 1 the part of a room on which you stand; 2 one level of a building; **flaw**

floppy disk *noun* a small computer disk made of plastic on which information and programs are stored

flour *noun* powder made from grain and used for making bread and cakes; **floury** *adjective;* **flower**

F

flow *verb* to run or spread smoothly; to pour; **flow** *noun;* **flowing** *adjective;* ▣ **floe**

flowchart also **flow diagram** *noun* a drawing in which shapes, lines, and arrows are used to show the order of the steps or the actions needed to do something or to solve a problem

fog *noun* very thick mist; **foggy** *adjective*

fold *verb* to turn or bend one part of something on to another part of it; **fold** *noun*

follow *verb* **1** to come or go after somebody or something; **2** to go in the same direction; **3** to understand; **follower** *noun*

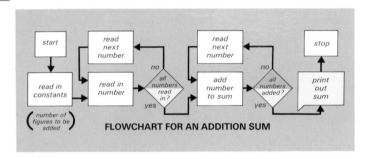

FLOWCHART FOR AN ADDITION SUM

¹**flower** *noun* the part of a plant which makes the seeds and is usually coloured; ▣ **flour**

²**flower** *verb* to produce flowers; ▣ **flour**

flown *see* FLY

flue *noun* a narrow passage up which smoke or heat passes; the inside of a chimney; ▣ **flew**

flute *noun* a musical instrument which you blow

¹**fly** *verb* (**flies, flying, flew, flown**) **1** to move through the air using wings or in a machine; **2** to go quickly

²**fly** *noun* a small insect with wings

fond *adjective* **1** loving; **2 to be fond of** to have a great liking or love for; **fondly** *adverb*

food *noun* something for eating

¹**fool** *noun* a silly person; **foolish** *adjective;* **foolishly** *adverb*

²**fool** *verb* **1** to deceive or trick; **2** to speak or behave in a silly way

foot *noun (plural* **feet***)* **1** the part of the body at the end of the leg, on which a person or an animal stands: **footpath, footstep, footwear; 2** the lowest or bottom part of anything; **3** a measure of length equal to 12 inches or about 0.305 metres *(see last page)*

football *noun* a game in which two teams kick a ball and try to get goals; **footballer** *noun*

for *preposition* **1** meant to belong to, be given to, or be used in this way; **2** in order to reach, get, or have; **3** as a sign of; instead of; **4** in support of; **5** because of; **6** at the price of; **7** the length or distance of; ◼ **fore, four**

forbid *verb* (**forbids, forbidding, forbade** *or* **forbad, forbidden**) to tell somebody not to do something

force *noun* **1** strength or power; **2** a group of specially trained people; **force** *verb*

fore *adjective, adverb* front; in or near the front part; ◼ **for, four**

forecast *verb* to say what you think will happen; **forecast** *noun*

forehead *noun* the part of the face above the eyes and below the hair

foreign *adjective* of or from another country; **foreigner** *noun*

forest *noun* a large area of land covered with trees and bushes

forever, also **for ever** *adverb* always; for all time

foreword *noun* a short piece at the beginning of a book, not written by the author; ◼ **forward**

forget *verb* (**forgets, forgetting, forgot, forgotten**) not to remember; to no longer have the memory of something

forgive *verb* (**forgives, forgiving, forgave, forgiven**) to say or feel that you are no longer angry about something and will not punish somebody

fork *noun* **1** an instrument with a handle at one end and two or more points at the other; **2** a place where something divides, or one of the divided parts

¹form *noun* **1** shape or appearance; **2** a kind or sort; **3** a special paper on which certain things must be written down; **4** a long wooden seat without a back; **5** a class in a school

²form *verb* **1** to take shape or appear; **2** to make; **3** to make up

fort *noun* a strong building which can protect people from attack; ◼ **fought**

fortnight *noun* two weeks

fortune *noun* **1** whatever happens in the future to a person by good or bad luck; **2** a great amount of money; **fortunate** *adjective;* **fortunately** *adverb*

forty *adjective, noun* the number 40; **fortieth** *adjective, adverb (see last page)*

¹forward also **forwards** *adverb* **1** towards the front in the direction you are facing; **2** to an earlier time; **3 look forward to** to think something will be pleasant; **forward** *adjective;* ◼ **foreword**

²forward *verb* to send on letters or parcels to a new address; ◼ **foreword**

fought *see* FIGHT; ◼ **fort**

found *see* FIND

fountain *noun* a stream of water that shoots straight up into the air from a pipe

F

four *adjective, noun* the number 4; **fourth** *adjective, adverb (see last page);* ■ **for, fore**

fourteen *adjective, noun* the number 14; **fourteenth** *adjective, adverb (see last page)*

fox *noun (female* **vixen***, young* **cub***)* a small wild animal like a dog, with a bushy tail and reddish fur

fraction *noun* a very small piece or amount; a part of a whole number

frame *noun* **1** the rods and bars which are fitted together to make something or round which something is built: **framework; 2** the pieces of wood, plastic, or metal round a picture; **frame** *verb*

free *adjective* **1** able to do what you like; not tied up or in prison; **2** not costing any money; given away; **3** not busy; not being used; **free** *verb;* **freedom** *noun*

freeze *verb* (**freezes, freezing, froze, frozen**) **1** to harden or become solid as a result of great cold; **2 deep freeze** to keep and store food by freezing it

freezer *also* **deep freeze** *noun* a large refrigerator for frozen food

frequency *noun* **1** the number of times something happens or is repeated during a certain amount of time; **2** a particular number of radio waves per second at which a radio signal is broadcast

fresh *adjective* **1** new or different; **2** newly made; **3** newly picked, grown, or supplied; **4** not preserved in tins, bottles, etc; not frozen;

5 clean or pure; **6** not tired; healthy; **freshness** *noun;* **freshly** *adverb*

Friday *noun* the sixth day of the week

fridge *see* REFRIGERATOR

friend *noun* a person you like and enjoy talking to and going out with; somebody who is kind and helpful; **friendliness** *noun;* **friendly** *adjective;* **friendship** *noun*

frighten *verb* to make somebody afraid

fro *see* TO AND FRO

frog *noun* a small animal that can live in water and on land and has long back legs for swimming and jumping

common frog

from *preposition* **1** beginning at; **2** given or sent by; **3** out of; **4** using; **5** because of

front *noun* **1** the position directly before somebody or something; **2** the surface or part facing forwards, outwards, or upwards; **3** the most forward or important position; **4 in front of** in the position facing forward; whilst somebody is present; **front** *adjective*

frost *noun* white powdery ice that forms on outside surfaces when the weather is very cold; **frosty** *adjective*

frown *verb* to draw your eyebrows down and wrinkle your forehead when angry or worried; **frown** *noun*

froze *see* FREEZE

frozen *see* FREEZE

fruit *noun* the part of a tree or bush that contains seeds and is often sweet and used for food

fry *verb* to cook in hot fat or oil

fuel *noun* material that is used for producing heat or power by burning

full *adjective* holding as much or as many people, objects, liquids, etc, as possible; **fully** *adverb*

full stop *noun* a point (.) showing the end of a sentence or a shortened form of a word

fully grown also **full grown** *adjective* completely developed; not going to get any larger

fun *noun* amusement and enjoyment

funeral *noun* all the things concerned with burying a dead person

a type of fungus – field mushrooms

fungus *noun (plural* **fungi** *or* **funguses***)* a type of plant without flowers, leaves, or green colouring matter

funny *adjective* **1** amusing; **2** strange; unusual

fur *noun* the soft hair that covers the body of animals such as bears, rabbits, cats, etc; **furry** *adjective;* ■ **fir**

furniture *noun* all the things used in a house or room such as beds, chairs, tables, etc

further *see* FAR

furthest *see* FAR

fuse *noun* a short thin piece of wire placed in something electrical, which melts if too much power is used and prevents fires or other damage

¹**future** *noun* **1** the time that will come; **2** things that will happen to somebody or something

²**future** *noun, adjective* an action that will happen later: **future tense**

an electrical fuse

galaxy *noun* a very large group of stars

gale *noun* a strong wind

gallon *noun* a measure for liquids equal to eight pints or 4.55 litres *(see last page)*

gallop *noun* the fastest movement of a horse; **gallop** *verb*

game *noun* **1** something you play, with rules which tell you what to do; **2** wild animals or birds which are hunted for food

gander *noun* a male goose

gang *noun* a group of people who go around together

gaol *see* jail; ▪**goal**

gap *noun* an empty space; a narrow opening

garage *noun* a place where cars are kept or repaired

garden *noun* a piece of land, near a house or in a public place, on which flowers, trees, and vegetables may be grown; **garden** *verb;* **gardener** *noun;* **gardening** *noun*

gas *noun (plural* **gases***)* **1** a substance like air, which is not solid or liquid; **2** a substance like this which is used for heating and cooking

gate *noun* a sort of door which closes an opening in a fence or wall

gather *verb* to come or bring together

gauge (*say* gage) *noun* an instrument for measuring such things as the amount of rain or the width of wire

gave *see* GIVE

gaze *verb* to look steadily at something for a long time; **gaze** *noun*

gear *noun* **1** a set of toothed wheels in an engine or a machine, which helps to control the power, speed, or direction of movement; **2** clothes

geese *see* GOOSE

general *adjective* about, for, or by everybody or everything

generally *adverb* usually

generous *adjective* ready to give money or be helpful or kind; **generously** *adverb*

gentle *adjective* kind and friendly; soft and quiet; **gentleness** *noun* **gently** *adverb*

gentleman *noun* a man who behaves well and can be trusted

geography *noun* the study of the world and its countries, seas, rivers, towns, etc; **geographer** *noun;* **geographical** *adjective;* **geographically** *adverb*

gerbil *noun* a small jumping animal like a large mouse, often kept as a pet

this modern tyre pressure gauge still shows the pressure reading when removed from the tyre

germs – as seen through a microscope

germ *noun* a very small creature living on food or dirt or in the body, so causing disease

German measles *noun* a disease in which red spots appear for a short time on your body

get *verb* (**gets, getting, got**) **1** to have; to receive; **2** to obtain or buy; to take; **3** to become; **4** to make happen; **5** to cause somebody to do something; **6** to arrive; **7** to catch an illness; **8 have got to** must

ghost *noun* the spirit of a dead person or animal which appears again; **ghostly** *adjective*

giant *noun* a very big, strong man who is written about in fairy stories; **giant** *adjective*

gift *noun* something which is given; a present

gipsy also **gypsy** *noun* a member of a race of people who travel from place to place

giraffe *noun* an animal with a very long neck and legs and a yellowish coat with dark spots

girl *noun* a young female person

give *verb* (**gives, giving, gave, given**) **1** to hand something over to somebody; **2** to let somebody have something; **3** to pay; **4** to cause to

experience; **5** to produce or supply; **6** to show; to tell in words; **7** to do an action

glad *adjective* pleased and happy; **gladly** *adverb;* **gladness** *noun*

glance *verb* to look quickly; **glance** *noun*

glass *noun* **1** a hard clear material used for windows; **2** a drinking container made of this material

glasses *noun* two pieces of specially shaped glass held in a frame and worn in front of the eyes to help somebody to see better

glider *noun* a plane that flies on a current of air

glove *noun* a covering for the hand

glow *verb* **1** to give out heat and/or light without flames or smoke; **2** to look or feel warm or excited; **glow** *noun*

¹**glue** *noun* a sticky substance used for joining things together

²**glue** *verb* (**glues, gluing or glueing, glued**) to join with glue

gnaw (*say* naw) *verb* to keep biting something until it is worn away; ■ **nor**

go *verb* (**goes, going, went, gone**) **1** to leave; **2** to travel or move; **3** to reach; **4** to do or start something; **5** to have a usual or proper place; **6** to work properly; **7** to become; **8** to wear out; to disappear; to die

goal *noun* the place where the ball must go for a point to be won in football, hockey, etc: **goalkeeper**; ■ **gaol**

G

goat *noun (young* **kid**) an animal like a sheep, that has horns and gives milk and a hairy sort of wool

god *noun* **1** (feminine **goddess**) a being to whom people pray because they feel he or she has power over men and the world; **2 God** the being to whom Christians, Jews, and Muslims pray

goes *see* GO

going *see* GO

gold *noun* **1** a yellow metal that costs a lot of money and is used for making coins, jewellery, etc; **2** the colour of this metal; **gold, golden** *adjective*

goldfish *noun* a small fish that is often kept as a pet

golf *noun* a game in which a small hard ball is hit with special **golf clubs** into holes on a **golf course**; **golfer** *noun*

gone *see* GO

¹good *adjective* (**better, best**) **1** having the right qualities; **2** kind; helpful; **3** well-behaved; **4** useful or suitable; **5** enjoyable; **6** able to do something; **7** large in size, amount, etc; **8** used in greetings: **Good morning, Goodbye**; **goodness** noun

²good *noun* what is right or useful

goods *noun* things which are bought, sold, or owned

goose *noun (plural* **geese**) *(male* **gander**, *young* **gosling**) a large bird with webbed feet

gooseberry *noun* a small round green berry that grows on a bush

gorilla *noun* a large animal that looks like a man, is very strong, and lives in Africa; ■**guerrilla**

gosling *noun* a young goose

got *see* GET

government *noun* the people who rule a country

grab *verb* (**grabbed**) to take hold of something with a sudden, rough movement; **grab** *noun*

gradual *adjective* happening slowly and little by little; **gradually** *adverb*

grain *noun* **1** a seed of rice, wheat, etc; **2** a small piece

gram *noun* a measure of weight equal to 0.035 ounces *(see last page)*

gramophone *noun* a record player: **gramophone record**

grand *adjective* very large and fine

grandchild *noun (plural* **grandchildren**) the child of your child: **granddaughter, grandson**

grandparent *noun* the father or mother of your father or mother: **grandfather, grandmother**

grape *noun* a small round juicy fruit, usually green or dark purple, that grows in bunches and is used for making wine

grapefruit *noun* a large yellow fruit that is like an orange but not as sweet

grapefruit – a citrus fruit

66

graphics *noun* information in the form of pictures, especially those that can be seen on a computer screen

grass *noun* a green plant that grows close to the ground and has thin leaves that cattle eat; **grassy** *adjective*

grasshopper *noun* a jumping insect which makes a sharp noise by rubbing parts of its body together

¹**grate** *noun* the bars and frame which hold the wood, coal, etc, in a fireplace; ◼ **great**

²**grate** *verb* 1 to rub food on a hard rough surface so as to break it into small pieces; 2 to make a sharp unpleasant sound; **grater** *noun;* **grating** *noun;* ◼ **great**

grateful *adjective* feeling or showing thanks to somebody; **gratefully** *adverb*

¹**grave** *noun* the place in the ground where a dead person is buried

²**grave** *adjective* serious; **gravely** *adverb*

gravity *noun* the natural force by which things are attracted to the Earth

gravy *noun* a sauce made from the juice which comes out of meat as it cooks

grease *noun* oil or fat; **grease** *verb;* **greasy** *adjective*

great *adjective* 1 very large, important, etc; 2 very good, enjoyable, or pleasant; 3 unusually good at something; **greatly** *adverb;* ◼ **grate**

great-grandchild *noun* the son or daughter of a grandchild: **great-granddaughter, great-grandson**

great-grandparent *noun* the father or mother of a grandparent: **great-grandfather, great-grandmother**

greed *noun* a wish to obtain more of something than you need, such as food or money; **greedy** *adjective*

green *noun* 1 a colour between yellow and blue, which is that of leaves and grass; 2 a smooth piece of grass used for a special purpose; **green** *adjective;* **greenish** *adjective*

greengrocer *noun* a person who sells vegetables and fruit

a greenhouse

greenhouse *noun* a building made of glass, used to protect growing plants

greet *verb* to welcome with words or actions; **greeting** *noun*

grew *see* GROW

grey *noun* a colour like black mixed with white which is that of ashes and of rain clouds; **grey** *adjective;* **greyish** *adjective*

grin *noun* a wide smile that shows your teeth; **grin** *verb*

grip *verb* (**gripped**) to take a very tight hold of something; **grip** *noun*

G

groan *verb* to make a deep low sound to show you are in pain or are very sad; **groan** *noun*

grocer *noun* a person who sells foods, like flour, sugar, rice, and other things for the home, such as matches and soap

ground *noun* **1** the surface of the Earth; **2** soil; earth

group *noun* a number of people or things placed together; a set; **group** *verb*

grow *verb* (**grows, growing, grew, grown**) **1** to get bigger, taller, or longer; **2** to live and be able to develop; **3** to cause to or allow to grow; **4** to become; **growth** *noun*

grown-up *noun* a fully grown person; **grown-up** *adjective*

grubby *adjective* dirty

grunt *noun* a short deep rough sound like that of a pig; **grunt** *verb*

guarantee *noun* a promise to repair or replace something if it is faulty; **guarantee** *verb*

¹guard *noun* **1** a person who guards; **2** somebody in charge of a train; **3** something which covers and protects: **fireguard, mudguard**

²guard *verb* to watch over and keep safe; **guardian** *noun*

guerrilla also **guerilla** *noun* a person who fights secretly against the government or against an army; ■ **gorilla**

guess *verb* to say something is correct or not correct without really knowing; **guess** *noun*

guest *noun* a person you invite to stay in your home; a visitor

guide *noun* something or somebody that shows the way or gives directions; **guide** *verb*; **guidance** *noun*

guilt *noun* knowing you have done wrong; **guiltily** *adverb*; **guiltless** *adjective*; **guilty** *adjective*

guinea pig *noun* a small furry animal, often kept as a pet

an electric guitar

guitar *noun* a musical instrument with six strings, played by plucking

¹gum *noun* the part of the mouth in which your teeth are fixed

²gum *noun* **1** a substance used to stick things together; **2** a sweet

gun *noun* a weapon from which bullets are fired

gutter *noun* an open pipe at the edge of a roof or a channel at the side of the road to carry away water

gymnastics, gym *noun* the training of the body by exercises; **gymnasium** *noun*; **gymnast** *noun*

gypsy *see* GIPSY

habit *noun* **1** something you always do; **2** a special kind of clothing, especially that worn by monks and nuns

had *see* HAVE

haddock *noun* a common sea fish that is eaten

hadn't *see* HAVE

hail *noun* little balls of ice that fall from the clouds; **hail** *verb*

hair *noun* the fine threads that grow from the skin of a person or animal: **hairbrush, haircut, hairdresser; hairy** *adjective;* ■ **hare**

¹half *noun, pronoun (plural* **halves)** one of the two equal parts into which something is or could be divided; ½; 50%; **half** *adjective;* **halfway** *adjective, adverb*

²half *adverb* **1** partly; not completely; **2 half past** thirty minutes after

hall *noun* **1** a large room in which meetings, dances, etc, can be held; **2** the space just inside the front door of a house, from which the rooms open; ■ **haul**

Hallowe'en also **Halloween** *noun* the night of 31st October

ham *noun* meat from a pig's leg

hammer *noun* a tool with a heavy metal head for hitting in nails, or for breaking things; **hammer** *verb*

a claw hammer

hamster *noun* a small furry animal with pockets in its cheeks for storing food that is often kept as a pet

¹hand *noun* **1** the movable part at the end of the arm, including the fingers, with which you hold things; **2** a pointer or needle on a clock or machine; **handful** *noun*

²hand *verb* to give from your own hand into somebody else's

handbag *noun* a small bag for money and personal things

handkerchief *noun (plural* **handkerchiefs** *or* **handkerchieves)** a piece of cloth or thin soft paper for drying the nose, eyes, etc

¹handle *noun* a part of something for holding it or for opening it: **handlebars**

²handle *verb* **1** to feel or move with your hands; **2** to deal with; to control

handsome *adjective* good-looking and attractive; **handsomely** *adverb*

¹hang *verb* (**hangs, hanging, hung**) **1** to fix something at the top so that the lower part is free; **2** to be in such a position

²hang *verb* (**hangs, hanging, hanged**) to kill or die, as a punishment for a crime, by dropping with a rope round the neck

happen *verb* **1** to take place; to be; **2** to do by chance; **happening** *noun*

happy *adjective* feeling very pleased; giving pleasure; **happily** *adverb;* **happiness** *noun*

H

harass *verb* to annoy or trouble somebody; **harassment** *noun*

harbour *noun* an area of sheltered water where ships are safe from rough seas

harvest *noun* **1** the time of year when crops are picked; **2** the amount picked; **harvest** *verb*

has *see* HAVE

hasn't *see* HAVE

a harbour wall keeps out rough seas so that boats can be moored safely

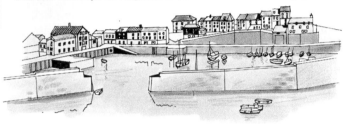

¹**hard** *adjective* **1** firm, solid, and not easily broken, pressed down, bent, etc; **2** difficult to do or understand; **harden** *verb*

²**hard** *adverb* **1** with great effort; **2** a lot; very much

hardly *adverb* almost not at all; only just

hardware *noun* **1** goods for the home and garden, such as pans, tools, etc; **2** the machines that make up a computer

hare *noun (young* **leveret***)* an animal like a rabbit, with long ears and long back legs that make it able to run fast; **hair**

harm *noun* damage; wrong; **harm** *verb;* **harmful** *adjective;* **harmfully** *adverb;* **harmfulness** *noun*

harp *noun* a large musical instrument with strings, played by stroking or plucking with the hands; **harpist** *noun*

hat *noun* a covering placed on top of the head

hate *verb* to have a strong dislike for something or somebody; **hate** *noun;* **hateful** *adjective;* **hatred** *noun*

haul *verb* to pull hard; **hall**

haunt *verb* to appear in a place as a ghost

have *verb* **(has, having, had, haven't, hasn't, hadn't)** **1** also **have got** to possess or own; **2** to receive or take; **3** to enjoy or experience; **4** to cause to be done; **5 had better** ought to; **6 have to** also **have got to** must

hay *noun* grass that has been cut and dried and is used as food for horses, sheep, and cows: **haystack, haymaking**

he *pronoun* **(him, himself)** that male person or animal

70

¹**head** *noun* **1** the part of the body which contains the eyes, ears, nose and mouth, and the brain − in man on top of the body, in other animals in front: **headache, headband, headfirst; 2** the chief person; a ruler or leader; **3** the front side of a coin which often has a picture of the ruler's head: *heads or tails?;* **4** the top or front part of something; **5 head over heels** turning over in the air headfirst

²**head** *verb* **1** to be at the front or in charge of something; **2** to strike a ball with the head; **header** *noun*

headmaster feminine **headmistress** *noun* the teacher in charge of a school

headphones *noun* a piece of apparatus made to fit over the ears, for listening to a radio, tape recorder, etc

headphones

heal *verb* to make or become better; ▣**heel**

health *noun* **1** the state of being well, without any illness; **2** the condition of the body; **healthily** *adverb;* **healthiness** *noun;* **healthy** *adjective*

heap *noun* a pile or mass of things one on top of another; **heap** *verb*

hear *verb* (**hears, hearing, heard**) **1** to receive and understand by using the ears; **2** to get news of; to be told; ▣**here**

heart *noun* **1** the organ inside the chest which pumps the blood round the body: **heartbeat, heart attack; 2** the centre of your feelings; your true nature; **3** a playing card with one or more figures of this shape printed on it in red; **4** the centre or middle of something; **heartless** *adjective;* **hearty** *adjective*

¹**heat** *verb* to make or become warm or hot; **heater** *noun*

²**heat** *noun* **1** hotness; warmth; **2** a part of a race or competition to decide who will be in the final

heaven *noun* the place where God or the gods are said to live and where good people are believed to go after they die

heavy *adjective* **1** of great weight, and not easy to move or lift; **2** of unusual force or amount; **heavily** *adverb;* **heaviness** *noun*

hectare (**say** hektair) *noun* a measure of land equal to 10,000 square metres or about 2.47 acres *(see last page)*

hedge *noun* a row of bushes or small trees acting as a fence

hedgehog *noun* a small insect-eating animal which comes out only at night. It rolls itself into a ball and sticks up sharp spines when it is afraid

H

71

heel *noun* **1** the back part of the foot; **2** the part of a shoe, sock, etc, that covers this; the raised part of a shoe underneath the foot; heal

height *noun* how tall or high something is

heir *(say* air*)* feminine **heiress** *noun* a person who gets money, property, or a title when somebody dies; air

held *see* HOLD

helicopters play a vital role in mountain and air-sea rescue

helicopter *noun* a type of aircraft which is made to fly by a set of large fast-turning metal blades, and which can land in a small space, take off straight from the ground, and hover in the air

hell *noun* the place where the Devil is said to live and where bad people are believed to go after they die

hello used as a greeting

helmet *noun* a hard covering to protect the head, worn by soldiers, policemen, etc

¹help *verb* **1** to do part of the work for somebody; to be of use; **2** to avoid or prevent; **3** to serve food or drink; **helper** *noun*

²help *noun* **1** the act of helping; **2** something or somebody that helps; **helpful** *adjective;* **helpfully** *adverb;* **helpfulness** *noun*

hem *noun* the sewn bottom edge of a skirt, dress, etc; **hem** *verb*

hen *noun (male* **cock***; young* **chick***)* a female chicken often kept for its eggs on farms

¹her *adjective* belonging to her

²her *see* SHE

herd *noun* a group of animals of one kind that live and feed together; **herd** *verb*

here *adverb* **1** at, in, or to this place; **2** at this point of time; hear

herring *noun* a fish which swims in large shoals in the sea and is eaten for food

hers *pronoun* that/those belonging to her

herself *see* SHE

hibernate *verb* to be in or to go into a state like a long sleep during the winter, as some animals do; **hibernation** *noun*

hide *verb* **(hides, hiding, hid, hidden)** to put or keep out of sight; to make or keep secret

hi-fi *noun* tape recorders, record players, and other equipment for reproducing sound very clearly

high *adjective, adverb* **1** at a point well above the ground; **2** important; chief; **3** near the top of the set of sounds that the ear can hear

high chair *noun* a chair with long legs and a tray, at which a baby or small child can sit

hijack *verb* to force the driver of a plane, train, etc, to take you somewhere or give you something; **hijacker** *noun*

hill *noun* a raised piece of ground; a small mountain: **uphill, downhill; hilly** *adjective*

him *see* HE; ▣ **hymn**

himself *see* HE

Hindu *noun* a person who follows **Hinduism**, the main religion of India

hip *noun* the fleshy part of either side of the human body above the legs

hippopotamus *noun (plural* **hippopotamuses** *or* **hippopotami, hippos)** a large animal with a thick skin, that lives near water

¹his *adjective* belonging to him

²his *pronoun* that/those belonging to him

history *noun* the study of past events; **historical** *adjective;* **historically** *adverb*

¹hit *verb* (**hits, hitting, hit**) to strike; to come against something with force

²hit *noun* **1** a blow; a stroke; **2** a successful song, film, play, etc

hive also **beehive** *noun* a place where bees live, like a small hut or box

hobby *noun* an enjoyable activity you do in your free time

hockey *noun* a game played by two teams of eleven players each, on a field with sticks and a ball

hog *noun* a male pig

hold *verb* (**holds, holding, held**) **1** to keep or support with the hands; **2** to contain; **3** to possess; **4** to arrange and give an event, such as a party; **hold** *noun;* **holder** *noun*

hole *noun* **1** an empty space or opening within something; **2** the home of a small animal; ▣ **whole**

holiday *noun* a time of rest from work or school

hollow *adjective* having an empty space inside; not solid

holly *noun* a small tree with dark green prickly leaves and red berries

hologram *noun* a picture produced by lasers; **holograph** *verb;* **holography** *noun*

holy *adjective* of God and religion

home *noun* the house or place where somebody lives; **home** *adjective;* **homeless** *adjective* **homelessness** *noun*

honest (*say* onest) *adjective* not telling lies or deceiving people; fair and true; **honestly** *adverb;* **honesty** *noun*

honey *noun* the sweet sticky material produced by bees

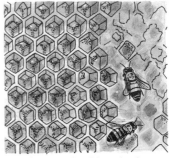

a honeycomb, with worker bees

H

73

honour (*say* onor) *noun* great respect; **honour** *verb*; **honourable** *adjective*

hood *noun* **1** a covering for the head and neck usually fastened to the back of a coat; **2** a folding cover over a car, pram, etc

hoof *noun* (*plural* **hoofs** *or* **hooves**) the hard foot of certain animals, such as horses and cows

¹hook *noun* a curved piece of metal, plastic, etc, for catching something on or hanging things on

²hook *verb* **1** to catch with a hook; **2** to hang on or fasten with a hook

hoop *noun* a round band of wood or metal; a ring

hop *verb* (**hopped**) **1** to jump on one leg; **2** to move along by jumping, like some birds and small creatures

hope *verb* to wish for and expect; **hope** *noun*; **hopeful** *adjective*; **hopefully** *adverb*; **hopeless** *adjective*; **hopelessly** *adverb*

horizon *noun* the place where the sky seems to meet the Earth or sea; **horizontal** *adjective*

horn *noun* **1** one of two hard pointed growths on the top of the heads of some animals such as cattle, sheep, and goats; **2** the material that these growths are made of; **3** a musical instrument that you blow; **4** an instrument in a car, bus, etc, that makes a noise to warn people; **horned** *adjective*; **hornless** *adjective*

horrendous *adjective* really terrible; causing great fear

horrible *adjective* very unkind, unpleasant, or ugly; **horribly** *adverb*

horror *noun* great shock, fear, and dislike; **horrid** *adjective*; **horridly** *adverb*; **horridness** *noun*

horse *noun* a large strong animal with a mane, tail, and hooves, that people ride and use for pulling and carrying heavy things; **horseback, horsehair, horseshoe**

hose *also* **hosepipe** *noun* a piece of rubber or plastic tube that can direct water onto fires, a garden, etc

hospital *noun* a place where ill people stay and have treatment

host *feminine* **hostess** *noun* a person who receives and looks after guests

hot *adjective* (**hotter**) **1** having a lot of heat; **2** having a burning taste; **hotness** *noun*

hotel *noun* a building where people can stay if they pay

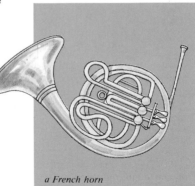

a French horn

hour (*say* our) *noun* a measure of time; sixty minutes; **hourly** *adverb*;  **our**

house *noun* a building for people to live in: **household, housekeeper, housewife, housework**

House of Commons *noun* the lower, but more powerful, of the two parts of the British Parliament

House of Lords *noun* the upper, but less powerful, of the two parts of the British Parliament

hover *verb* to stay in the air in one place

hovercraft *noun* (*trademark*) a sort of boat that moves over land or water by means of a strong force of air underneath

how *adverb* **1** in what way or by what means; **2** in what condition of health or mind; **3** by what amount

howl *noun* a long loud cry like that made by wolves and dogs; **howl** *verb*

hug *verb* (**hugged**) to hold tightly in the arms; **hug** *noun*

huge *adjective* very big; **hugeness** *noun*

hum *verb* (**hummed**) **1** to make a buzzing sound like a bee; **2** to sing with the lips closed; **hum** *noun*

¹human *adjective* of or like a person

²human also **human being** *noun* a man, woman, or child, not an animal

humour *noun* the ability to laugh at things or make other people laugh; **humorous** *adjective*

this road sign shows a hump-back bridge ahead

hump *noun* a lump or round part which sticks out

hundred *adjective, noun* the number 100; **hundredth** *adjective, adverb* (*see last page*)

hung *see* HANG

hunger *noun* the wish or need for food; **hungrily** *adverb*; **hungry** *adjective*

hunt *verb* **1** to chase and kill animals and birds either for food or sport; **2** to search for; **hunt** *noun*; **hunter** *noun*

hurricane *noun* a violent wind storm

hurry *verb* to move or do something quickly; **hurry** *noun*

hurt *verb* (**hurts, hurting, hurt**) to cause pain and/or injury; to damage; **hurtful** *adjective*

husband *noun* the man to whom a woman is married

hut *noun* a small building, often made of wood

hutch *noun* a small box or cage for keeping rabbits in

hydrogen *noun* a colourless gas that is lighter than air and burns very easily

hyena *noun* a wild animal like a dog, that has a cry like a laugh

hymn *noun* a song to or about God;  **him**

hyphen *noun* a short line (-) that can join words or parts of words

I *pronoun* (**me, myself**) the person speaking

ice *noun* water which has frozen to a solid; **icy** *adjective*

ice cream *noun* a sweet frozen mixture, usually containing milk products and eggs

icicle *noun* a pointed stick of ice formed when running water freezes

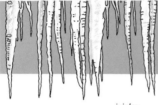

icicles

icing *noun* a sweet and either creamy or hard covering for cakes, biscuits, etc

idea *noun* a picture in the mind; a thought

ideal *adjective* perfect; the best possible

identical *adjective* exactly the same

identify *verb* to say who somebody is or what something is; **identification** *noun;* **identity** *noun*

idle *adjective* **1** not working; not doing anything; **2** lazy; **idleness** *noun;* **idly** *adverb;* ▣**idol**

idol *noun* **1** a statue worshipped as a god; **2** somebody who is greatly loved or admired; ▣**idle**

i.e. that is to say

if *conjunction* on condition that; whether

ignorant *adjective* not knowing much; not having been taught; **ignorance** *noun*

ignore *verb* to take no notice of; to pretend somebody or something is not there

¹ill *adjective* not well

²ill *adverb* (**worse, worst**) badly, cruelly, or unpleasantly: *The child has been ill-treated*

illness *noun* a disease; sickness

illustration *noun* a picture to go with the words of a book, a speaker, etc; **illustrate** *verb*

imagine *verb* **1** to form a picture of something in the mind; **2** to suppose or have an idea about; **imaginary** *adjective;* **imagination** *noun*

immediate *adjective* done or needed at once; **immediately** *adverb*

impatient *adjective* not able to wait for something to happen; **impatience** *noun;* **impatiently** *adverb*

important *adjective* powerful; of great value; **importance** *noun;* **importantly** *adverb*

impossible *adjective* not possible; not able to be done; **impossibility** *noun;* **impossibly** *adverb*

impress *verb* to cause strong good feelings; to have a strong effect on the mind; **impression** *noun;* **impressive** *adjective*

improve *verb* to make or get better; **improvement** *noun*

in *preposition, adverb* **1** contained or surrounded by something; within; inside; **2** during; at the time of; ▣**inn**

inch *noun* a measure of length equal to 1/12 of a foot or about 0.025 metres *(see last page)*

include *verb* to have or put in as a part; to contain

increase *verb* to make or become larger in amount or number; **increase** *noun;* **increasingly** *adverb*

incredible *adjective* too strange or good to be believed; **incredibly** *adverb*

indeed *adverb* really; certainly

independent *adjective* not needing other things or people; **independence** *noun;* **independently** *adverb*

indigestion *noun* illness or pain caused by the stomach not being able to deal with the food which has been eaten

indigo *noun* a dark purple-blue colour

indoor *adjective* done, used, etc, indoors

indoors *adverb* to, in, or into the inside of a building

industry *noun* a particular sort of work, usually employing lots of people and using machines; **industrial** *adjective*

infant *noun* a very young child

infect *verb* to put disease into a person's body; **infection** *noun;* **infectious** *adjective*

influence *verb* to have an effect on

inform *verb* to tell; **information** *noun*

initial *noun* a large letter at the beginning of a name, used to stand for the name

inject *verb* to give medicine through the skin, with a needle; **injection** *noun*

injure *verb* to hurt; **injury** *noun*

ink *noun* coloured liquid used for writing or drawing; **inky** *adjective*

in-laws *noun* the father and mother, and sometimes other relatives, of the person somebody has married

inn *noun* a pub or small hotel; ▣ **in**

inner *adjective* inside; closest to the centre

input *verb* to put data into a computer; **input** *noun*

insect *noun* a small creature with six legs and a body divided into three parts, such as an ant or fly

an insect — atlas moth

¹inside *noun* the area within something else; that part that is nearest to the centre, or that faces away from other people or from the open air

²inside *preposition, adjective, adverb* in; on or to the inside of something

instead *adverb* in place of somebody or something

instruct *verb* **1** to teach; **2** to order; **instruction** *noun*

instrument *noun* **1** a tool; **2** an object such as a piano, horn, etc, played to give music

77

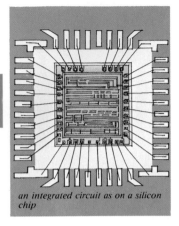
an integrated circuit as on a silicon chip

integrated circuit *noun* a tiny electronic circuit on a single computer chip

intelligence *noun* the ability to learn and understand; **intelligent** *adjective*

intend *verb* to plan to do something; **intention** *noun*

interest *noun* wanting to know more about something; getting pleasure from studying something; **interest** *verb;* **interesting** *adjective;* **interestingly** *adverb*

interfere *verb* to get in the way; to prevent somebody from doing something; **interference** *noun*

interrupt *verb* to stop something continuing; to break in on somebody who is already speaking; **interruption** *noun*

into *preposition* to the inside of; in

introduce *verb* **1** to make two people known for the first time to each other; **2** to bring in a new thing; **introduction** *noun*

invent *verb* to make up or produce something new; **invention** *noun;* **inventor** *noun*

invisible *adjective* not able to be seen

invite *verb* to ask somebody to do something or go somewhere, such as to a party; **invitation** *noun*

inwards *adverb* towards the inside

¹iron *noun* **1** a useful silver-white metal; **2** a heavy metal object with a handle, pointed at the front and flat underneath, used for making clothes smooth: **ironing board**

²iron *verb* to make smooth with an iron

irritate *verb* **1** to annoy; **2** to make sore and uncomfortable; **irritation** *noun*

is *see* BE

island *noun* a piece of land surrounded by water

isn't *see* BE

it *pronoun* (**itself**) **1** that thing; **2** that person or animal whose sex is not known or not thought important

itch *verb* to feel or cause a soreness which you want to scratch; **itch** *noun;* **itchy** *adjective*

its *adjective* belonging to it; ■ **it's**

it's it is; it has; ■ **its**

itself *see* IT

ivory *noun* **1** a hard white substance of which elephants' tusks are made; **2** the creamy colour of ivory

ivy *noun* a plant which climbs up walls and has shiny leaves

jack *noun* **1** an apparatus for lifting something heavy, such as a car, off the ground; **2** also **knave** any of the four playing cards with a picture of a man, that comes between the 10 and the queen

jackal *noun* a wild animal like a dog

jacket *noun* a short coat

jail also **gaol** *verb* to put in prison; *noun* a prison

¹jam *verb* (**jammed**) **1** to pack tightly into a small space; to push or press together; **2** to get stuck

²jam *noun* a mass of people or things jammed together

³jam *noun* sweet food made of fruit boiled in sugar, for spreading on bread

January *noun* the first month of the year

jar *noun* a container like a bottle with a short neck and wide mouth

javelin *noun* a light throwing spear used in sport

throwing the javelin

jaw *noun* either of the two face bones which hold the teeth

jazz *noun* a type of music with a strong beat

jealous *adjective* **1** wanting to get what somebody else has; **2** being afraid of losing what you have; **jealously** *adverb;* **jealousy** *noun*

jeans *noun* strong cotton trousers that are often blue

jelly *noun* a soft food that shakes when moved

jersey *noun* a sweater

jet *noun* **1** a type of aircraft that has a **jet engine; 2** a narrow stream of liquid, gas, etc, forced through a small hole

Jew *noun* a person belonging to the worldwide group descended from the people of ancient Israel and practising their religion; **Jewish** *adjective*

jewel *noun* a precious stone, used as an ornament

jewellery or **jewelry** *noun* ornaments with jewels

jigsaw puzzle or **jigsaw** *noun* a picture made up of pieces which have to be fitted together

job *noun* **1** a piece of work; **2** regular work for which you are paid

jockey *noun* a person who rides in horse races

jog *verb* (**jogged**) **1** to run slowly and steadily; to run like this to keep fit; **2** to shake or push slightly; **jog** *noun;* **jogger** *noun;* **jogging** *noun*

¹join *verb* **1** to fasten together; to connect; **2** to become a member of a group

J

²join *noun* a place where two things are joined

joint *noun* **1** a join; a thing used for making a join; **2** a place where two or more bones fit together; **3** a large piece of meat

joke *noun* anything said or done to cause amusement; **joke** *verb*; **jokingly** *adverb*

journey *noun (plural journeys)* a trip of some distance

joy *noun* great happiness

joystick *noun* a lever in a control box that is connected to a computer to move figures, pictures, etc, about on the screen of a VDU, especially in computer video games

¹judge *verb* **1** to act as a judge; **2** to give a decision about somebody or something in a competition; **3** to give an opinion about

²judge *noun* **1** the person who has the power to decide questions brought before a court of law; **2** a person who decides who has won a competition; **judgement, judgment** *noun*

jug *noun* a pot for liquids, with a handle and a lip for pouring

juggle *verb* to keep several things in the air at the same time, throwing them up and catching them; **juggler** *noun*

juice *noun* the liquid part of fruit, vegetables, and meat; **juiciness** *noun*; **juicy** *adjective*

July *noun* the seventh month of the year

¹jump *verb* **1** to move your body suddenly and quickly off the ground, into the air, or over something; **2** to make a quick sudden movement

²jump *noun* **1** an act of jumping; **2** something that you jump over, such as in a race

jumper *noun* a knitted piece of clothing for the upper body, pulled on over the head

June *noun* the sixth month of the year

jungle *noun* a thick tropical forest

junior *adjective* **1** younger; **2** of lower importance or position; **junior** *noun*

Jupiter (top right) and four of its moons

Jupiter *noun* the largest planet of the solar system

¹just *adjective* fair and honest; **justice** *noun*

²just *adverb* **1** exactly; **2** very near the present time; **3** hardly; almost not; **4** only

J

kaleidoscope *noun* a tube fitted with mirrors and pieces of coloured glass which shows coloured patterns when turned

kangaroo *noun (young* **joey***)* an animal which jumps along on large back legs and carries its young in a special pocket

a red kangaroo with a joey in its pouch

keen *adjective* eager to do something; liking to do something; **keenly** *adverb;* **keenness** *noun*

keep *verb* **(keeps, keeping, kept) 1** to have without the need of returning; **2** to have or hold for some time; **3** to take care of; **4** to own; to have the use of; **5** to cause to continue, to stay, or to remain

kennel *noun* a small house for a dog

kerb *noun* a line of raised stones separating the footpath from the road

ketchup *noun* a sauce, made usually of tomatoes, for flavouring food

kettle *noun* a pot with a lid, handle, and spout for heating water

key *noun* **1** a metal instrument for locking or unlocking a door, winding a clock, etc: **keyhole, key ring; 2** a part of a piano, typewriter, etc, that is pressed with the finger: **keyboard; 3** something that explains or helps you to understand, such as the list of symbols or abbreviations on a map; **4** a set of musical notes with a certain starting note

kick *verb* **1** to hit with the foot; **2** to move the feet backwards and forwards; **kick** *noun;* **kicker** *noun*

kid *noun* **1** a young goat; **2** a child or young person

kidnap *verb* to take somebody away and ask for money in return for bringing him or her back safely; **kidnapper** *noun*

kill *verb* to cause somebody or something to die; **killer** *noun*

kilogram also **kilo** *noun* a measure of weight equal to 1,000 grams or 2.21 pounds *(see last page)*

kilometre *noun* a measure of length equal to 1,000 metres or 0.62 miles *(see last page)*

¹kind *(say* **kynd***) noun* a group that are alike; type; sort

²kind *adjective* helpful; gentle and wanting to do good; **kindness** *noun*

K

king *noun* **1** the male ruler of a country: **kingdom**; **2** any of the four playing cards with a picture of a king

kipper *noun* a smoked salted herring used for food

kiss *verb* to touch with the lips as a greeting or sign of love; **kiss** *noun*

kitchen *noun* a room used for cooking

kite *noun* a very light frame covered with paper or cloth for flying at the end of a long string

kitten *noun* a young cat

knee *noun* the middle joint of the leg

kneel *verb* (**kneels, kneeling, knelt**) to go down on the knees

knew *see* KNOW; 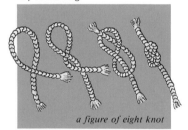 **new**

knife *noun* (*plural* **knives**) a blade fixed in a handle for cutting

knight – a chess piece; the horse's head symbolises a soldier on horseback

knight *noun* **1** a man given the title 'Sir' by the king or queen of England; **2** a soldier on horseback serving a ruler; ▪ **night**

knit *verb* (**knits, knitting, knitted** *or* **knit**) **1** to make a sort of cloth or a piece of clothing by joining threads using long **knitting needles**; **2** to join together closely; **knitter** *noun*; **knitting** *noun*

knob *noun* a round lump, handle, or control button; **knobbly** *adjective*

¹knock *verb* **1** to strike something so that it makes a noise; **2** to hit hard

²knock *noun* a sound caused by knocking

a figure of eight knot

¹knot *noun* **1** a fastening formed by tying two ends of something together; **2** a hard mass in wood where a branch has come off a tree; **3** a measure of the speed of a ship, about 1,852 metres or about 6,076.12 feet per hour; ▪ **not**

²knot *verb* (**knotted**) to make a knot in or join with knots; ▪ **not**

know *verb* (**knows, knowing, knew, known**) **1** to have in the mind; **2** to have learnt; **3** to have seen, heard, etc, before; to recognise somebody or something; **knowledge** *noun*; ▪ **no**

knuckle *noun* a finger joint

label *noun* a piece of paper or other material fixed to something, on which is written what it is, where it is to go, etc; **label** *verb*

lace *noun* **1** a string for fastening the edges of something together: **shoelaces**; **2** a cloth made from cotton or silk, with a pattern of holes in it

ladder *noun* a frame of two bars or ropes of equal length joined by shorter bars that form steps for climbing

lady *noun* **1** a polite way of saying woman; **2 Lady** the wife of a Lord or knight; the daughter of an earl, duke, etc

ladybird *noun* a small round beetle, usually red with black spots

laid *see* LAY

lain *see* LIE; 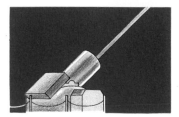 **lane**

lake *noun* a large mass of water surrounded by land

lamb (*say* lam) *noun* a young sheep

lamp *noun* an instrument for giving light

¹land *noun* **1** the solid dry part of the Earth's surface; **2** a country

²land *verb* to come to, bring to, or put on land

landing *noun* the level space or passage at the top of stairs

lane *noun* **1** a narrow, often winding, road; **2** any of the parallel parts into which wide roads are divided; **lain**

language *noun* **1** the words people use in speaking or writing; **2** a particular system of signs and symbols for use in a computer

lantern *noun* a light in a glass case that usually has a handle for carrying it

large *adjective* more than usual in size, number, or amount; big; **largely** *adverb;* **largeness** *noun*

lark *noun* a small light brown bird with long pointed wings

argon laser beam – for measuring the distance to the moon

laser *noun* an apparatus with a very strong, very narrow beam of light used to cut materials, send messages, etc

¹last *adjective, adverb, pronoun* **1** after all others; **2** the one before now; most recent

²last *verb* to continue

late *adjective, adverb* arriving, developing, happening, etc, after the expected time; **lateness** *noun*

lately *adverb* recently

laugh *verb* to make a sound to show that you are pleased, happy, amused, etc; **laugh** *noun;* **laughter** *noun*

L

launching the American space shuttle

launch *verb* **1** to set a boat into the water; **2** to send a rocket into space: **launching pad, launching site**

launderette *noun* a place where the public may wash clothes in machines that work when coins are put into them

laundry *noun* **1** a place where clothes are washed and ironed; **2** clothes, sheets, etc, that need washing or have just been washed

lava *noun* very hot liquid rock that comes out of the top of a volcano

lavatory *noun* **1** a large seatlike bowl connected to a drain, used for passing body waste; **2** a room or building containing this

law *noun* a rule made by the government that everybody must follow; **lawful** *adjective;* **lawyer** *noun*

lawn *noun* a stretch of smooth ground covered with short grass: **lawn mower**

¹lay *verb* **(lays, laying, laid)**
1 to place or set; to put in a certain position; **2** to produce an egg or eggs

²lay *see* LIE

layer *noun* a thickness of some material laid over something or put between two things

lazy *adjective* not wanting to work; **lazily** *adverb;* **laziness** *noun*

¹lead *(say like* need) *verb* **(leads, leading, led) 1** to show somebody the way; to guide; **2** to be the chief person in doing something; to be first, especially in a race or competition; **leader** *noun*

²lead *(say like* need) *noun* **1** the first or front place; a guiding example; **2** the chief acting part in a play or film; **3** also **leash** a length of leather, chain, etc, tied to a dog to control it; **4** a wire that carries electrical power

³lead *(say like* dead) *noun* **1** a soft heavy metal, sometimes used as a covering for roofs; **2** the black substance in the middle of pencils; ▣ **led**

leaf *noun (plural* **leaves***)* one of the flat parts of a plant that grow from a stem or branch

leak *noun* a hole or crack through which a gas or liquid may pass in or out; **leak** *verb;* **leaky** *adjective;* ▣ **leek**

¹lean *verb* **(leans, leaning, leant** *or* **leaned) 1** to bend forwards, backwards, sideways, or towards; **2** to rest something against or on another

²lean *adjective* without much fat; thin; **leanness** *noun*

84

leap *verb* (leaps, leaping, leapt *or* leaped) to jump; **leap** *noun*

learn *verb* (learns, learning, learned *or* learnt) **1** to get knowledge or skill; **2** to find out; **learner** *noun;* **learning** *noun*

least *noun, adjective, adverb* **1** the smallest thing, amount, etc; **2** *see* LITTLE

leather *noun* animal skin treated for use

¹**leave** *verb* (leaves, leaving, left) **1** to go away from; **2** to allow something to stay somewhere; **3** to let things stay as they are

²**leave** *noun* a short time away from work

leaves *see* LEAF

led *see* ¹LEAD; ▓ ³**lead**

leek *noun* a vegetable like an onion, with a long white fleshy stem; ▓ **leak**

¹**left** *noun, adjective* the side or direction opposite to right

²**left** *see* LEAVE

leg *noun* **1** the part of the body on which an animal walks and which supports its body; **2** the part of a piece of clothing that covers the leg; **3** one of the pieces of wood, metal, or plastic on which a table, chair, etc, stands

legal *adjective* allowed by the law; **legally** *adverb*

lemon *noun* **1** a type of fruit like an orange but with a light yellow skin and sour juice; **2** a light bright yellow colour; **lemon** *adjective*

lemonade *noun* a drink tasting of lemons and containing bubbles of gas

lend *verb* (lends, lending, lent) to give somebody the use of something, such as money or a car for a short time, after which he or she must give it back; **lender** *noun*

length *noun* the measurement from one end of something to the other; **lengthen** *verb;* **lengthy** *adjective*

this fisheye lens creates a curved, slightly distorted picture

lens *noun (plural* **lenses***)* a piece of glass or plastic with curved surfaces, used in cameras, telescopes, microscopes, glasses, etc, for seeing things clearly

lent *see* LEND

Lent *noun* the forty days before Easter, during which many Christians give up some of their usual pleasures

leopard *noun (female* **leopardess***)* a large meat-eating wild animal of the cat family, that is yellowish with black spots

leotard *noun* a piece of clothing that fits tightly, worn by dancers, acrobats, etc

less *noun, adjective, adverb* **1** a smaller amount; not so much; **2** *see* LITTLE

lesson *noun* **1** part of a school day, when a pupil or class studies a subject; **2** something that we must learn

let *verb* (**lets, letting, let**) **1** to allow to do or happen; **2** to give the use of a room, a building, land, etc, in return for money; **3** **let's** let us; used when you ask somebody to do something with you

letter *noun* **1** a written or printed message sent to somebody, usually in an envelope; **2** one of the signs we use in writing

lettuce *noun* a garden plant with large pale green leaves which are used in salads

¹level *adjective* **1** having a surface which is the same height above the ground all over; **2** flat; smooth; **3** equal

²level *verb* (**levelled**) to make or become flat

³level *noun* a place or position of a particular height

lever *noun* a long bar used for lifting or moving something heavy

leveret *noun* a young hare

library *noun* **1** a room or a building that contains books that may be looked at or borrowed: **public library**; **2** a collection of books

licence *noun* a written or printed paper which allows you to do something: **driving licence**; ▇ **license**

license *verb* to give or get permission to do something; ▇ **licence**

lick *verb* to move the tongue across something in order to taste, clean, make wet, etc; **lick** *noun*

lid *noun* **1** the top of a box or other hollow container, that can be taken off; **2** an eyelid

¹lie *verb* (**lies, lying, lay, lain**) **1** to have your body in a flat resting position on something such as the ground or a bed; **2** to be or stay in a certain place

²lie *noun* something said which is not true; **lie** *verb*

life *noun* (*plural* **lives**) **1** the active force that makes humans, animals, and plants able to grow and produce young ones, and that makes them different from stones, machines, objects, etc; **2** the time that humans, animals, and plants are alive; **3** the way somebody lives or spends their time; **4** activity; strength; cheerfulness

¹lift *verb* to pick up; to pick up and put in a higher place; to raise

²lift *noun* **1** an apparatus in a building for taking people and goods from one floor to another; **2** a free ride in a vehicle

lift-off *noun* the start of the flight of a spacecraft

¹light *noun* **1** that which makes you able to see things; **2** something that gives out light such as a lamp or torch; **3** something that will set something else, especially a cigarette, burning

²light *adjective* **1** having light; not dark; bright; **2** not deep or dark in colour; pale

³light *verb* (**lights, lighting, lit** *or* **lighted**) **1** to make a fire, match, etc, start to burn; **2** to give light to something

⁴light *adjective* of little weight; not heavy; **lightly** *adverb*; **lightness** *noun*

lighten *verb* to make or become brighter or less dark; **lightening** *noun;* ◨ **lightning**

lighthouse *noun* a tower with a powerful flashing light that guides ships or warns them of dangerous rocks

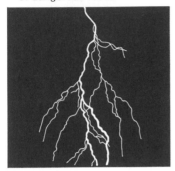

forked lightning

lightning *noun* a powerful flash of light in the sky, usually followed by thunder; ◨ **lightening**

light year *noun* a unit of length in astronomy equal to the distance that light travels in one year in a vacuum; 9,460 thousand million kilometres (about 5,878 thousand million miles)

¹like *verb* **1** to be fond of; to find pleasant; **2** to wish; **liking** *noun*

²like *adjective, preposition* **1** in the same way as; of the same kind; **2** for example; **likeness** *noun;* **likewise** *adverb*

likely *adjective* **1** expected; **2** suitable

lilac *noun* a tree with pinkish purple or white flowers giving a sweet smell

lily *noun* a plant with large white flowers

limb (*say* lim) *noun* a part of the body, such as an arm or a leg

lime *noun* a fruit like a small green lemon

¹limp *verb* to walk as if your leg or foot has been hurt; **limp** *noun*

²limp *adjective* not stiff or firm

line *noun* **1** a long very thin mark which can be drawn on a surface; **2** a piece of string, wire, or thin cord; **3** a set of people or things one after the other or beside each other; a row

lion *noun (female* **lioness,** *young* **cub***)* a large wild animal of the cat family. The male has a thick mane over the head and shoulders

a lion cub

lip *noun* **1** one of the two soft pink edges of the mouth: **lipstick; 2** the edge of something such as a cup

liquid *noun* a substance not solid or gas, that flows and has no fixed shape

list *noun* a set of names of things written one after the other, so as to remember them

L

87

listen *verb* to try to hear;
listener *noun*

lit *see* LIGHT

litre *noun* a measure of liquid
equal to 1.759 pints *(see last
page)*

litter *noun* **1** waste paper and
other things thrown away;
2 a group of young animals
born at the same time

¹little *adjective* small; not big;
young

²little *adjective, adverb, noun*
(less, least) 1 not much; not
enough; **2** a small amount,
but at least some

¹live (*say* liv) *verb* **1** to be alive;
to have life; **2** to have your
home somewhere; to stay in
a place or at a house; **3** to
keep yourself alive by eating
food or by working

²live (*say like* dive) *adjective*
1 having life; not dead;
2 seen and/or heard as it
happens; not recorded: *a live
television programme;*
3 carrying free electricity
which can kill anyone who
touches it

lives (*say like* dives) *see* LIFE

lizard *noun* a reptile with a
rough skin, four legs, and a
long tail

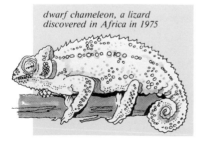

*dwarf chameleon, a lizard
discovered in Africa in 1975*

¹load *noun* things that are
carried by train, ship, or lorry

²load *verb* **1** to put a full load
on or in something; **2** to put
bullets into a gun or film into
a camera

loaf *noun (plural* **loaves***)* bread
shaped and baked in one
large piece

lobster *noun* a sea animal with
a shell, eight legs, and a pair
of powerful claws

local *adjective* in or near a
certain place, especially the
place or area in which you
live

lock *noun* an apparatus for
closing and fastening
something by means of a
key; **lock** *verb*

log *noun* a thick piece of wood
from a tree

lollipop *noun* a sweet on
a stick

lonely *adjective* unhappy
because of being on your
own or without friends;
loneliness *noun*

¹long *adjective* **1** measuring a
great distance or time from
one end to the other;
2 covering a certain distance
or time

²long *adverb* for a long time

³long *verb* to want very much;
longing *noun, adjective;*
longingly *adverb*

long-playing record *noun*
an LP

long wave *noun* radio
broadcasting on waves of
1,000 metres or more in
length

look *verb* **1** to try to see; to
use your eyes; **2** to seem to
be; **look** *noun*

loop *noun* a ring made by a piece of rope, string, etc, crossing itself

loose *adjective* **1** not tied up, shut up, etc; **2** not firmly fixed; not tight; **loosely** *adverb;* **loosen** *verb;* **looseness** *noun;* ◼**lose**

lord *noun* **1** a man who rules people; a master; **2 Lord** a title for a man of high position

lorry also **truck** *noun* a large motor vehicle for carrying goods

a container lorry

lose *verb* (**loses, losing, lost**) **1** not to keep; not to have something any more; not to find; **2** not to win; not to do well; ◼**loose**

lost *adjective* not able to find your way

lot *noun* a large number or amount; much

loud *adjective* being or producing much sound; not quiet; noisy; **loudly** *adverb;* **loudness** *noun*

loudspeaker also **speaker** *noun* an apparatus that turns electrical current into sound

love *noun* **1** a strong warm feeling of liking somebody or something very much; **2** a person who is loved; **lovable** *adjective;* **love** *verb;* **loving** *adjective;* **lovingly** *adjective*

lovely *adjective* **1** beautiful, attractive, etc; **2** very pleasant; **loveliness** *noun*

low *adjective* **1** near the ground; not high; **2** not loud; soft; not high in sound; **lower** *verb;* **lowness** *noun*

loyal *adjective* true to our friends, group, country, etc; faithful; **loyally** *adverb*

LP also **album, long-playing record** *noun* a record which turns fairly slowly and plays for a long time

luck *noun* good or bad things which happen to you by chance; fate; **luckily** *adverb;* **lucky** *adjective*

luggage *noun* the cases and bags that you take with you when you travel

lukewarm *adjective* not much hotter than cool

lump *noun* **1** a mass of something solid without a special size or shape; **2** a hard swelling on the body

lunar *adjective* of the moon; made for use on or around the moon: **lunar module**

lunch *noun* a meal eaten in the middle of the day

lung *noun* either of the two breathing organs in the chest of humans and certain other creatures

luxury *noun* **1** great comfort; **2** something not necessary and not often had or done but which is very pleasant

lying *see* LIE

L

macaroni *noun* a food made of thin tubes of pasta

machine *noun* an instrument or apparatus that uses power (such as electricity) to do work; **machinery** *noun*

mackerel *noun* a sea fish with green and dark blue stripes on its back

mad *adjective* **(madder)** **1** having a sick mind; **2** very foolish; **3** angry

made *see* MAKE; maid

magazine *noun* a thin book with a paper cover which contains articles or stories, pictures, and advertisements, and which is sold usually every week or month

magic *noun* **1** the use of spells, spirits, secret forces, etc, to try to control events; **2** the skill used by a conjurer who produces unexpected results by tricks; **magical** *adjective;* **magician** *noun*

magnet *noun* an object, such as a piece of iron, steel, etc, that can draw iron towards it; **magnetic** *adjective;* **magnetism** *noun*

magpie *noun* a noisy black and white bird which often takes small bright objects

maid *noun* a female servant; ▪made

¹mail *noun* letters and anything else sent or received by post; ▪male

²mail *noun* armour made of pieces or rings of metal; ▪male

main *adjective* chief; first in importance or size: **main road; mainly** *adverb;* ▪mane

mainframe *noun* a large powerful computer that can do many jobs at the same time

maintain *verb* to keep in good condition; **maintenance** *noun*

¹make *verb* **(makes, making, made) 1** to produce or form something, especially by work or action; **2** to earn, get, or win; **3** to force or cause a person to do something or a thing to happen; **maker** *noun*

this electro-magnet makes use of electricity and magnetism to lift an old car

²**make** *noun* the type to which a set of man-made objects belongs, especially the name of the makers

male *noun* a boy or a man; any person or animal of the sex that does not give birth to young; **male** *adjective;* ■ **mail**

mammal *noun* an animal that feeds its young on milk from the mother's body

¹**man** *noun (plural* **men)** **1** a fully grown human male; **2** a human being; **3** also **mankind** the human race

²**man** *verb* **(manned)** to provide with people for operation: *to man the guns*

manage *verb* **1** to succeed in dealing with something; **2** to control or be in charge of something or somebody; **management** *noun;* **manager** *noun*

mane *noun* the long hair on the back of a horse's neck, or around a lion's face; ■ **main**

man-made *adjective* made by people; not growing or produced by nature

manner *noun* the way in which anything is done or happens

manners *noun* the way you behave, especially the correct way to behave when you are with other people

many *adjective, pronoun, noun* **(more, most)** a great number

map *noun* **1** a drawing of the Earth's surface or of a part of it, showing the shape of countries, the position of towns, the height of land, etc; **2** a plan of the stars in the sky or of the surface of the moon or a planet

glass marbles

M

marble *noun* **1** a hard stone that can be polished to make it smooth and shiny and that can be used for building; **2** a small hard glass ball used in the game of **marbles**

¹**march** *verb* to walk with a regular step like a soldier

²**march** *noun* **1** the act of marching; **2** a piece of music that can be marched to

March *noun* the third month of the year

margarine *noun* a food made from animal or vegetable fats, used instead of butter

¹**mark** *noun* **1** a spot or line on something by which it can be recognised or which spoils its natural colour or appearance; **2** an object, sign, letter, or number that shows something, such as how well somebody has done a piece of work

²**mark** *verb* **1** to make or put a mark on something, especially one that spoils the appearance; **2** to give a mark to a person, piece of work, etc

market *noun* a place where people bring goods to sell

marmalade *noun* a type of jam made from oranges

marry *verb* **1** to become the husband or wife of somebody; **2** to join two people as husband and wife; **marriage** *noun*

Mars *noun* the planet that is fourth in order from the sun

martyr *noun* a person who dies for what he or she believes in, especially a religion

marvellous *adjective* wonderful

masculine *adjective* concerning boys or men

mask *noun* a covering for the face which hides, protects it, etc; **masked** *adjective*

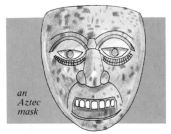

an Aztec mask

mass *noun* **1** a quantity or heap of something; **2** a large number of people or things

master *noun* a person in control of people, animals, or things; the chief person

mat *noun* a small piece of material for covering part of a floor or for putting under an object such as a plate

¹match *noun* a short thin stick with one end covered by chemicals that catch fire when rubbed or struck against a rough surface

²match *verb* to be like or suitable for use with something else

³match *noun* **1** something that is like or that is suitable to be used with something else; **2** a game or sports event between two teams or people

¹mate *noun* **1** a friend; **2** one of a male-female pair of animals

²mate *verb* to join together as a pair to have young

material *noun* **1** anything from which something can be made; **2** cloth from which clothes, curtains, etc, can be made

mathematics also **maths** *noun* the study or science of numbers; **mathematical** *adjective;* **mathematician** *noun*

¹matter *noun* **1** the material that makes up the world and everything which can be seen or touched; **2** a subject to which you give attention; **3** a trouble or cause of pain, illness, etc

²matter *verb* to be important

mattress *noun* a large bag filled with soft material, on which you sleep

may *verb* **(might) 1** to be possible or likely to: *She may come, or she may not;* **2** to have permission to do something: *May I come in?* **3** used to show a hope that something will happen: *May the best team win!* ■ **might** Used correctly, *may have* and *might have* mean different things. Compare: *he may have* (= perhaps he was) *been drowned/he might have been* (= but he was not) *drowned*

May *noun* the fifth month of the year

maybe *adverb* perhaps

mayor *noun* the chief person of a city or town

me *see* I

meal *noun* an amount of food eaten at one time

¹mean *adjective* not generous; not willing to share something or help; **meanly** *adverb;* **meanness** *noun*

²mean *verb* (**means, meaning, meant**) **1** to be the same as; to have as a meaning; **2** to plan or want to do or say something

meaning *noun* the idea that is intended to be understood

measles *noun* an infectious disease that causes a fever and small red spots on the face and body

¹measure *noun* **1** a unit used for calculating amount, size, weight, etc; **2** an instrument used for measuring: **tape measure**

²measure *verb* **1** to find the size, weight, amount, etc, of something; **2** to be of a certain size; **measurement** *noun*

meat *noun* the parts of an animal's body that are eaten; ▣ **meet**

medal *noun* a piece of metal in the shape of a coin, cross, etc, given to somebody for something he or she has done, such as a brave action

Montreal Winter Olympics gold medal

or for winning a race; ▣ **meddle**

meddle *verb* to interest yourself in something that is nothing to do with you; to interfere; **meddler** *noun;* **meddlesome** *adjective;* ▣ **medal**

media *noun* the newspapers, television, and radio

medicine *noun* **1** a substance used for treating disease; **2** the science of treating and understanding diseases; **medical** *adjective;* **medically** *adverb*

medium *adjective* of middle size, amount, etc

medium wave *noun* radio broadcasting on waves of about 200 to 700 metres in length

meet *verb* (**meets, meeting, met**) **1** to come together; **2** to get to know or be introduced to somebody for the first time; **meeting** *noun;* ▣ **meat**

melon *noun* a large very juicy round or oval fruit with a thick skin

melt *verb* to become or cause to become liquid

member *noun* a person who belongs to a club, group, etc: **Member of Parliament**

memorise *verb* to learn by heart

memory *noun* **1** the ability to remember things; **2** something remembered; **3** the part of a computer in which information is stored

men *see* MAN

mend *verb* to put something back into its proper condition

menu *noun* **1** a list of the foods that are available in a restaurant or at a meal; **2** a list of the choices that are available in a computer program

mercury *noun* a silver-white metal that is liquid at ordinary temperatures and is used in thermometers

Mercury *noun* the planet that is nearest to the sun

mercy *noun* kindness shown by somebody who has the power to hurt or punish; **merciful** *adjective;* **merciless** *adjective*

a mermaid

mermaid *noun* an imaginary creature with the head and body of a woman and a fish's tail instead of legs

merry *adjective* full of laughter; cheerful, happy; **merrily** *adverb;* **merriness** *noun*

mess *noun* a dirty or untidy state; **messy** *adjective*

message *noun* a spoken or written piece of information passed from one person to another

messenger *noun* a person who brings a message

mess up *verb* **1** to make something dirty or untidy; **2** to do something badly

met *see* MEET

metal *noun* one of a group of usually solid shiny substances such as tin, gold, silver, and iron

meteor *noun* a small piece of matter in space that glows as it falls into the Earth's atmosphere

meteorite *noun* a meteor that has fallen onto the Earth

metre *noun* a measure of length equal to 39.37 inches; **metric** *adjective (see last page)*

metric system *noun* a system of measurement that uses the metre for measuring length and the kilogram for measuring weight

mice *see* MOUSE

microcomputer also **micro** *noun* a small computer that fits on a table or desk and can be used at home or at school

a microcomputer

microphone *noun* an instrument for recording sounds or carrying them over a distance, or for making sounds louder

microprocessor *noun* the integrated circuit that controls a microcomputer

microscope *noun* an instrument that makes very small close objects look larger

microwave *noun* **1** radio waves of very short length; **2** also **microwave oven** an oven in which food is cooked very quickly by microwaves entering the food

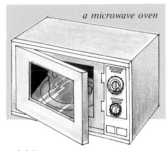
a microwave oven

midday *noun* the middle of the day; 12 o'clock in the day

middle *noun* the part, point, or position which is an equal distance from the two ends or sides of something; **middle** *adjective*

middle-aged *adjective* neither old nor young

midnight *noun* 12 o'clock at night

¹**might** **1** *see* MAY; **2** to be possible or likely to: *Jane might come later, but I don't think she will.* ■ **may**

²**might** *noun* power; strength; force

mile *noun* a measure of length or distance equal to 1,760 yards or 1.609 kilometres *(see last page)*

¹**milk** *noun* a white liquid produced by female mammals for feeding their young

²**milk** *verb* to take milk from a cow, goat, or other animal

milkman *noun* (*plural* **milkmen**) someone who delivers milk to people's houses

Milky Way *noun* the galaxy to which the sun and solar system belong

mill *noun* **1** a place where grain is made into flour; **2** a place, such as a factory, where something is produced or made; *a steel mill*; **3** a small machine in which something, such as coffee, can be ground into smaller pieces

million *adjective, noun* the number 1,000,000; a thousand thousand; **millionth** *adjective (see last page)*

¹**mince** *verb* to cut food, especially meat, into very small pieces; **mincer** *noun*

²**mince** *noun* minced meat

mincemeat *noun* a mixture of spices and dried fruits such as raisins and currants that is used as a filling for **mince pies**

¹**mind** *noun* **1** thoughts; a person's way of thinking or feeling; **2** *make up your mind* to reach a decision

²**mind** *verb* **1** to be careful of; to take notice of; **2** to dislike or to have a reason against something; **3** to take care or charge of; look after

¹**mine** *pronoun* that or those belonging to me

²**mine** *noun* a hole, usually under the ground, from which coal, gold, tin, etc, are dug; **mine** *verb*; **miner** *noun*

a coal miner

mineral *noun* any of various usually solid substances that are formed naturally in the ground, such as stone, coal, and salt

mineral water *noun* **1** water that comes from a natural spring and contains minerals, often drunk for health reasons; **2** a drink with a sweet taste and a little gas in it

minibus *noun* a small bus

¹**minute** (*say* min-it) *noun* one of the sixty parts into which an hour is divided

²**minute** (*say* my-newt) *adjective* very small; tiny

mirror *noun* a piece of glass with a silvery back in which you can see things reflected

mischief *noun* naughty behaviour, such as playing tricks on people; **mischievous** *adjective*

miss *verb* **1** to fail to hit, catch, find, meet, see, etc; **2** to discover that somebody or something is lost or is not there; to realise that something is not where it should be; **3** to feel sorry or unhappy because somebody or something is not there

Miss *noun* a title placed before the name of a girl or a woman who is not married

mist *noun* thin cloud near the ground; thin fog; **misty** *adjective*

¹**mistake** *verb* (**mistakes, mistaking, mistook, mistaken**) to have a wrong idea about somebody or something; to understand wrongly

²**mistake** *noun* a wrong thought, act, etc; something done, said, believed, etc, as a result of wrong thinking or understanding

mitt *noun* a glove that leaves the ends of the fingers bare

mitten *noun* a type of glove having one part for all of the fingers and one part for the thumb

mix *verb* **1** to put different things together so that the separate parts no longer have a separate shape, appearance, etc, or cannot easily be separated; **2 mix up** to mistake one thing for another; to confuse in your mind; **mixer** *noun*; **mixture** *noun*

moan *verb* **1** to make a low sound of pain; **2** to complain; **moan** *noun*

moat *noun* a deep ditch, often filled with water, surrounding a castle

model *noun* **1** a small copy of something or a small object, such as a building, which is to be made in a large size; **2** a person whose job is to wear clothes and to show them to possible buyers; **3** a person who is painted by an artist or photographed by a photographer; **4** an object, such as a car, which is one of a number of objects of a standard pattern; **model** *verb*

modern *adjective* of the present time; not old

module *noun* **1** a part of a space vehicle that can be used on its own without the rest of the vehicle: **command module, lunar module; 2** a part of a school course, treating a particular subject

¹**mole** *noun* a small animal with soft fur, that digs holes in the ground

²**mole** *noun* a small dark spot on the skin

³**mole** *noun* a spy

moment *noun* **1** a period of time too short to measure; **2** the time for doing something

Monday *noun* the second day of the week

money *noun* metal coins or paper notes with their value printed on them, used in buying and selling

monk *noun* one of a group of men who live together and have given their lives to a religion

monkey *noun* any of several types of long-tailed active tree-climbing animals, belonging to that class most like humans

monster *noun* a creature that is unusual in shape or qualities, and that is often very large and ugly

month *noun* one of the twelve parts into which the year is divided; about four weeks

moon *noun* a body that moves round a planet, especially the body that moves round the Earth once every twenty eight days, and can be seen in the sky at night: **moonlight**

¹**moor** *noun* a wide open area covered with rough grass or bushes; ■ **more**

the most successful British airship, R100, at mooring mast

²**moor** *verb* to fasten (a boat, an airship, etc) to land, the sea bed, etc, by means of ropes, an anchor, etc; ■ **more**

M

97

mop *noun* a long stick with threads of thick string or a sponge on one end for washing floors or dishes

more *adjective* **1** *see* MANY, MUCH; **2 more or less** nearly; about; **moor**

morning *noun* **1** the first part of the day from sunrise until midday; **2** the part of the day from midnight until midday; **mourning**

mosquito *noun (plural* **mosquitoes***)* a small fly that pricks the skin and then drinks blood

moss *noun* a small flat green or yellow plant that grows in a thick furry mass on damp surfaces; **mossy** *adjective*

most *see* MANY, MUCH

moth *noun* an insect like a butterfly but not usually so brightly coloured, that flies mainly at night and is attracted by lights

mother *noun* **1** a woman who has children; **2** a female animal that has young

¹motor *noun* a machine that changes power, especially electrical power, into movement

an outboard motor for a small boat

²motor *adjective* driven by an engine: **motorboat, motorbike, motorcycle**

motorist *noun* a person who drives a car

motorway *noun* a very wide road for fast long-distance vehicles

mountain *noun* a very high hill

mourn *verb* to be very sad, especially for somebody who is dead; **mourning** *noun;* **morning**

mouse *noun (plural* **mice***)* a small furry animal with a long tail

mouth *noun* **1** the opening in the face through which an animal or person eats and makes sounds; **2** an opening: *the* **mouth** *of the cave*

move *verb* **1** to go from one place to another; **2** to change the position of something; to put something in a different place; **3** to cause a person to have certain feelings, such as sadness; **movable, moveable** *adjective;* **move** *noun;* **movement** *noun*

mow *verb* (**mows, mowing, mowed, mown** *or* **mowed**) to cut grass; **mower** *noun*

Mr *noun* a title placed before the name of a man

Mrs *noun* a title placed before the name of a married woman

Ms *noun* a title placed before the name of a woman instead of Mrs or Miss

much *adjective, noun, adverb* (**more, most**) **1** a large quantity or amount; **2** often

mud *noun* very wet sticky earth or soil; **muddy** *adjective*

muddle *noun* a confused, untidy, or mixed-up state; **muddle** *verb*

¹mug *noun* a big cup usually with straight sides and a handle, that is not normally used with a saucer

²mug *verb* **(mugged)** to attack and rob somebody, as in a dark street; **mugger** *noun;* **mugging** *noun*

mule *noun* an animal that is a cross between a horse and a donkey

a mule

multiply *verb* **1** to increase a number by a certain number of times; **2** to increase; to make more; **multiplication** *noun*

mum, mummy *noun* mother

mumble *verb* to speak in a way that is not clear or is hard to hear

mumps *noun* an infectious disease which causes swelling of the neck

murder *verb* to kill somebody on purpose; **murder** *noun;* **murderer** *noun*

muscle *noun* one of the pieces of elastic material in the body that tighten to produce movement; **mussel**

museum *noun* a building where interesting objects are kept and shown to the public

mushroom *noun* a fungus that can be eaten

musical symbols

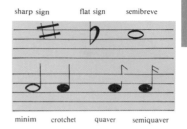
sharp sign   flat sign   semibreve

minim   crotchet   quaver   semiquaver

music *noun* **1** sounds arranged in pleasant patterns and tunes produced by singing or playing instruments; **2** a written set of musical notes; **musical** *adjective*

musician *noun* somebody who plays a musical instrument

Muslim also **Moslem** *noun* a person of the religion started by Mohammed

mussel *noun* a type of shellfish; ▦**muscle**

must *verb* **(mustn't) 1** to have to because it is necessary; **2** to be sure or likely to

mustard *noun* a hot-tasting yellow powder used in cooking, or a thick mixture of this powder with water, eaten with food

mutton *noun* the meat from a sheep

my *adjective* belonging to me

myself *see* **I**

mystery *noun* something strange that cannot be easily explained

nail *noun* **1** a thin piece of metal with a point at one end and a flat head at the other for hammering into a piece of wood or other material; **2** a fingernail or toenail; **nail** *verb*

naked *adjective* **1** not wearing any clothes; **2** not covered: *a naked flame*

name *noun* the word or words that somebody or something is called by; **name** *verb*

narrow *adjective* **1** small from one side to the other; not wide; **2** almost not enough or only just successful: *a narrow escape;* **narrowness** *noun*

nasty *adjective* unpleasant; unkind; ugly; **nastily** *adverb;* **nastiness** *noun*

natural *adjective* **1** to do with nature; not made by people; **2** usual; normal; **naturally** *adverb*

nature *noun* **1** the qualities which make somebody or something different from others; the character of somebody or something; **2** the whole world and everything in it that is not made or changed by people, such as the mountains, sea, sky, animals, and plants

naughty *adjective* badly behaved; not obeying a parent, teacher, set of rules, etc; **naughtily** *adverb;* **naughtiness** *noun*

navy *noun* **1** the ships, people, etc, which make up the power of a country for war at sea; **2** a dark blue colour

near *adjective, adverb, preposition* not far from in distance, time, etc; close

nearly *adverb* almost but not quite

neat *adjective* showing care in appearance; liking order; clean and tidy; **neatly** *adverb;* **neatness** *noun*

nebula *noun* a large cloud of gas and dust in space

necessary *adjective* something that must be had or done; **necessarily** *adverb*

neck *noun* **1** the part of the body between the head and shoulders; **2** the narrow part of something that is shaped like this part of the body: *the neck of a bottle*

a jewelled necklace

necklace *noun* a string of jewels or beads worn round the neck

need *verb* (**needn't**) **1** to want or not have something necessary or very useful; **2** **need to** to have to; **need** *noun*

needle *noun* **1** a long thin pointed piece of metal with a hole in one end, for carrying thread through material in sewing; **2** a thin pointed object: *a pine needle;* **3** any of various thin rods with points or hooks used in working with wool, cloth, etc: *knitting needles;* **4** the very small pointed jewel or piece of metal that touches a record as it turns and picks up the sound recorded on it

neighbour *noun* somebody who lives very near you

neither *adjective, pronoun, adverb* **1** not one and not the other of two; **2** also not

nephew the son of your brother or sister

Neptune *noun* the planet eighth in order from the sun

nerve *noun* any of the threadlike parts of the body that form a system to carry feelings and messages to and from the brain

nervous *adjective* slightly afraid; anxious; worried; **nervously** *adverb;* **nervousness** *noun*

nest *noun* **1** a hollow place built or found by a bird as a home; **2** the home of certain animals or insects; **nest** *verb*

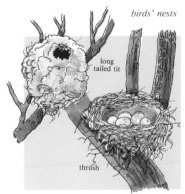

birds' nests

long tailed tit

thrush

net *noun* **1** a material of strings, wires, threads, etc, twisted, tied, or woven together with regular equal spaces between them: **network**; **2** any of various objects made from this, such as a fishing net or the goal in football

netball *noun* a game in which two teams of seven people try to score goals by throwing a large ball through a ring on a high post

nettle *noun* a wild plant covered with stinging hairs

neutral *adjective* **1** neither for nor against something; not taking sides; **2** in a position between opposites; not one thing or the other; **3** not electrically live; being the wire in a plug which is neither live nor earth

never *adverb* **1** not ever; not at any time; **2 never mind** do not worry, it does not matter

new *adjective* **1** not used by anyone before; **2** different from the earlier thing or things; not seen or known before; **newly** *adverb;* **newness** *noun;* ▪**knew**

news *noun* **1** new information; **2** any of the regular reports of recent events broadcast on radio and television

newsagent *noun* a person in charge of a shop selling newspapers and magazines

newspaper *noun* a paper printed usually daily or weekly, with news, notices, etc

newt *noun* a small animal that can live both on land and in water

next *adjective, adverb* **1** without anything coming between; **2** following nearest in time

nibble *verb* to eat with small bites

nice *adjective* good; kind; pleasant; **nicely** *adverb*

niece *noun* the daughter of your brother or sister

night *noun* the dark part of each day: **nighttime;** ◼ **knight**

nightingale *noun* a bird with a beautiful song

nightmare *noun* an unpleasant and frightening dream

nine *adjective, noun* the number 9; **ninth** *adjective, adverb (see last page)*

nineteen *adjective, noun* the number 19; **nineteenth** *adjective, adverb (see last page)*

ninety *adjective, noun* the number 90; **ninetieth** *adjective (see last page)*

no *adverb, adjective* **1** a word used in an answer to show that you refuse or do not agree with something; **2** not one; not any; ◼ **know**

noble *adjective* **1** belonging to the group of people who have titles, such as Lord and Lady: **nobleman; 2** brave and not selfish

nobody also **no one** *pronoun* not anybody; no person

nod *verb* **(nodded)** to bend the head forwards and down, especially to show agreement or give a greeting or sign; **nod** *noun*

noise *noun* a loud sound that is often unpleasant; **noisily** *adverb;* **noisy** *adjective*

none *pronoun* not one; not any; ◼ **nun**

nonsense *noun* something that has no meaning or that is not sensible

no one *see* nobody

nor *conjunction* used between the two or more choices after *neither* or *not: just warm, neither cold* **nor** *hot;* ◼ **gnaw**

normal *adjective* usual; expected; ordinary; **normally** *adverb*

north *noun* one of the four main points of the compass; the direction which is on the left of a person facing the rising sun; **north** *adjective, adverb;* **northerly** *adjective;* **northern** *adjective*

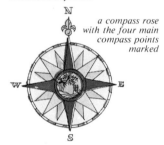

a compass rose with the four main compass points marked

northeast *noun* the direction of the point of the compass which is halfway between north and east

northwest *noun* the direction of the point of the compass which is halfway between north and west

nose *noun* **1** the part of the face above the mouth through which we breathe and with which we smell things; **2 turn up your nose at** to consider something not good enough to eat, take part in, etc

not *adverb* used for changing a word or sentence to one with the opposite meaning; ◼ **knot**

¹note *verb* to look or listen carefully and remember

²note *noun* **1** a single particular musical sound; **2** a reminder of something in writing: **notebook**; **3** a short letter or written message; **4** a piece of paper money

a note – a Jamaican dollar bill

nothing *pronoun* no thing; not any thing

¹notice *noun* **1** warning or information about something that is going to happen; **2** a written message

²notice *verb* to see, feel, hear, etc, something; **noticeable** *adjective*

nought *noun* the figure 0; zero *(see last page)*

noun *noun* a word that is the name of a person, place, animal, or thing

nova *noun* a star that suddenly becomes very bright

November *noun* the eleventh month of the year

now *adverb* at this time; at present

nowhere *adverb* not anywhere; in, at, or to no place

nuclear *adjective* using or to do with the energy that comes from splitting atoms or joining them together: **nuclear weapon, nuclear power**

number *noun* **1** a member of the system used in counting and measuring; a word or figure for one of these; **2** a quantity or amount; **number** *verb*

nun *noun* one of a group of women who live together and have given their lives to God; **none**

nurse *noun* a person who cares for the sick, hurt, old, or very young people; **nurse** *verb*

nursery *noun* **1** a place where small children are looked after for a short time; **2** a place where young plants and trees are grown for sale

nut *noun* **1** a dry fruit or seed with a hard shell; **2** a block, usually of metal, with a hole in the centre for screwing onto a bolt

nuts

Brazil nut

hazelnut

almond

pistachio

nylon *noun* a strong man-made material, often made into cloth or thread

oak *noun* a large tree with hard wood

oar *noun* a pole with a wide flat blade, used for rowing a boat

oats *noun* a plant which produces grain that can be eaten

obey *verb* to do what somebody tells you

¹object (*say* ob-*ject*) *noun* 1 a thing; 2 an aim or purpose

²object (*say* ob-ject) *verb* to be against something or somebody; **objection** *noun*

oblong *noun* a shape with four straight sides that is longer than it is wide

oboe *noun* a musical instrument that you blow

observatory *noun* a place from which the stars can be watched using a telescope

Mauna Kea observatory, Hawaii

observe *verb* to watch; to see; **observer** *noun*

obtain *verb* to get

occasion *noun* a particular or special time; a time when something happens; **occasional** *adjective;* **occasionally** *adverb*

occur *verb* (**occurred**) to happen; **occurrence** *noun*

ocean *noun* a very large sea

o'clock *adverb* used in telling the time to say what hour it is

October *noun* the tenth month of the year

odd *adjective* 1 strange; unusual; 2 not matching; not part of a set; left over; 3 not regular or planned: *odd jobs;* 4 **odd number** a number that cannot be divided by two; **oddly** *adverb*

of *preposition* 1 belonging to; 2 made from; 3 containing; 4 that is one or some from the whole or all; 5 connected or concerned with; to do with; ◼ **off**

off *adverb, preposition, adjective* 1 away; from a place or position; 2 so as not to be working or in use; 3 to or at a distance away; 4 no longer keen on or fond of: *He's off his food;* 5 no longer good to eat or drink; not fresh; 6 not going to happen after having been arranged; ◼ **of**

offend *verb* 1 to do wrong; 2 to cause somebody to feel annoyed or unhappy; **offence** *noun;* **offender** *noun;* **offensive** *adjective*

offer *verb* to say or show that you are ready to give or do something; **offer** *noun*

office *noun* 1 a place where business, or written work connected with a business, is done; 2 a part of the government: *the Foreign Office*

officer *noun* 1 a person who gives orders to others in the army, navy, etc; 2 a policeman

often *adverb* many times

oil *noun* any of several types of liquid used for burning, for making machines run easily, or for cooking; **oily** *adjective*

ointment *noun* a sticky substance that is rubbed on the skin to heal wounds

old *adjective* 1 used when asking or showing the age of somebody or something; 2 having lived, been in use, or continued for a long time; not young or new

on *preposition, adverb, adjective* 1 so as to be above or supported from below; at or covering the top; 2 attached to or touching; 3 towards; by; near to; 4 about; to do with; 5 at the time of; 6 by means of; using; 7 further; forwards; 8 in use; working; 9 happening or about to happen

once *adverb* 1 one time; 2 some time ago; 3 **all at once** suddenly; 4 **at once** immediately; at the same time

¹**one** *adjective, noun* the number 1 *(see last page)*; ▣ **won**

²**one** *pronoun* a single thing or person; any person; ▣ **won**

onion *noun* a round white vegetable with a strong smell, that is much used in cooking

only *adjective, adverb* 1 having no others in the same group; 2 and nothing more; and no one else: *Only the goalkeeper can handle the ball*

onto *preposition* to a position or point on

¹**open** *adjective* 1 not shut; 2 not surrounded by other things; 3 not covered; not fastened; 4 ready for business: *The bank is open*

²**open** *verb* 1 to make or become open; 2 to start or cause to start

operation *noun* 1 a state of working; the way a thing works; 2 a carefully planned action or activity; 3 an act of using instruments on a person's body in order to set right or cut out a diseased part; **operate** *verb*

opinion *noun* that which a person thinks about something

opponent *noun* somebody who is on the opposite side in a fight, game, argument, etc

opportunity *noun* a chance or time to do something

¹**opposite** *noun* a person or thing that is as different as possible from another

²**opposite** *adjective* 1 as different as possible; 2 facing

or *conjunction* 1 and not; 2 used to show that there is a choice

orange *noun* 1 a round sweet juicy fruit with a reddish yellow peel; 2 a colour between red and yellow; **orange** *adjective*

105

planets orbiting the sun

O

orbit *noun* the path of one thing, such as a planet, moon, or satellite, round another in space; **orbit** *verb;* **orbital** *adjective*

orchard *noun* a place where fruit trees are grown

orchestra *noun* a large group of people who play music together on different instruments; **orchestral** *adjective*

order *noun* **1** neatness; tidiness; **2** fitness for working or use; **3** a special way in which a group of people, objects, etc, are arranged: *alphabetical* **order***;* **4** the condition in which laws and rules are obeyed; **5** a command to do something; **6** a request to supply something; **7 in order that** so that; **8 in order to** with the purpose of; so as to; **order** *verb*

ordinary *adjective* not unusual; common; **ordinarily** *adverb;* **ordinariness** *noun*

organ *noun* **1** a part of an animal or plant that has a special purpose; **2** a musical instrument consisting of pipes through which air is forced to make the sounds

origin *noun* a place or time at which something begins; a starting point

original *adjective* **1** earliest; first; **2** new; different from others; not copied; **originally** *adverb*

ornament *noun* an object that we keep for its beauty; **ornamental** *adjective*

ostrich *noun* a very large bird with long legs and a long neck, that runs very quickly but cannot fly

other *adjective, pronoun* the remaining one or ones of a set; a different one from that spoken of

otherwise *adverb* **1** apart from that; **2** if not

otter *noun* an animal with dark brown fur that swims well and eats fish

ought *verb* **1** should; **2** will probably

ounce *noun* a measure of weight equal to 1/16 of a pound or about 28.35 grams *(see last page)*

our *adjective* belonging to us; ▣**hour**

ours *pronoun* that or those belonging to us

ourselves *see* WE

out *adverb* **1** in or to the open air, the outside, etc; away from the inside or centre; **2** not at home; **3** no longer in a game; **4** no longer lit or shining

outdoor *adjective* existing, happening, done, or used not in a building

outdoors *adverb* in the open air; not in a building

outer space *noun* space beyond the Earth's atmosphere; space between the stars

outing *noun* a pleasure trip

output *noun* something that is produced; the quantity of things produced

¹**outside** *noun* the part furthest from the centre

²**outside** *adverb, preposition, adjective* **1** in, on, or to the outside; out; **2** not in a building; in the open air

outwards *adverb* towards the outside

oval *adjective* shaped like an egg; **oval** *noun*

oven *noun* a box that can be made hot to cook food in

over *adverb, preposition* **1** directly above; **2** completely or partly covering; **3** to or on the other side of; across; **4** downwards from an upright position; **5** right through; from the beginning to the end; **6** more; more than; **7** remaining; **8** finished; at an end

overalls *noun* loose clothes worn over other clothes to keep them clean

overflow *verb* to be so full that the contents flow over the edges; **overflow** *noun*

owe *verb* **1** to have to pay; **2** to feel grateful to somebody for what he or she has done for us or given to us

owing to *preposition* because of

owl *noun* a bird with large eyes that flies at night

¹**own** *adjective, pronoun* **1** belonging to the particular person spoken of and to nobody else; **2 on your own** alone or without help

²**own** *verb* to have; to possess; **owner** *noun*

ox *noun (plural* **oxen***)* a male cow that has been prevented from breeding and that is used for pulling vehicles and for heavy work on farms

oxygen *noun* a colourless gas that is present in the air and is needed by plants and animals in order to live

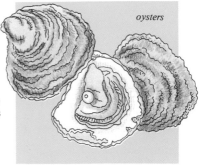

oysters

oyster *noun* a shellfish that is used for food and whose shell sometimes contains a pearl

¹**pack** *noun* **1** a number of things put together; **2** a group of animals, such as wolves, that hunt together

²**pack** *verb* **1** to put things into containers; **2** to crush or crowd together into a space

package *noun* a parcel

packet *noun* a small parcel or container

pad *noun* **1** a mass of soft material used to protect something or make it more comfortable, or to fill out a shape; **2** a number of sheets of paper fastened together along one edge

¹**paddle** *noun* a short pole with a wide flat end used for pushing and guiding a small boat, such as a canoe

²**paddle** *verb* **1** to move a boat through water using a paddle; **2** to walk about in shallow water; **3** to swim about in water as a dog or duck does

¹**page** *noun* one side of a sheet of paper in a book, newspaper, etc

²**page** *noun* a boy servant

paid *see* PAY

pail *noun* a bucket;  pale

pain *noun* a feeling of hurt or suffering; **painful** *adjective;* **painfully** *adverb;* ■ pane

¹**paint** *verb* **1** to put on a surface, such as a wall; **2** to make a picture using paint; **painter** *noun*

²**paint** *noun* liquid colouring matter for putting or spreading on a surface

painting *noun* a painted picture

pair *noun* **1** two things that are alike or of the same kind, and are used or thought of together; **2** something made up of two parts that are alike and which are joined and used together: *a **pair** of trousers;* ■ pear

palace *noun* a very large grand house in which an important person, such as a king or queen, lives

pale *adjective* rather white or light in colour; not bright; **paleness** *noun;* ■ pail

¹**palm** *noun* the inside part of a hand between the fingers and the wrist

²**palm** *noun* usually a very tall tree with large leaves at the top and no branches

a tropical palm tree

pan *noun* a round metal container with a handle, used in cooking food

pancake *noun* a very thin cake made from batter and cooked in a frying pan

pane *noun* a flat piece of glass in a window; ■ pain

pansy *noun* a small plant with wide flat flowers

pant *verb* to breathe quickly, taking short breaths, especially after exercise or in great heat

pantomime *noun* a play, usually telling an old story, which includes singing and dancing

pantry *noun* a small room where food is kept

pants *noun* underpants or trousers

paper *noun* 1 material made in the form of sheets from very thin threads of wood or cloth, used for writing or printing on, covering parcels or walls, etc; 2 a newspaper

parachute *noun* an apparatus consisting of a large piece of material which is fastened to people or objects dropped from aircraft in order to make them fall slowly

parachute

parallel *adjective* running side by side but staying the same distance apart: *parallel lines*

parcel *noun* a thing or things wrapped in paper and tied or fastened for posting or carrying

parent *noun* a father or mother

¹**park** *noun* 1 a large garden or grass place in a town, used by the public; 2 a piece of land with grass and trees round a large country house

²**park** *verb* to stop or leave a vehicle for a time

parliament *noun* the group of people who make the laws of a country: **Member of Parliament (MP)**

parrot *noun* a brightly coloured tropical bird that has a curved beak and can be taught to copy human speech

¹**part** *noun* 1 any of the pieces that make up a whole; some of a thing; 2 a share in some activity: *take **part** in;* 3 a character acted by an actor in a play or film; the words and actions of an actor in a play or film

²**part** *verb* to separate or no longer be together

participle *noun* one of two forms of a verb which may be used with other parts of a verb or as adjectives: **present participle, past participle**

particular *adjective* separate or different from others; special; **particularly** *adverb*

parting *noun* the line on the head where the hair is parted

partly *adverb* in some way but not completely

partner *noun* one or two, or sometimes more, people who share in the same activity; **partnership** *noun*

party *noun* 1 a meeting of people, usually by invitation, to eat, drink, and enjoy themselves; 2 a group of people doing something together; 3 a group of people having the same political opinions

¹**pass** *verb* **1** to reach and move beyond; **2** to go forward, through, across, over, or between; **3** to give: *Please pass the bread;* **4** to succeed in an examination or test; **5** to go by: *several years passed;* ▤past

²**pass** *noun* **1** an act of passing something, such as the ball in various sports; **2** a way by which one may pass, especially through mountains; **3** a printed piece of paper, which shows that one is permitted to do a certain thing; **4** a successful result in an examination

passage *noun* **1** a narrow and often long connecting way or path, especially inside a building; **2** a part of a speech or of a piece of writing or music

passenger *noun* a traveller in a vehicle

a British passport

passport *noun* a small book or card with your photograph and information about you in it, which you need if you are travelling abroad

¹**past** *noun* the time before the present; ▤passed

²**past** *adjective* to do with or belonging to the past; in the past; ▤passed

³**past** *preposition, adverb* **1** after: *ten past seven;* **2** up to and beyond; ▤passed

⁴**past** *noun, adjective* talking about an action that has already happened: *past tense;* ▤passed

pasta *noun* a food made from flour and water that is formed into many different shapes

¹**paste** *noun* **1** a thin mixture used for sticking paper; **2** a soft mixture that is easily shaped or spread

²**paste** *verb* to stick with paste

pastry *noun* a baked mixture of flour, fat, and milk or water that is used for pies and flans

pat *verb* **(patted)** to touch or strike gently with the palm of the hand; **pat** *noun*

¹**patch** *noun* **1** a piece of material used to cover a hole or a damaged place; **2** a part of a surface that is different from the space round it

²**patch** *verb* to cover a hole with a patch

path *noun* a track for walking or riding along

¹**patient** (*say* payshunt) *adjective* able to bear trouble or pain without complaining or to wait for something calmly; **patience** *noun;* **patiently** *adverb*

²**patient** (*say* payshunt) *noun* a sick person who is being treated by a doctor or nurse

pattern *noun* **1** a regularly repeated arrangement of shapes and colours; **2** something that can be copied and used as a guide for making something

pause *verb* to stop for a short time; **pause** *noun;* ▣ **paws**

pavement *noun* a hard path at the side of a road

paw *noun* an animal's foot with nails or claws; ▣ **poor, pore, pour**

¹pay *verb* **(pays, paying, paid)** to give money for something bought, work done, etc; **payment** *noun*

²pay *noun* money received for work

pea *noun* a round green seed eaten as a vegetable

peace *noun* **1** a state or time in which there is no war or fighting; **2** calmness; quietness; **peaceful** *adjective;* **peacefully** *adverb;* ▣ **piece**

peach *noun* a round fruit with soft yellowish red skin, sweet juicy flesh, and a large rough seed

peaches

peacock *noun* **1** *(female* **peahen/** the male of a large bird **(peafowl)** whose long tail feathers can be spread out to show beautiful colours and patterns; **2** a butterfly with large colourful wings

peal *noun* a ringing noise, or loud noise: *a **peal** of bells;* **peal** *verb;* ▣ **peel**

pear *noun* a sweet juicy fruit that is narrower at the stalk end; ▣ **pair**

pearl *noun* a hard silvery white ball formed inside shellfish, especially oysters, which is very valuable as a jewel

pebble *noun* a small stone

peck *verb* to eat or strike at something with the beak

peculiar *adjective* strange; odd; unusual

¹pedal *noun* a part of a machine which can be pressed with the foot to control or move the machine

²pedal *verb* **(pedalled)** to work the pedals of a machine; to move a machine by using pedals

¹peel *verb* to remove or lose the peel or an outer covering; ▣ **peal**

²peel *noun* the outer covering of a fruit or vegetable; ▣ **peal**

peep *verb* to look at something quickly and secretly; **peep** *noun*

¹peer feminine **peeress** *noun* **1** a person of high position, such as an **earl** or a **duke**; **2** a person who has the right to sit in the British House of Lords

²peer *verb* to look at something very carefully or hard

peg *noun* **1** a short piece of metal, plastic, etc, fixed to a wall or door for hanging coats and hats on; **2** a wooden or plastic clip for fastening wet washing to a line

¹pen *noun* a small place with a fence round it for keeping animals in

²pen *noun* an instrument for writing or drawing with ink

pence *see* PENNY

pencil *noun* a narrow pointed instrument containing a thin stick of lead or coloured material, for writing or drawing

penguin *noun* a large black and white seabird that swims well but cannot fly

jackass (blackfooted) penguin

penknife *noun (plural* **penknives***)* a small knife with one or more folding blades

penny *noun (plural* **pence** *or* **pennies***)* a small coin. In Britain, 100 pence equal one pound

pension *noun* money paid regularly to somebody who has reached the age when he or she can stop working

people *noun* men, women, and children; human beings

pepper *noun* **1** a hot-tasting spice used for flavouring food; **2** a green or red vegetable that can be eaten cooked or raw

per *preposition* for each; during each; ■**purr**

perfect *adjective* of the very best possible kind; without any faults; **perfection** *noun*; **perfectly** *adverb*

perform *verb* **1** to act, dance, play a musical instrument, etc, in front of an audience; **2** to do something; to carry out a piece of work; **performance** *noun*; **performer** *noun*

perfume *noun* a sweet smell; a pleasant smelling liquid that is put on the skin

perhaps *adverb* it may be; possibly

period *noun* a length of time

permanent *adjective* lasting for a long time or for ever; **permanently** *adverb*

permit *verb* **(permitted)** to allow; **permission** *noun*

person *noun* a man, woman, or child; a human being

personal *adjective* belonging to, or for, one person; of your own: *a personal letter*; **personally** *adverb*

persuade *(say* perswade*) verb* to cause somebody to do or to believe something

pet *noun* **1** an animal you look after and keep in your house; **2** a favourite person

petal *noun* one of the usually coloured leaflike parts of a flower

petrol *noun* a liquid used for producing power in car engines

PG *noun, adjective* a film that can be watched by anybody but for which you should ask your parents' permission if you are under 15

phantom *noun* a ghost

pharaoh *noun* a ruler of ancient Egypt

pheasant *noun* a large bird with a long tail

P

112

phone *noun* a telephone;
phone *verb*

photograph also **photo** *noun*
a picture obtained with a
camera and film; **photograph**
verb; **photographer** *noun;*
photographic *adjective*

phrase *noun* a group of words
that does not make a full
sentence

physical *adjective* **1** of or
about the body: **physical
education; 2** of or about the
natural world

physics *noun* the science of
matter and natural forces,
such as light, heat, and
sound

a grand piano

piano *noun (plural* **pianos***)* a
large musical instrument that
is played by pressing keys
which cause hammers to hit
wires; **pianist** *noun*

pick *verb* **1** to choose; **2** to
take up or pull off with the
fingers

¹picnic *noun* a meal eaten
outside, usually away from
home

²picnic *verb* **(picnicked)** to
have a picnic; **picnicker** *noun*

picture *noun* **1** a painting,
drawing, or photograph;
2 the pictures the cinema

pie *noun* a pastry case filled
with meat or fruit, baked
usually in a deep dish

piece *noun* **1** a part of
something; a part which is
separated from a whole; **2** a
single object: *a **piece** of
furniture;* ■ **peace**

pig *noun (male* **hog,** *female*
sow, *young* **piglet***)* a short-
legged animal with a curly
tail and thick skin, kept on
farms for food

pigeon *noun* a quite large
short-legged bird

piglet *noun* a young pig

pile *noun* a heap of things on
top of one another; **pile** *verb*

pill *noun* a small ball of solid
medicine to be swallowed

pillar *noun* a tall upright usually
round post made of concrete,
stone, etc

pillar-box also **postbox** *noun*
a box in the street with a
hole to post letters in

pillow *noun* an oblong cloth
bag filled with soft material,
for supporting the head in
bed: **pillowcase**

pilot *noun* **1** a person who flies
an aircraft; **2** a person who
guides ships in and out of a
harbour; **pilot** *verb*

pimple *noun* a small raised
diseased spot on the skin;
pimply *adjective;* **pimpled**
adjective

pin *noun* a short thin stiff
pointed piece of metal for
fastening cloth, paper, etc;
pin *verb*

P

¹pinch *verb* **1** to press tightly and often painfully between the thumb and finger or between two hard surfaces; **2** to steal

²pinch *noun* an amount that can be picked up between the thumb and a finger; a small amount

¹pine *verb* to become thin and weak slowly, through disease or unhappiness

²pine *noun* a tall tree with thin sharp leaves (**pine needles**), that bears cones

a pineapple growing

pineapple *noun* a large yellow juicy tropical fruit with thin stiff leaves on top

pink *noun, adjective* pale red; **pinkish** *adjective*

pint *noun* a measure of liquid equal to about 0.568 of a litre *(see last page)*

¹pip *noun* a small fruit seed

²pip *noun* a short high-sounding note, as given on the radio to tell the time

pipe *noun* **1** a tube for carrying a liquid or gas; **2** a small tube with a bowl-shaped container at one end, for smoking tobacco; **3** a tube-shaped musical instrument, played by blowing

pirate *noun* **1** a person who robs a ship at sea; **2** a person who uses or sells the work of other people such as books, records, or videos without permission or payment; **piracy** *noun*

pistol *noun* a small gun

pit *noun* **1** a hole, usually in the ground; **2** a coal mine

¹place *noun* **1** a particular area, part of space, or position; **2** a position in the result of a competition, race, etc; ■**plaice**

²place *verb* to put in a certain place or position; ■**plaice**

plaice *noun* a flat bony sea fish; ■**place**

¹plain *adjective* **1** easy to see, hear, or understand; **2** simple; without decoration; **plainly** *adverb;* ■**plane**

²plain *noun* a large area of flat land; ■**plane**

plait *(say* plat*) noun* a length of something, especially hair, made by twisting three or more pieces over and under one another; **plait** *verb*

plan *noun* **1** a carefully worked out arrangement for something to be done in the future; **2** a drawing of a building or room showing the shape, measurements, etc; **plan** *verb*

plane *noun* an aeroplane; ■**plain**

planet *noun* a large body in space that moves round a sun

planetarium *noun* a building containing a machine that throws spots of light onto a surface to show the movements of the stars and planets

¹**plant** *verb* to put plants or seeds in the ground to grow

²**plant** *noun* **1** a living thing that has leaves and roots and grows, usually in the ground; **2** the buildings and machines used in making something; a factory

plaster *noun* **1** a soft mixture that hardens when dry and is spread on walls to give a smooth surface; **2** a piece of sticky tape put on the body to protect a wound; **3** also **plaster cast** a special covering for protecting a broken bone in an arm, leg, etc, while it heals

plastic *noun* a man-made material that can be made into different shapes

Plasticine *noun (trademark)* a soft substance like clay, that comes in many colours, and is used for making small models, shapes, etc

plate *noun* **1** a flat dish from which food is eaten or served; **2** a flat thin piece of metal

platform *noun* **1** a raised floor or stage; **2** a raised surface along the side of the track at a railway station

¹**play** *noun* a story performed in a theatre or on the radio or television

²**play** *verb* **1** to have fun; to take part in a game: **playground**; **2** to perform a part in a film or play; **3** to make sounds on a musical instrument; **4** to reproduce the sounds recorded on a record, cassette, etc; **player** *noun*; **playful** *adjective*; **playfully** *adverb*

pleasant *adjective* enjoyable; nice; **pleasantly** *adverb*

please *verb* **1** to make somebody happy; **2** used to make a request more polite; **pleasure** *noun*

plenty *noun* a large quantity or number; enough; **plentiful** *adjective*

plough (*say like* cow) *noun* a farming tool for breaking up and turning over soil and earth; **plough** *verb*

an Eastern musical instrument played by plucking – a sitar

pluck *verb* **1** to pull the feathers off a bird; **2** to play a musical instrument by pulling the strings and letting go quickly

plug *noun* **1** a plastic object with metal pieces that connects a television set, iron, vacuum cleaner, etc, to an electrical socket; **2** something used for blocking a hole, especially a round piece of rubber or plastic for stopping water from running out of a sink or bath

plum *noun* a sweet juicy fruit with a smooth skin and large stone; the tree on which this grows

plumber *noun* somebody who fits and mends water pipes, central heating, etc

plus *preposition* with the addition of; and

Pluto *noun* the planet furthest from the sun

p.m. after midday (short for *post meridiem*)

pocket *noun* a small flat cloth bag sewn into or onto a piece of clothing

poem *noun* a piece of writing in patterns of lines and sounds, expressing something in powerful or beautiful language

poet *noun* a person who writes poems; **poetic** *adjective*

poetry *noun* poems

¹point *noun* 1 a sharp end; 2 the importance or purpose of something said or done; 3 an exact moment; 4 a mark or position on a compass, measuring instrument, etc; 5 a single quantity used in deciding the winner in a game, quiz, etc; a mark

²point *verb* to hold out a finger, a stick, etc, in a direction; to show where something is with the finger; **pointer** *noun*

¹poison *noun* a substance that harms or kills if it is taken into the body; **poisonous** *adjective*

²poison *verb* to give poison to; to harm or kill with poison

French flag flying from a flagpole

poke *verb* to push a pointed thing into or at somebody or something; **poke** *noun*

¹pole *noun* a long often thin round stick or post: **flagpole, telegraph pole**

²pole *noun* 1 either end of an imaginary straight line (**axis**) round which a solid round mass, such as the Earth, turns; 2 either of the points at the ends of a magnet where its power is greatest

police *noun* a body of men and women whose duty is to protect people and buildings, to make everyone obey the law, to catch criminals, etc: **police force, policeman, police station, policewoman**

¹polish *verb* to make something smooth and shiny by rubbing

²polish *noun* a liquid, paste, etc, used in polishing a surface

polite *adjective* having good manners; **politely** *adverb;* **politeness** *noun*

politics *noun* the study of government; how countries should be governed; **political** *adjective*

pond *noun* an area of water smaller than a lake

pony *noun* a small horse

pool *noun* 1 a small area of water; a pond; 2 a small amount of any liquid poured or dropped on a surface; 3 a swimming pool

116

poor *adjective* **1** having very little money; **2** low in quality or quantity; not good; **3** needing kindness; unlucky; ■ **paw, pore, pour**

¹pop *noun* a sudden noise like the sound of the top being pulled out of a bottle

²pop *noun* modern popular music and songs

Pope *noun* head of the Roman Catholic Church

poppy *noun* a plant that has a milky juice in its stem and bright, usually red flowers

popular *adjective* liked by many people

porcupine

porcupine *noun* a small short-legged animal that has long stiff prickles on its back and sides and is larger than a hedgehog

pore *noun* any of the tiny holes in the skin through which you sweat; ■ **paw, poor, pour**

pork *noun* meat from a pig

porridge *noun* a soft breakfast food made by boiling oats in milk or water

¹port *noun* a harbour or a town with a harbour

²port *noun* the left side of a ship or aircraft as you face forward

porter *noun* a person who carries luggage at railway stations, airports, etc

position *noun* **1** the place where somebody or something is or stands; **2** the place where somebody or something belongs; the proper place; **3** the way or manner in which somebody or something is placed or moves, stands, sits, etc; **4** a condition or state; **5** a job

possess *verb* to have or own **possession** *noun*

possible *adjective* that may exist, happen, or be done; **possibility** *noun;* **possibly** *adverb*

¹post *noun* a strong thick upright pole or bar made of wood, metal, etc, fixed into the ground or some other base especially as a support: **gatepost**

²post *noun* the system for collecting, carrying, and delivering letters, parcels, etc: **postman, post office, postwoman**

³post *verb* to send something by post

⁴post *noun* **1** a special place of duty, especially on guard or on watch; **2** a job

postage stamp *noun* a stamp for sticking on things to be posted

P

one of the first postage stamps, a Penny Black

POSTAGE
ONE PENNY

117

postcard *noun* a small card, often with a picture on one side, on which a message may be written and sent by post

poster *noun* a large printed notice or drawing put up in a public place

postpone *verb* to put off until a later time or day; **postponement** *noun*

pot *noun* a container, especially a round one, made from baked clay, metal, etc

potato *noun (plural* **potatoes***)* a vegetable with a thin usually brown skin that is cooked and served in many ways

pottery *noun* pots, dishes, etc, made from baked clay

pound *noun* **1** a measure of weight equal to about 0.454 kilograms; **2** the standard unit of money in Britain, which is divided into 100 pence

pour *verb* **1** to flow or make a liquid flow; **2** to rain hard and steadily; ■ **paw, poor, pore**

powder *noun* a substance in the form of very small dry grains; **powdery** *adjective*

power *noun* **1** strength, force, or energy; **2** the ability to do something; **3** a person, group, government, etc, that has control; **powerful** *adjective*

practice *noun* the doing of something; ■ **practise**

practise *verb* to do something regularly or over and over again, especially in order to become better at it; ■ **practice**

praise *verb* to speak well of; to say that you admire; **praise** *noun*

pram *noun* a four-wheeled vehicle for a baby which is pushed by hand

prawn *noun* a shellfish that looks like a large shrimp

pray *verb* to speak, often silently, to God or a god; ■ **prey**

prayer *noun* the act of praying; what you say when you are praying

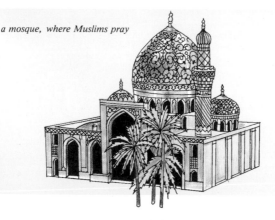

a mosque, where Muslims pray

118

preach *verb* to give a religious talk; **preacher** *noun*

precede *verb* to come before or in front

precious *adjective* very valuable

prefer *verb* **(preferred)** to like better; **preference** *noun*

pregnant *adjective* about to have a baby; **pregnancy** *noun*

prehistoric *adjective* to do with or belonging to time in history before there were written records

prepare *verb* to get ready or make something ready; **preparation** *noun*

preposition *noun* a word like *to, for, on, by,* etc; a word that is put in front of a noun to show where, when, how, etc

¹present (*say* prez-*ent*) *noun* a gift

²present (*say pree*-zent) *verb* to give; to offer

³present (*say* prez-*ent*) *adjective* **1** in the place talked of; there; here; **2** existing or happening now

⁴present (*say* prez-*ent*) *noun* the present time; this time

⁵present (*say* prez-*ent*) *noun, adjective* talking about an action that is happening now: **present tense**

preserve *verb* to keep safe or in good condition; **preservation** *noun*

president *noun* **1** the head of government in many countries that do not have a king or queen: *the **President** of France;* **2** the head of a business, company, bank, club, etc

¹press *verb* **1** to push firmly and steadily; **2** to make flat or smooth, as by ironing; **pressure** *noun*

²press *noun* **1** an act of pressing something; **2** newspapers and magazines in general; **3** a machine for printing books, newspapers, etc

pretend *verb* **1** to act in a deceiving way; **2** to imagine as a game

¹pretty *adjective* pleasing to look at; **prettily** *adverb;* **prettiness** *noun*

²pretty *adverb* quite though not completely; fairly

prevent *verb* to stop something from happening; **prevention** *noun*

prey *noun* an animal that is hunted by another; ■ **pray**

price *noun* an amount of money for which a thing is bought or sold

prick *verb* to make a very small hole or wound in something with a sharp-pointed object

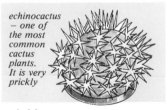

echinocactus – one of the most common cactus plants. It is very prickly

prickle *noun* a small sharp part of a plant or animal; **prickly** *adjective*

pride *noun* **1** the feeling of having a good opinion of yourself or being satisfied with yourself; being proud; **2** a group of lions

priest *noun* a person trained for various religious duties

primary *adjective* earliest; first

primary school *noun* a school for children aged between five and eleven

prime minister *noun* the head of government

primrose *noun* a pale yellow flower that grows in the spring

prince *noun* the son or grandson of a king or queen

princess *noun* **1** a daughter or granddaughter of a king or queen; **2** the wife of a prince

¹print *noun* **1** a mark on a surface showing the shape, pattern, etc, of the thing pressed into it: **footprint**; **2** printed letters; **3** a photograph printed from film

²print *verb* **1** to make a book, magazine, etc, by putting words and pictures on paper using a special machine; **2** to make or copy a photograph on paper from film; **3** to write without joining the letters

printer *noun* **1** a person whose job is printing; **2** a machine for making photographic prints; **3** a machine connected to a computer, for printing out paper copies of programs, data, etc

printout *noun* information produced and printed on paper by a computer

prism *noun* a block of clear glass that breaks up light into its separate colours

prison *noun* a large building where criminals are kept locked up; **prisoner** *noun*

private *adjective* belonging to or to do with one person or one group of people; not for everybody; **privacy** *noun;* **privately** *adverb*

privilege *noun* a right or favour which only one person or a few people can have

prize *noun* something of value given to the winner of a competition, game, etc; a reward for doing well or for good work

probably *adverb* almost but not quite certainly; likely

problem *noun* a difficulty that needs attention; a question for which an answer is needed

procession *noun* a line of people or vehicles moving slowly forwards

¹produce (*say pro-duce*) *verb* **1** to show or bring out; **2** to make or cause to exist; **product** *noun;* **production** *noun*

²produce (*say prod-uce*) *noun* something produced, especially by growing or farming

professor *noun* a senior teacher at a university

a prism, which divides light into its different parts

120

profit *noun* money you get when you sell something for more than it cost to buy or make; **profitable** *adjective;* ■ prophet

¹**program** *noun* a set of instructions for a computer; ■ programme

²**program** *verb* (programmed) to provide a computer with a program; ■ programme

programme *noun* 1 a list of things to be done or that will happen; 2 a show, story, etc, on radio or television; ■ program

promise *verb* to say that you will or will not do something; **promise** *noun*

pronoun *noun* a word, like *he, she, it, they,* etc, that is used instead of using a noun again

pronounce *verb* to make the sound of a letter or a word; **pronunciation** *noun*

proof *noun* a way of showing that something is true

propel *verb* to drive or push something forward; **propulsion** *noun*

propeller *noun* a set of specially shaped blades that turn rapidly to drive an aeroplane or ship

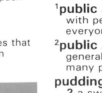

a ship's propeller

proper *adjective* suitable; correct; right; **properly** *adverb*

property *noun* 1 something that is owned; 2 land, buildings, or both together

prophet *noun* a person directed by God to make known God's wishes or to teach a religion; ■ profit

protect *verb* to keep safe; to prevent somebody or something from being hurt or damaged; **protection** *noun*

protein *noun* a substance in food that is needed to build up the body and to keep it healthy

proud *adjective* having a high opinion of yourself or of something connected with yourself; **proudly** *adverb*

prove *verb* to show that something is true

provide *verb* to supply

prune *noun* a dried plum

pub also **public house** *noun* a building where alcohol may be bought and drunk

¹**public** *adjective* for or to do with people in general; for everyone to use

²**public** *noun* 1 people in general; 2 **in public** with many people present

pudding *noun* 1 a dessert; 2 a sweet food made with pastry, rice, bread, etc, and served hot; 3 a meat dish boiled with a pastry cover

puddle *noun* a small pool of water, especially rainwater

puff *noun* a sudden rush of air, smoke, etc

pull *verb* 1 to draw something along behind; 2 to move or draw something towards yourself

P

121

pullover *noun* a jumper

pump *noun* a machine for forcing a liquid or gas into or out of something; **pump** *verb*

pumpkin *noun* a large round dark yellow vegetable

punch *verb* to strike hard with the fist; **punch** *noun*

puncture *noun* a small hole, especially in a tyre; **puncture** *verb*

punish *verb* to cause somebody to suffer for a fault or crime; **punishment** *noun*

¹**pupil** *noun* a person, especially a child, who is being taught

²**pupil** *noun* the small round opening in the middle of your eye, that looks black and which can grow larger or smaller

puppet *noun* **1** a small toy figure of a person or an animal that can be made to move by pulling wires or strings; **2** also **glove puppet** a hollow cloth figure into which you put your hand to move the figure with your fingers

puppy also **pup** *noun* a young dog

pure *adjective* without anything mixed with it; clean; **purely** *adverb*

purple *noun* a dark colour between red and blue; **purple** *adjective;* **purplish** *adjective*

purpose *noun* a reason for doing something

purr *noun* a low sound produced by a cat when it is pleased; **purr** *verb;* ■**per**

purse *noun* a small bag for carrying money

push *verb* to press somebody or something forward, away, or to a different position; **push** *noun*

pushchair *noun* a light folding chair on wheels for pushing a small child about

put *verb* **(puts, putting, put)** to move, place, or fix somebody or something in, on, or to a certain place

¹**puzzle** *verb* to be difficult to understand; **puzzled** *adjective*

²**puzzle** *noun* **1** something that you cannot understand or explain; a difficult question to answer; **2** a game, toy, or apparatus in which parts must be fitted together correctly: **crossword puzzle, jigsaw puzzle**

pyjamas *noun* a loose shirt and trousers that you wear in bed

pyramid *noun* a solid object or shape with straight flat triangular sides that slope upwards and meet in a point at the top

Egyptian pyramids at Giza

quack *noun* the sound that ducks make; **quack** *verb*

quality *noun* **1** how good something is; **2** something typical of a person or thing

quantity *noun* the amount of something or the number of things

²question *verb* **1** to ask a question; **2** to raise doubts about somebody or something; **questioner** *noun*

question mark *noun* the mark (?) used in writing or printing at the end of a sentence that asks a question

a traffic queue

quarrel *noun* an argument; **quarrel** *verb*

quart *noun* a measure of liquid equal to ¼ of a gallon, 2 pints, or about 1.136 litres *(see last page)*

quarter *noun* **1** one of four parts of anything; ¼; **2** 15 minutes before or after the hour: *quarter past; quarter to*

queen *noun* **1** a female ruler of a country or the wife of a king; **2** any of the four playing cards with a picture of a queen, that comes between the jack and the king

queer *adjective* strange; unusual; **queerly** *adverb*

¹question *noun* **1** a sentence which asks something and needs an answer; **2** a problem; something to be talked about

¹queue *noun* a line of waiting people, cars, etc; ■**cue**

²queue *verb* to form or join a line while waiting; ■**cue**

quick *adjective* fast; not slow; soon finished; **quickly** *adverb*

quiet *adjective* **1** having or making very little noise; **2** calm; peaceful; **quiet** *noun;* **quietly** *adverb;* **quietness** *noun;* ■**quite**

quilt *noun* a thick cover for a bed

quite *adverb* **1** completely; perfectly; **2** rather; ■**quiet**

quiz *noun* a competition or game in which questions are asked

quotation mark *noun* either of a pair of marks ('') or ('') showing the beginning and end of words said or written by somebody else

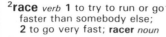

rabbit *noun (male* **buck**, *female* **doe)** a small long-eared animal of the hare family that lives in a burrow

¹race *noun* a competition to see who can do something fastest

²race *verb* **1** to try to run or go faster than somebody else; **2** to go very fast; **racer** *noun*

³race *noun* a group of people or animals of the same shape, colour, size, etc; **racial** *adjective;* **racially** *adverb*

rack *noun* a frame with bars, hooks, etc, for holding things: **luggage rack**

¹racket, **racquet** *noun* a network, usually of nylon, stretched in a frame with a handle, for hitting the ball in games such as tennis

²racket *noun* a loud noise

a radar screen – used to help pilots to land safely, especially in bad weather

radar *noun* a way of finding the position of solid objects, such as ships, aeroplanes, etc, by using radio waves

radiate *verb* to send out light or heat

radiation *noun* **1** the sending out of heat, light, etc; **2** the giving off of harmful rays from a radioactive substance

radiator *noun* **1** an apparatus for sending out heat in a house; **2** an apparatus for cooling the engine of a car

¹radio *noun* **1** the sending or receiving of sounds through the air by electrical waves; **2** an apparatus to receive sounds sent out in this way

²radio *verb* to send through the air by electrical waves

radioactive *adjective* giving out energy or rays; **radioactivity** *noun*

rag *noun* **1** a small piece of old cloth; **2** an old worn out piece of clothing

rail *noun* **1** a fixed bar to hang things on or for protection; **2** one of the pair of metal bars along which a train runs: **railway**

rain *noun* water falling in drops from the clouds: **raindrop**, **rainwater**; **rain** *verb;* **rainy** *adjective;* ■ **reign, rein**

rainbow *noun* an arch of different colours that sometimes appears in the sky after it has rained

raincoat *noun* a waterproof coat

raise *verb* to lift, push, or move up; to make lighter

raisin *noun* a dried grape

rake *noun* a gardening tool consisting of a row of teeth at the end of a long handle, for levelling soil, gathering up leaves, etc; **rake** *verb*

ram *noun* a male sheep

RAM also **random access memory** *noun* a type of computer memory that holds information and programs

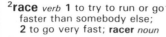R

124

ran *see* RUN

random *adjective* made or done without a fixed plan; by chance; **randomly** *adverb*

rang *see* RING

range *noun* 1 a line of mountains or hills; 2 the distance that a gun can fire; 3 a set of different objects of the same kind

rapid *adjective* very fast; **rapidly** *adverb*

rare *adjective* not happening often; not often seen; **rarely** *adverb*

¹**rash** *noun* a set of red spots on the skin, caused by illness

²**rash** *adjective* acting quickly without thinking enough of what might happen; **rashly** *adverb*

raspberry *noun* a soft sweet red berry; the bush on which this grows

rat *noun* a long-tailed animal with strong sharp teeth, related to but larger than the mouse

rather *adverb* 1 a little; quite: *rather* cold weather; 2 sooner; more willingly: *I'd* **rather** *play tennis than swim*

¹**rattle** *verb* to make a lot of quick little noises

²**rattle** *noun* a baby's toy that makes a rattling noise when it is shaken

baby's bell rattle

raw *adjective* not cooked; ■**roar**

ray *noun* a line of light, heat, or other form of energy

razor *noun* a sharp instrument for shaving

reach *verb* 1 to stretch out your hand or arm; 2 to be big enough to touch; to stretch out as far as; 3 to get to; to arrive at

read *verb* (**reads, reading, read**) to look at and understand printed or written words; ■**reed**

ready *adjective* 1 prepared; in the right way or order for use; 2 willing; **readily** *adverb*

real *adjective* actual; true; not imagined; ■**reel**

realise *verb* to understand and believe something as a fact; **realisation** *noun*

really *adverb* in fact; truly

reason *noun* 1 what makes you decide to do something; why something happens; 2 the power to think and understand; **reasonable** *adjective;* **reasonably** *adverb*

receipt (*say* re-seet) *noun* a written or printed note saying that something has been paid for or that something has been received

receive *verb* to get something given or sent to you; **receiver** *noun*

recent *adjective* having happened only a short time ago; **recently** *adverb*

recipe (*say* resipee) *noun* a set of instructions for cooking food

R

recognise *verb* **1** to know again somebody or something you have met before; **2** to agree that something is true; **recognisable** *adjective;* **recognition** *noun*

¹record (*say* re-kord) *verb* **1** to write down so that it will be known; **2** to keep sounds or pictures so that they can be heard or seen again; **recording** *noun*

²record (*say* rek-ord) *noun* **1** information that is written down and kept; **2** the best yet done; **3** also **gramophone record, disc** a circular piece of plastic on which sound is recorded: **record player**

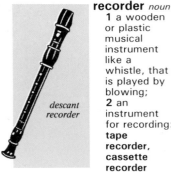

recorder *noun* **1** a wooden or plastic musical instrument like a whistle, that is played by blowing; **2** an instrument for recording: **tape recorder, cassette recorder**

descant recorder

red *noun* the colour of blood; **red** *adjective;* **reddish** *adjective;* **redness** *noun*

reduce *verb* to get or make smaller or less; **reduction** *noun*

reed *noun* a grasslike plant that grows in wet places; ■ **read**

reel *noun* a round object on which cotton, wire, fishing line, recording tape, etc, can be wound; ■ **real**

reflect *verb* to throw back light, heat, sound, or a picture; **reflection** *noun*

refrigerator also **fridge** *noun* a machine in which food or drink can be kept cool

refuse *verb* not to allow; not to accept, do, or give

register *noun* a list of names; **register** *verb;* **registration** *noun*

regret *verb* (**regretted**) to be sorry about something

regular *adjective* **1** done or happening at fixed times; **2** normal; proper; correct; **regularly** *adverb*

reign (*say* rane) *verb* **1** to be king or queen; **2** to exist noticeably: *quietness reigned;* **reign** *noun;* ■ **rain, rein**

rein *noun* a long narrow band of leather by which a horse is controlled; ■ **rain, reign**

reindeer *noun* a deer with long branching horns

reject (*say* re-ject) *verb* to refuse to accept; to throw away; **reject** (*say* ree-ject) *noun;* **rejection** *noun*

rejoice *verb* to feel or show great joy

related *adjective* of the same family or kind

relation *noun* a member of your family

relative *noun* a relation

relax *verb* **1** to make or become less active; to stop worrying; **2** to make or become less stiff or tight; **relaxation** *noun*

release *verb* **1** to set free; to allow to come out; **2** to allow a new film or a record to be shown to or bought by the public; **release** *noun*

reliable *adjective* fit to be trusted; **reliably** *adverb*

relief *noun* **1** a feeling of comfort at the ending of worry or pain; **2** help for people in trouble: **famine relief**; **relieve** *verb*

religion *noun* **1** belief in one or more gods; **2** a particular set of beliefs and the worship, behaviour, etc, connected with them; **religious** *adjective*

rely *verb* **1** to depend on something or on something happening; **2** to trust somebody or trust somebody to do something

remain *verb* to stay or be left behind after others have gone; **remainder** *noun*

remark *noun* something said; an opinion; **remark** *verb*

remarry *verb* to marry for a second time; to marry again

remember *verb* to keep in the memory; to not forget

remind *verb* to cause somebody to remember; **reminder** *noun*

remove *verb* to take away; to take off; **removal** *noun*

¹rent *noun* money paid regularly for the use of a house, office, etc

²rent *verb* to have the use of or allow somebody to use a house, room, etc, in return for money

¹repair *verb* to mend

²repair *noun* **1** mending; **2 in good/bad repair** in good/bad condition

repeat *verb* to say or do again; **repeat** *noun*; **repetition** *noun*

replace *verb* **1** to put something back in its place; **2** to take the place of somebody or something; **replacement** *noun*

reply *verb* to answer; **reply** *noun*

report *verb* to give the story of; to say what has taken place; **report** *noun*; **reporter** *noun*

reproduce *verb* **1** to produce young; **2** to make a copy of; **reproduction** *noun*

a grass snake – a type of reptile found in England and Wales

reptile *noun* a cold-blooded animal, such as a snake, tortoise, or crocodile, that has a body covered in scales

request *verb* to ask politely; **request** *noun*

rescue *verb* to save from harm or danger; to set free; **rescue** *noun*; **rescuer** *noun*

research *noun* the study of a subject, so as to learn new facts; **research** *verb*

respect *noun* **1** admiration; feeling of honour; **2** attention; care; **respect** *verb*

R

response *noun* an answer or reply; an action done in answer to something

responsible *adjective* **1** having the duty of looking after somebody or something, so that you can be blamed if things go wrong; **2** able to be trusted; **responsibility** *noun*; **responsibly** *adverb*

¹rest *noun* **1** freedom from anything tiring; sleep; **2** a support; **rest** *verb*; **restful** *adjective*; **restless** *adjective*

²rest *noun* what is left

restaurant *noun* a place where food is sold and eaten

result *noun* **1** what happens because of an action or event; an effect; **2** a person's or team's success or failure in an examination, match, etc: *the football results*

retire *verb* to stop working at your job, usually because of old age; **retired** *adjective*; **retirement** *noun*

return *verb* **1** to come or go back; **2** to give or send back; **return** *noun*

revolution *noun* **1** one complete circular movement round a fixed point; a full turn of a wheel or other object; **2** a complete change; **3** the changing of a government by force

reward *noun* something received or given for work, service, finding something, etc

rewind *verb* to wind film, tape, etc, back onto a reel; **rewind** *noun*

rhinoceros also **rhino** *noun* a large heavy thick-skinned animal, with either one or two horns on its nose

rhubarb *noun* a garden plant with thick juicy stems that can be eaten

rhyme *noun* **1** a word that ends with the same sound as another; **2** a short and not serious poem or piece of writing, using words that rhyme; **rhyme** *verb*

rhythm *noun* a regular pattern of beats in music, poetry, etc; **rhythmic, rhythmical** *adjective*; **rhythmically** *adverb*

ribbon *noun* a long narrow band of cloth used for tying things, for ornament, etc

rice *noun* a food grain grown in hot wet places, with seeds that can be cooked and eaten

rice growing in paddy fields

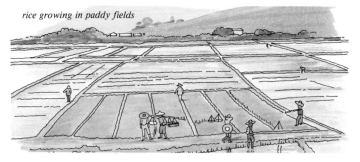

128

rich *adjective* **1** having a lot of money or property; **2** valuable and beautiful; **3** containing a lot of a particular thing; full of goodness and colour: *rich food*; **riches** *noun*; **richly** *adverb*; **richness** *noun*

rid *verb* (**rids, ridding, rid**) **1** to make free of; **2 get rid of** to free yourself from something; to drive or give away

riddle *noun* **1** a difficult and amusing question to which you must guess the answer; **2** something you cannot understand

¹ride *verb* (**rides, riding, rode, ridden**) **1** to travel along, controlling and sitting on a horse, bicycle, etc; **2** to travel on a horse; **rider** *noun*

²ride *noun* a journey on an animal, in a vehicle, etc

rifle *noun* a gun fired from the shoulder, with a long barrel

¹right *noun, adjective* the side or direction opposite to left;  **rite, write**

²right *adjective* **1** good; proper; **2** correct; true;  **rite, write**

³right *noun* **1** what is good; **2** something a person can have or do because of the law;  **rite, write**

⁴right *adverb* **1** towards the right; **2** directly; straight; **3** properly; correctly; **4** all the way;  **rite, write**

rind (*say* rynd) *noun* the thick outer covering of certain fruits, foods, etc

¹ring *noun* **1** a circle; **2** a circular band; something shaped like a circle: **key ring**; **3** a metal band worn on the finger; **4** any closed-in space

where things are shown or performed, as in a circus or for boxing;  **wring**

a signet ring has a person's initials on it

²ring *verb* to put or make a ring round something;  **wring**

³ring *verb* (**rings, ringing, rang, rung**) **1** to cause a bell to sound; **2** to make a sound like a bell; **3** to telephone; **4 ring a bell** to remind you of something; **ring** *noun*;  **wring**

rinse *verb* to wash in clean water to remove soap, dirt, etc; **rinse** *noun*

rip *noun* a long tear; **rip** *verb*

ripe *adjective* fully grown and ready to be eaten

¹rise *verb* (**rises, rising, rose, risen**) to go up; to get higher; to increase

²rise *noun* **1** an increase in wages, prices, etc; **2** the act of growing greater or more powerful

¹risk *noun* a danger; a chance of losing something; **risky** *adjective*

²risk *verb* **1** to place in danger; **2** to take a chance

rite *noun* a ceremony, especially one that is religious;  **right, write**

129

river *noun* a wide natural stream of water

road *noun* a smooth broad prepared track for wheeled vehicles; ▣**rode**

roar *noun* a deep loud continuing sound; **roar** *verb*; ▣**raw**

roast *verb* to cook meat or other foods by dry heat in an oven or over a fire

rob *verb* (**robbed**) to take money, goods, etc, from a person or place when it is not yours; to steal from; **robber** *noun*; **robbery** *noun*

robin also **robin redbreast** *noun* a fat little bird, with a brown back and a red breast

robot *noun* **1** a machine that can do some human work; **2** an imaginary machine figure that acts as if alive

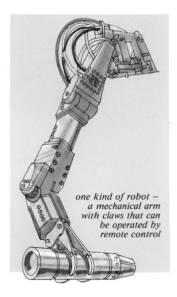

one kind of robot – a mechanical arm with claws that can be operated by remote control

¹**rock** *noun* **1** stone forming part of the Earth's surface; **2** a large separate piece of stone; **3** a hard sticky sweet made in long round bars; **rocky** *adjective*

²**rock** *verb* to move backwards and forwards or from side to side

³**rock** *noun* a kind of popular modern music played on electric instruments and with a strong beat

rocket *noun* **1** a kind of firework that shoots high into the air and lets out coloured flames; **2** a machine of this kind driven by burning gases, used for aircraft and spacecraft

rod *noun* a long thin stiff stick of wood, metal, etc

rode *see* RIDE; ▣**road**

role *noun* the part taken by somebody in a play or film; ▣**roll**

¹**roll** *noun* **1** a flat piece of some material rolled into a tube shape; **2** a small loaf of bread for one person; ▣**role**

²**roll** *verb* **1** to turn over and over, round and round, or from side to side; **2** to move steadily and smoothly along as if on wheels; **3** to form into a circular shape by curling round and round; **4** to make flat by passing something over and over: **rolling pin**; **5** to make a long deep sound: *the drums* **rolled**; ▣**role**

Roman Catholic *noun* a member of the branch of the Christian religion (**Roman Catholic Church**) which has the Pope as its head; **Roman Catholic** *adjective*

thatchers at work using straw to make a thatched roof

roof *noun* **1** the outside covering on top of a building; **2** the top covering of a tent, vehicle, etc; **3 the roof of the mouth** the bony upper part of the inside of the mouth

room *noun* **1** a division of a building, with its own walls, floor, and ceiling; **2** space which could be filled or is enough for any purpose

root *noun* **1** the part of a plant that grows down into the soil; **2** the part of a tooth, hair, or organ that holds it to the body; ■ **route**

rope *noun* a strong thick cord made of twisted threads

¹rose *noun* a sweet-smelling flower with prickly stems; the bush on which this grows

²rose *see* RISE

rot *verb* **(rotted)** to decay or go bad; **rot** *noun*; **rotten** *adjective*

rough *adjective* **1** not smooth; **2** violent; stormy; **3** done or made quickly and not yet in finished form: *a rough drawing*; **roughly** *adverb*; **roughen** *verb*

¹round *adjective* **1** shaped like a circle or a ball; **2** curved

²round *adverb, preposition* **1** with a circular movement or movements; spinning in a circle; **2** in a circular position; surrounding a central point; **3** all over the place; in or into all parts; **4** so as to face the other way; **5 all the year round** during the whole year

³round *noun* **1** one stage, period, or game in a competition or sport; **2** a regular journey to many houses, offices, etc: *a paper round;* **3** a complete slice of bread

roundabout *noun* **1** a circular machine on which you can ride, usually at a fairground; **2** a circular place where several roads meet or cross

rounders *noun* a ball game in which a player hits the ball and then runs round the sides of a square

route *noun* a way planned or followed from one place to another; ■ **root**

¹row *(say like* no*) noun* a neat line of people or things side by side

²row *(say like* now*) noun* a quarrel; a loud noise; **row** *verb*

³row *(say like* no*) verb* to move through the water with oars; **row** *noun*; **rower** *noun*

royal *adjective* for, belonging to, supported by, or connected with a king or queen; **royally** *adverb*

rub *verb* **(rubbed)** to slide something to and fro or round and round against another; **rub** *noun*

131

rubber *noun* 1 a substance, made from chemicals or from the juice of a tropical tree, which keeps out water and springs back into position after being stretched; 2 a piece of this substance used for removing pencil marks; **rubbery** *adjective*

rubbish *noun* 1 waste material to be thrown away; 2 silly remarks; nonsense

rude *adjective* not polite; **rudely** *adverb*; **rudeness** *noun*

rug *noun* 1 a thick floor mat; 2 a large warm woollen covering to wrap round yourself when travelling or camping

rugby also **rugby football, rugger** *noun* a type of game played with an oval ball, by teams of thirteen (**rugby league**) or fifteen (**rugby union**) men

ruin *verb* to destroy and spoil completely; **ruin** *noun*

an ancient ruined city – Inca ruins at Machupicchu, Peru

¹rule *noun* 1 an order, law, etc, that tells you what you must or must not do; 2 government; 3 **as a rule** usually; generally

²rule *verb* 1 to have and use the highest power over a country, people, etc, especially as a government; 2 to draw a straight line

ruler *noun* 1 a person who rules; 2 a long narrow piece of hard material with straight edges for measuring things or drawing lines

rumour *noun* something that people tell each other but that may not be true

¹run *verb* (**runs, running, ran, run**) 1 to move on your legs faster than walking; 2 to move quickly; 3 to work or cause to work: *the car runs well;* 4 to flow, pour, drip, etc; 5 to stretch; to continue: *The road runs beside the river;* 6 to be in charge of a shop, business, etc

²run *noun* 1 the action of running; 2 a journey; 3 a point won in cricket

¹rung *noun* one of the bars that form the steps of a ladder

²rung *see* RING

runway *noun* an area with a specially prepared hard surface, on which aircraft land and take off

rush *verb* to hurry; to act quickly; **rush** *noun*

rust *noun* the reddish brown substance that forms on iron when it has been wet; **rust** *verb*; **rusty** *adjective*

132

¹**sack** *noun* **1** a large bag used for storing or moving goods: **sackful; 2** the taking away of someone's job by an employer

²**sack** *verb* to take somebody's job away

sad *adjective* (**sadder**) feeling, showing, or causing sorrow; unhappy; **sadly** *adverb;* **sadness** *noun*

saddle *noun* a leather seat that fits on the back of a horse or on a bicycle, for a rider to sit on

¹**safe** *adjective* out of danger; not able to be hurt; protected; **safely** *adverb;* **safety** *noun*

²**safe** *noun* a box or cupboard with thick metal sides and a lock, used to protect money, jewellery, etc

said *see* SAY

¹**sail** *noun* **1** a piece of cloth fixed on a ship to move it through the water by the force of the wind; **2** a short trip in such a ship; **3 set sail** to begin a trip at sea; ▣ **sale**

²**sail** *verb* **1** to travel on water; **2** to direct a ship or boat on water; **sailor** *noun;* ▣ **sale**

salad *noun* a mixture of vegetables or fruits, served cold

sale *noun* **1** an act of selling; **2** a time when goods are sold at lower prices than usual; ▣ **sail**

salmon *noun* a large fish of the northern seas with silvery skin and yellowish pink flesh, which swims up rivers to breed

¹**salt** *noun* a very common colourless or white solid substance used to preserve food, improve its taste, etc; **salty** *adjective*

²**salt** *verb* **1** to add salt to; to put salt on; **2** to preserve with salt

same *adjective* **1** like something else in every way; alike in almost every way; not different or changed; **2** being always only one single thing, person, etc

sand *noun* a loose material of very small fine grains, found along coasts and in deserts; **sandy** *adjective*

sandal *noun* a light open shoe with bands to hold it on the foot

sandwich *noun* two slices of bread with some other food between them

sang *see* SING

sank *see* SINK

sardine *noun* a small sea fish used as food

sat *see* SIT

S

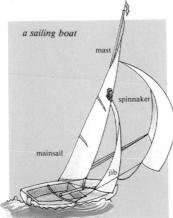

a sailing boat

mast

spinnaker

mainsail

jib

satchel *noun* a small bag of strong cloth or leather for carrying books on your shoulder or back

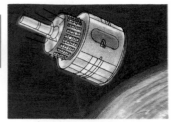

Meteosat – a satellite used in weather forecasting

satellite *noun* **1** a small body moving round a planet; **2** a man-made object that travels round the Earth, moon, etc

satisfy *verb* **1** to make happy; to please; **2** to be or give enough for; **satisfying** *adjective;* **satisfaction** *noun;* **satisfactory** *adjective*

Saturday *noun* the seventh day of the week

Saturn *noun* a planet surrounded by large rings that is sixth in order from the sun

sauce *noun* any of various kinds of usually cooked liquids put on or eaten with food; ■**source**

saucepan *noun* a deep round metal cooking pot with a handle and a lid

saucer *noun* a small plate made for setting a cup on

sausage *noun* a thin eatable tube of animal skin filled with a mixture of meat, cereal, spices, etc: **sausage roll**

save *verb* **1** to make safe from danger; **2** to keep for later use; **3** to use less; to stop waste; **saver** *noun;* **savings** *noun*

¹saw *noun* a tool for cutting materials, having a thin flat blade with a row of V-shaped teeth on the edge; ■**sore**

²saw *verb* (**saws, sawing, sawed, sawn** *or* **sawed**) to cut with a saw; ■**sore**

³saw *see* SEE; ■**sore**

say *verb* (**says, saying, said**) **1** to pronounce a sound, word, etc; to speak; **2** to give an opinion, etc, ask a question, etc, using words; **3 that is to say** also i.e. in other words; **saying** *noun*

scab *noun* a hard mass of dried blood which forms over a wound while it is healing; **scabby** *adjective*

¹scale *noun* one of the small nearly flat stiff pieces covering the skin of some animals, especially fish and reptiles

²scale *noun* **1** a set of marks on a measuring instrument such as a ruler or a thermometer; **2** a rule or set of numbers comparing measurements on a map or model with actual measurements; **3** a set of musical notes going up or down in order

³scale also **scales** *noun* a weighing machine

⁴scale *verb* to climb up

scampi *noun* large prawns

scar *noun* a mark remaining on the skin or an organ from a wound, cut, etc; **scar** *verb*

scare *verb* 1 to cause sudden fear to somebody; 2 to become afraid; **scare** *noun;* **scared** *adjective*

scarecrow *noun* a figure in the shape of a man, set up in a field to keep birds away from the crops

scarf *noun (plural* **scarfs** *or* **scarves)** a piece of cloth for wearing round the neck, head, or shoulders

scarlet *noun* a very bright red colour; **scarlet** *adjective*

scatter *verb* 1 to cause a group of people or things to separate widely; 2 to spread widely in all directions

scene *noun* 1 a short part of a play, film, etc; 2 the place where something happens; 3 a view of a place; ■ **seen**

scenery *noun* 1 the set of painted backgrounds and other articles used on a theatre stage; 2 a view of the countryside

scent *noun* 1 a liquid with a nice smell; perfume; 2 a smell; ■ **cent, sent**

schedule *(say* **shedule)** *noun* a timetable of things to be done

¹school *noun* a place where people go to learn: **school boy, school girl, schoolwork**

²school *noun* a large group of one kind of fish, whale, etc

science *noun* 1 the study of knowledge which can be made into a system and which usually depends on seeing and testing facts and making general natural laws; 2 a branch of such knowledge, such as chemistry, physics, or biology; **scientific** *adjective;* **scientist** *noun*

scissors *noun* two sharp blades having handles at one end with holes for the fingers, fastened at the centre so that they open in the shape of the letter X and cut when they close: **pair of scissors**

scold *verb* to speak angrily, especially to blame; **scolding** *noun*

scone *(say* **skon** *or* **skohn)** *noun* a small soft round cake

scooter *noun* 1 a child's vehicle, pushed by one foot touching the ground; 2 also **motor scooter** a low bicycle-like vehicle with an engine, two small wheels, and usually a wide curved front to protect the legs

a motor scooter

scorch *verb* to burn something slightly, usually so there is a brown mark; **scorch** *noun*

score *noun* the number of points, runs, goals, etc, made in a game, sport, etc; **score** *verb*

135

scrape *verb* **1** to rub with something hard or sharp; **2** to hurt or damage in this way; **scrape** *noun*

¹scratch *verb* to rub and tear or mark with something pointed or rough

²scratch *noun* a mark or small wound made by scratching

scream *verb* to cry out loudly on a high note; **scream** *noun*

screen *noun* **1** a flat surface on which films or slides are shown; **2** the front surface of a television, VDU, or other instrument on which pictures and information can be shown; **3** a covering frame used for protecting people from cold or heat, for hiding something from view, etc

¹screw *noun* an object like a nail with a raised edge (thread) going round and round it which helps to hold it in place

²screw *verb* **1** to fasten with one or more screws; **2** to turn or tighten a screw or something that moves in the same way

scribble *verb* to write carelessly or in a hurry; **scribble** *noun*

scrub *verb* (**scrubbed**) to clean by hard rubbing, as with a stiff brush; **scrub** *noun*

sea *noun* the great body of salty water that covers much of the Earth's surface: **seabird, seashell, seashore, seaside, seaweed;** ▣**see**

¹seal *noun* a large fish-eating animal having broad flat limbs (**flippers**) for swimming

²seal *noun* a small piece of paper, wax, etc, which is fixed across an opening, and which must be broken in order to open it

³seal *verb* **1** to make or fix a seal onto something; **2** to fasten or close tightly and firmly

seam *noun* a line of stitches joining two pieces of cloth, leather, etc, at or near their edges; **seamless** *adjective;* ▣**seem**

search *verb* to look at, through, into, etc, to try to find something; **search** *noun*

season *noun* **1** one of the four parts of the year – spring, summer, autumn, or winter; **2** a period of time each year for a particular activity: *the football* **season**

seat *noun* **1** a place for sitting; **2** a thing to sit on; **3 take/ have a seat** please sit down

¹second *noun* **1** a length of time equal to 1/60 of a minute; **2** a moment; a very short time

²second *adjective, adverb, noun, pronoun* the one after the first; 2nd *(see last page)*

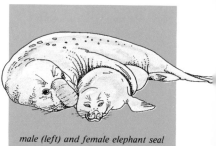

male (left) and female elephant seal

secret *noun* something known to only you or just a few other people; **secret** *adjective;* **secretly** *adverb*

secretary *noun* a person with the job of preparing letters, keeping records, arranging meetings, etc, for others; **secretarial** *adjective*

see *verb* (**see, seeing, saw, seen**) **1** to use the eyes; to have or use the power of sight; **2** to look at; **3** to understand or recognise; **4** to visit, call upon, or meet;  sea

seed *noun* the part of a plant from which a new plant can grow; **seedless** *adjective*

seek *verb* (**seeks, seeking, sought**) to make a search for; to try to find or get

seem *verb* to appear to be; ▪ seam

seen *see* SEE; ▪ scene

a seesaw

seesaw *noun* a board for children to sit on at opposite ends, balanced so that when one end goes up the other goes down

self *noun* (*plural* **selves**) your own person

selfish *adjective* concerned with or thinking about yourself and not caring for others; **selfishly** *adverb;* **selfishness** *noun*

self-service *noun, adjective* the system in many restaurants, shops, garages, etc, in which buyers collect what they want and then pay at special desks

sell *verb* (**sells, selling, sold**) to give to another for money; **seller** *noun;* ▪ cellar

send *verb* (**sends, sending, sent**) to cause or order a person or thing to go or be taken to a place, in a direction, etc; **sender** *noun*

senior *adjective* **1** older; **2** of higher position or importance; **senior** *noun*

¹**sense** *noun* **1** one of the five powers by which we see, smell, hear, feel, or taste; **2** good understanding and reasonable ideas: **common sense; sensation** *noun;* **sensitive** *adjective*

²**sense** *verb* to feel; to know through the senses

sensible *adjective* reasonable; having good sense; **sensibly** *adverb*

sent *see* SEND; ▪ cent, scent

sentence *noun* a group of words that forms a statement, question, etc, contains a verb and usually a subject, and (in writing) begins with a capital letter and ends with one of the marks .!?''

¹**separate** (*say* sepparayt) *verb* **1** to set or move apart; to go in different directions; **2** to make, become, or keep in different places

²**separate** (*say* sepprut) *adjective*
1 not the same; different;
2 apart; not joined or shared
with another; **separately**
adverb; **separation** *noun*

September *noun* the ninth
month of the year

sergeant *noun* a position in
the army or police force

serial *noun* a story appearing in
parts; ■**cereal**

series *noun* a group of things
coming one after the other

serious *adjective* **1** not
cheerful; not joking or funny;
2 important; **seriously** *adverb*

servant *noun* a person who
works for another as a cook,
gardener, maid, etc

serve *verb* **1** to work or do a
useful job; **2** to give food to
people; **3** to look after
somebody buying something;
4 to begin play in tennis,
badminton, etc, by hitting the
ball to the other player;
5 serve somebody right to be
a fair punishment for
somebody

service *noun* **1** work or duty
done for somebody;
2 attention to buyers in a
shop or to guests in a hotel,
restaurant, etc; **3** a religious
ceremony; **4** a useful
business or job that usually
does not produce goods:
postal service, train service

¹**set** *verb* (**sets, setting, set**)
1 to put in a place; **2** to give
a piece of work for
somebody to do; **3** to put
into a position, arrange: *set
the table;* **4** to put into
action; to make something
happen; **5** to pass
downwards out of sight: *The
sun is **setting***

²**set** *noun* **1** a group of things
thought of together; **2** an
electrical apparatus,
especially a radio or television

settee *noun* a long seat for
more than one person, with a
back and usually arms

settle *verb* **1** to go and live in a
place; **2** to bring or place
down, often in a comfortable
position; **3** to sink or come
down, usually to a position of
rest; **4** to decide on; to fix or
arrange; **settlement** *noun;*
settler *noun*

seven *adjective, noun* the
number 7; **seventh** *adjective,
adverb (see last page)*

seventeen *adjective, noun* the
number 17; **seventeenth**
adjective, adverb (see last page)

seventy *adjective, noun* the
number 70; **seventieth**
adjective, adverb (see last page)

several *adjective, pronoun* more
than two but fewer than
many; some but not many

severe *adjective* **1** not kind or
gentle; strict; **2** hard;
difficult; **severely** *adverb*

sew *verb* (**sews, sewing,
sewed, sewn**) to join or
fasten cloth, leather, paper,
etc, by stitching with thread;
to make or mend with needle
and thread: **sewing machine;**
■**so, sow**

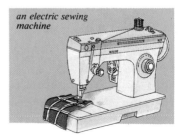

*an electric sewing
machine*

138

sex *noun* being male or female

¹shade *noun* **1** slight darkness; shelter from the sun or other light; **2** something that keeps out light: **lampshade**; **3** a slightly different colour: *light blue and a deeper* **shade**; **shady** *adjective*

²shade *verb* to shelter from direct light or heat

shadow *noun* a dark shape made by something when it blocks out light

shake *verb* (**shakes, shaking, shook, shaken**) **1** to move quickly up and down and to and fro; **2 shake hands with somebody** to take somebody's right hand in your own for a moment, moving it up and down, as a sign of greeting, goodbye, agreement, etc; **3 shake your head** to move your head from side to side to show 'no' or disapproval; **shake** *noun*; ■ **sheikh, sheik**

shall *verb* (**should, shan't** = shall not) **1** used with *I* and *we* to say what is going to happen: *I* **shall** *have finished my work by next Friday.* **2** used with *I* and *we* when asking a question or offering to do something: **Shall** *I get you a chair?*

shallow *adjective* not deep; not far from top to bottom

shame *noun* the painful feeling you have when you have done something wrong or silly

shampoo *noun* a liquid soap used for washing hair; **shampoo** *verb*

shan't *see* SHALL

shape *noun* the appearance or form of something seen; **shape** *verb*; **shaped** *adjective*; **shapeless** *adjective*

¹share *noun* the part belonging to or done by a person

²share *verb* **1** to use, pay, have, take part in, etc, with others or among a group; **2** to divide and give out in shares

shark *noun* a fierce flesh-eating fish that has several rows of sharp teeth, and can be dangerous to people

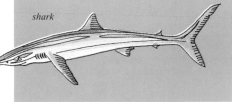

shark

sharp *adjective* **1** having a thin cutting edge; having a fine point; **2** quick and sensitive in thinking, seeing, hearing, etc: **sharp sighted**; **3** sudden and quick; **sharply** *adverb*; **sharpen** *verb*

shave *verb* to cut off hair close to the skin with a razor; **shave** *noun*

she *pronoun* (**her, herself**) that female person or animal

S

¹shed *noun* a lightly built hut, usually used for storing things

²shed *verb* (**sheds, shedding, shed**) to let fall or get rid of naturally, things such as leaves, hair, etc

sheep *noun* (*plural* **sheep**) (*male* **ram**, *female* **ewe**, *young* **lamb**) a grass-eating animal kept for its wool and meat

shield *noun* a broad piece of metal, wood, or leather once carried by soldiers to protect them from arrows, blows, etc

¹shine *verb* (**shines, shining, shone**) **1** to give off light; to look bright; **2** to direct a lamp, beam of light, etc

²shine *verb* (**shines, shining, shined**) to polish; to make bright by rubbing; **shiny** *adjective*

a famous ship –
Queen Elizabeth 2

sheet *noun* **1** a large four-sided piece of cloth used to cover a bed; **2** a piece of paper

sheikh, sheik (*say* shake) *noun* **1** an Arab chief or prince; **2** a Muslim religious teacher; ■ **shake**

shelf *noun* (*plural* **shelves**) a flat usually long and narrow board fixed against a wall or in a frame, for placing things on

shell *noun* a hard covering, as of an animal, egg, nut, etc: **shellfish**

¹shelter *noun* anything that protects, especially a building

²shelter *verb* to protect from harm; to give shelter to

shepherd feminine **shepherdess** *noun* a person who takes care of sheep in a field

ship *noun* a large boat

shirt *noun* a piece of clothing for the upper body, usually of light cloth with a collar and sleeves

shiver *verb* to shake, especially from cold or fear; **shiver** *noun*

shoal *noun* a large group of fish swimming together

¹shock *noun* **1** a violent force, as from a hard blow, crash, explosion, etc; **2** the strong feeling caused by something unexpected and usually very unpleasant; **3** the sudden violent effect of electricity passing through the body

²shock *verb* **1** to cause unpleasant or angry surprise

S

140

to somebody; **2** to give an electric shock to

shoe *noun* an outer covering for the foot, usually having a hard sole and a support under the heel

shone *see* SHINE

shook *see* SHAKE

¹shoot *verb* (**shoots, shooting, shot**) **1** to fire a weapon at and hit something or somebody; **2** to go fast or suddenly; **3** to kick, throw, etc, a ball in order to score in a game; **4** to make a photograph or film

²shoot *noun* a new growth from a plant, especially a young stem and leaves

shooting star also **falling star** *noun* a small meteor from space which burns brightly as it passes through the Earth's air

¹shop *noun* **1** a room or building where goods are regularly kept and sold: **shopkeeper; 2** a place where things are made or repaired

²shop *verb* (**shopped**) to buy things; **shopper** *noun;* **shopping** *noun*

shore *noun* the land along the edge of a large stretch of water; ▪sure

short *adjective* **1** not far from one end to the other; little in distance, length, or height; **2** lasting only a little time; **shortage** *noun;* **shorten** *verb*

shorts *noun* trousers ending above the knees

¹shot *noun* **1** an action of shooting a weapon; **2** a kick, throw, etc, of a ball intended to score a point; **3** a sending up of a space vehicle or rocket; **4** a chance to do something; a try

²shot *see* SHOOT

should *verb* (**shouldn't**) to have a duty to; ought to

shoulder *noun* **1** the part of the body at each side of the neck where the arms join; **2** either edge of a road outside the travelled part: **hard shoulder**

shout *verb* to speak or say very loudly; **shout** *noun*

shovel *noun* a long-handled tool with a broad blade for lifting and moving loose material such as earth or coal; **shovel** *verb*

¹show *verb* (**shows, showing, showed, shown**) **1** to offer for seeing; to allow or cause to be seen; **2** to appear; to be in or come into view; **3** to go with and guide or direct; **4** to explain; to make clear to by words or actions

²show *noun* **1** a collection of things for looking at; **2** a performance in a theatre, on radio or television, etc

shower *noun* **1** a short fall of rain or snow; **2** a fall of many small things or drops of liquid; **3** a washing of the body by standing under an opening from which water comes out in many small streams; an apparatus for this; **shower** *verb*

S

shown *see* SHOW

shrank *see* SHRINK

shrimp *noun* a small sea creature with long legs and a tail shaped like a fan

shrink *verb* (**shrinks, shrinking, shrank, shrunk** *or* **shrunken**) to make or become smaller, as from the effect of heat or water

shrug *verb* (**shrugged**) to lift and drop your shoulders, especially to show you do not know or do not care; **shrug** *noun*

shut *verb* (**shuts, shutting, shut**) to close; to move into a covered, blocked, or folded-together position

shuttlecock *noun* a small light object (*see* picture on page 12) for hitting across a net in a game of badminton

shy *adjective* (**shyer** *or* **shier**, **shyest** *or* **shiest**) nervous in the company of others; **shyly** *adverb*; **shyness** *noun*

sick *adjective* **1** ill; having a disease; **2** upset in the stomach so as to want to throw up what is in it; **sickness** *noun*

side *noun* **1** a more or less upright surface of something, not the top, bottom, front, or back; **2** the right or left part of the body, from the shoulder to the top of the leg; **3** an edge; **4** either of the two surfaces of a thin flat object; **5** a sports team

sideways *adverb, adjective* **1** with one side, and not the front or back, forward or up; **2** to or towards one side

sigh *verb* to let out a deep breath slowly and with a sound, usually showing that you are tired, sad, pleased, etc; **sigh** *noun*

sight *noun* **1** the sense of seeing; the power of the eye; **2** something that is seen; **3** something worth seeing, especially a place visited by tourists: *the **sights** of London;* ■ **site**

¹sign *noun* **1** a mark, symbol, or object which is seen and which means something to the person who sees it; **2** a board or other notice giving information, warning, directions, etc: **signpost**; **3** also **sign of the zodiac** any of the twelve divisions of the year named after groups of stars

signs of the zodiac

Aquarius
21 Jan – 19 Feb

Pisces
20 Feb – 20 March

Aries
21 March – 20 April

Taurus
21 April – 22 May

Gemini
23 May – 21 June

Cancer
22 June – 22 July

Leo
23 July – 22 Aug

Virgo
23 Aug – 22 Sept

Libra
23 Sept – 22 Oct

Scorpio
23 Oct – 21 Nov

Sagittarius
22 Nov – 22 Dec

Capricorn
23 Dec – 20 Jan

²sign *verb* to write your name; **signature** *noun*

142

¹signal *noun* **1** a sound, action, movement, or apparatus meant to warn, command, or give a message; **2** a sound, picture, or message sent by waves, as in radio or television

²signal *verb* **(signalled)** to give a signal

silence *noun* the state of not speaking or making a noise: complete quiet; stillness

silent *adjective* **1** not speaking; not using spoken expression; **2** free from noise; quiet; **silently** *adverb*

silk *noun* a fine thread which is produced by a type of caterpillar **(silkworm)** and made into thread for sewing or into cloth; the smooth soft cloth made from this; **silky** *adjective*

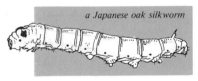

a Japanese oak silkworm

silly *adjective* not clever or reasonable; foolish; not serious

silver *noun* **1** a soft whitish precious metal that is used in ornaments and coins; **2** the colour of this metal; **silver** *adjective;* **silvery** *adjective*

similar *adjective* like or alike; of the same kind; partly or almost the same; **similarly** *adverb*

simple *adjective* **1** easy to understand or do; not difficult; **2** of the ordinary kind; not complicated; plain; **simply** *adverb*

sin *noun* something people think is a very bad act; something your religion teaches you is wrong; **sin** *verb*

since *adverb, preposition, conjunction* at a time between then and now; from then until now: *I haven't seen her since her illness*

sing *verb* **(sings, singing, sang, sung)** to make music, musical sounds, songs, etc, with the voice; **singer** *noun*

¹single *adjective* **1** the only one; not double; **2** not married; **3** for the use of only one person: *a single room*

²single *noun* a record with only one song on each side

¹sink *noun* a large basin in a kitchen, for washing dishes, clothes, vegetables, etc, in

²sink *verb* **(sinks, sinking, sank, sunk)** to go down below a surface, out of sight, or to the bottom

sip *verb* **(sipped)** to drink, taking only a little at a time into the front of the mouth; **sip** *noun*

sir *noun* a polite way of talking or writing to a man

sister *noun* **1** a girl or woman with the same parents as another person; **2** a nurse in charge of a ward of a hospital

sit *verb* **(sits, sitting, sat)** to rest in a position with the upper body upright and supported at the bottom of the back, as on a chair or other seat: **sitting room**

site *noun* **1** a place where something was or happened; **2** a piece of ground for building on; ■ **sight**

143

six *adjective, noun* **1** the number 6; **2** a cricket hit that counts as six runs; **sixth** *adjective, adverb (see last page)*

sixteen *adjective, noun* the number 16; **sixteenth** *adjective, adverb (see last page)*

sixty *adjective, noun* the number 60; **sixtieth** *adjective, adverb (see last page)*

size *noun* the bigness or smallness of anything

skate *noun* a special shoe or boot fitted with a metal blade or small wheels: **ice skates, roller skates; skate** *verb;* **skater** *noun*

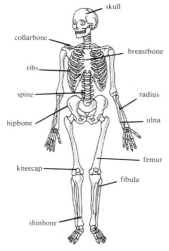

a human skeleton

skeleton *noun* the bones in a human or animal body

ski (*say* skee) *noun (plural* **skis***)* a long thin narrow piece of wood, plastic, or metal, curving up in front, that is fastened to a boot for travelling on snow; **ski** *verb;* **skier** *noun;* **skiing** *noun*

skill *noun* the ability to do something well; **skilful** *adjective;* **skilfully** *adverb;* **skilled** *adjective*

skin *noun* **1** the natural outer covering of an animal or human body, from which hair may grow; **2** a natural outer covering of some fruits and vegetables; peel

skinny *adjective* thin; without much flesh

skip *verb* **(skipped) 1** to move in a light dancing way, as with quick steps and jumps; **2** to pass over or leave out something; **3** to jump over a rope which is made to swing over your head and under your feet

skirt *noun* a piece of women's clothing that hangs from the waist

skull *noun* the bones of the head

sky *noun (plural* **skies***)* the upper air; the space above the Earth where clouds and the sun, moon, and stars appear

slap *verb* **(slapped)** to strike quickly with the flat part of the hand; **slap** *noun*

slave *noun* a person owned by another; a servant without freedom

sledge *noun* a small vehicle made for sliding along snow or ice

¹sleep *noun* the natural resting state of unconsciousness of the body; the state of not being awake; a period of time of this; **sleepy** *adjective*

²**sleep** *verb* (**sleeps, sleeping, slept**) to rest in sleep; to be naturally unconscious, as at night

sleeve *noun* a part of a piece of clothing for covering an arm; **sleeveless** *adjective*

slice *noun* a thin flat piece cut from something; **slice** *verb*

¹**slide** *verb* (**slides, sliding, slid**) to go smoothly over a surface

²**slide** *noun* **1** a slipping movement over a surface; **2** a track or apparatus for sliding down; **3** a square piece of framed film for passing strong light through to show a picture on a surface; **4** a small piece of thin glass to put an object on for seeing under a microscope

slight *adjective* small; not important; **slightly** *adverb*

¹**slip** *verb* (**slipped**) **1** to slide out of place or fall by sliding; **2** to make a slight mistake

²**slip** *noun* **1** an act of slipping or sliding; **2** a slight mistake; **3** a piece of woman's underwear not covering the arms or neck; **4** a small or narrow piece of paper

slipper *noun* a light shoe with the top made from soft material, for wearing indoors

slippery *adjective* difficult to hold or to stand, drive, etc, on without slipping

slit *verb* to make a long narrow cut or opening in; **slit** *noun*

slope *noun* a surface that slopes; a piece of ground going up or down; **slope** *verb*

¹**slow** *adjective* not moving or going on quickly; **2** taking a long time or too long; **3** not good or quick in understanding; **4** showing a time that is earlier than the true time; **slowly** *adjective*

²**slow** *verb* to make or become slower

slug *noun* a small plant-eating creature, related to the snail but with no shell, that often does damage to gardens

¹**smack** *verb* to strike loudly, as with the flat part of the hand

²**smack** *noun* an act of smacking; a hit

small *adjective* little in size, weight, force, importance, etc; **smallness** *noun*

smart *adjective* **1** neat and stylish in appearance; **2** clever; good or quick in thinking; **smartly** *adverb*

smash *verb* to break into pieces

¹**smell** *verb* (**smells, smelling, smelled** *or* **smelt**) **1** to have or use the sense of the nose; **2** to notice, examine, discover, or recognise by this sense; **3** to have a particular smell

²**smell** *noun* **1** the power of using the nose; **2** something that we discover through the nose

smile *noun* an expression of the face with the mouth turned up at the ends and the eyes bright, that shows amusement, happiness, etc; **smile** *verb*

¹**smoke** *noun* gas mixed with very small bits of solid material that can be seen in the air and is usually given off by burning; **smokeless** *adjective*; **smoky** *adjective*

S

145

²**smoke** *verb* **1** to suck or breathe in smoke from tobacco, as in cigarettes, a pipe, etc; **2** to give off smoke

smooth *adjective* having an even surface without sharply raised or lowered places, points, lumps, etc; not rough; **smooth** *verb;* **smoothly** *adverb*

snail *noun* a small animal with a soft body, no limbs, and a hard spiral shaped shell on its back

snake *noun* a reptile that has a long body with no limbs, a large mouth, and a fork-shaped tongue, usually feeding on other animals and sometimes with a poisonous bite

snatch *verb* to get hold of something quickly

sneeze *verb* to push air out of the lungs suddenly, making a noise through your nose and mouth; **sneeze** *noun*

sniff *verb* to draw air into the nose with a sound; to do this to discover a smell in or on something; **sniff** *noun*

snooker *noun* a billiards game played on a table with six pockets, with fifteen red balls and six balls of other colours

snore *verb* to breathe heavily and noisily through the nose and mouth while asleep

snow *noun* water frozen into small flat flakes that fall like rain in cold weather and may cover the ground thickly: **snowball, snowflake, snowman**

¹**so** *adverb* **1** in this way or that way; in the way shown or described; **2** in the same way; also; ■ **sew, sow**

²**so** *conjunction* in order that; therefore; ■ **sew, sow**

soak *verb* to remain or leave in a liquid, to become soft or completely wet; **soak** *noun;* **soaked** *adjective;* **soaking** *adjective, adverb*

soap *noun* a substance made from fats or oils, for use with water to clean the body or other things; **soapy** *adjective*

sock *noun* a covering of soft material for the foot and part of the lower leg

socket *noun* an opening, hollow place, or machine part that forms a holder or into which something fits: *an electric light* **socket**

sofa *noun* a comfortable seat with raised arms and a back and wide enough for usually two or three people

soft *adjective* **1** not hard or stiff; not firm against pressure; giving in to the touch; **2** smooth and pleasant to the touch; **3** quiet; not making much noise; **soften** *verb;* **softly** *adverb*

software *noun* the set of systems (in the form of programs rather than machine parts) which control the way a computer works

a snowflake as seen under a microscope

146

soil *noun* the top covering of the ground, in which plants grow

solar *adjective* **1** of the sun; **2** using the power of the sun's light and heat

solar system *noun* the sun together with all the bodies, such as the moon, planets, etc, going round it

sold *see* SELL

soldier *noun* a person in an army

¹sole *noun* **1** the bottom part of the foot on which you walk or stand; **2** the flat bottom part of a shoe not including the heel;  **soul**

²sole *noun* a flat fish with small eyes, fins, and mouth, often eaten as food;  **soul**

some *adjective, pronoun, adverb* **1** a little, few, or small number or amount: *I saw some people I knew;* **2** used when speaking about people or things without saying exactly which ones: *Come back some other time;*  **sum**

somebody *also* **someone** *pronoun* a person; some but no particular or known person

somehow *adverb* by some means; in some way not yet known

somersault (*say* **summer-sollt**) *noun* a jump or rolling movement backward or forward movement in which the feet go over the head before the body returns upright

turning somersaults in the air

solemn *adjective* done, made, etc, seriously; **solemnly** *adverb*

¹solid *adjective* **1** not needing a container to hold its shape; not liquid or gas; **2** having an inside filled up; not hollow; **3** made of one material all the way through

²solid *noun* a solid object; something that is not a gas or liquid

solve *verb* to find the answer to a puzzle, problem, etc

something *pronoun* a thing which is not known or not named

sometime *adverb* at some time in the past or future

sometimes *adverb* at times; now and then; occasionally

somewhere *adverb* in, at, or to, some place

son *noun* a person's male child;  **sun**

147

song *noun* **1** a short piece of music with words for singing; **2** the music-like sound of a bird

soon *adverb* within a short time

soot *noun* a black powder produced by burning, and carried into the air and left on surfaces by smoke; **sooty** *adjective*

soothe *verb* **1** to make less painful; **2** to make less angry, excited, or worried; to comfort or calm; **soothing** *adjective*

sore *adjective* painful or aching from a wound, infection, or hard use; **sore** *noun*; **soreness** *noun*; ■ **saw**

sorrow *noun* sadness; a cause of unhappiness

sorry *adjective* a polite way of saying that you are ashamed or unhappy because of things you have done and wish that you had not done them, or that you are sad because you cannot do what is wanted

¹sort *noun* a group of people, things, etc, all having certain qualities; a type; a kind; ■ **sought**

²sort *verb* to put things in order; to arrange; ■ **sought**

sought *see* SEEK; ■ **sort**

soul *noun* the part of a person that is not the body and is thought not to die; ■ **sole**

¹sound *noun* what is or may be heard; something that causes a sensation in the ear

²sound *verb* to make a sound; to produce an effect that can be heard

soup *noun* a liquid cooked food often containing small pieces of meat, fish, or vegetables

sour *adjective* having a taste that is not bitter, salty, or sweet

source *noun* where something comes from; ■ **sauce**

south *noun* one of the four main points of the compass; the right of a person facing the rising sun; **south** *adjective, adverb;* **southerly** *adverb;* **southern** *adjective*

southeast *noun* the direction of the point of the compass which is halfway between south and east

southwest *noun* the direction of the point of the compass which is halfway between south and west

¹sow (*say like* how) *noun* a fully grown female pig

²sow (*say* so) *verb* (**sows, sowing, sowed, sown** *or* **sowed**) to plant or scatter seeds on a piece of ground; **sower** *noun;* ■ **sew, so**

soya *noun* a plant that is grown for food from its seeds (**soya beans**) which produce oil and are rich in protein

space *noun* **1** what is outside the Earth's air; where stars, planets, moons, and other bodies move: **spaceman, spaceship; 2** an empty or open place; room; **3** an area or distance between objects

spacecraft *noun* a vehicle able to travel in space

space shuttle *noun* a rocket that can return to Earth like an aeroplane

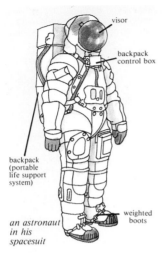

visor

backpack control box

backpack (portable life support system)

weighted boots

an astronaut in his spacesuit

spacesuit *noun* a suit for wearing in space, covering the whole body and provided with an air supply

spade *noun* **1** a tool like a shovel for digging earth, with a broad metal blade for pushing with the foot into the ground; **2** a playing card with one or more figures each shaped like a pointed leaf printed on it in black

spaghetti *noun* a food made of pasta in long strings, usually sold in dry form for making soft again in boiling water

spanner *noun* a metal hand tool for turning nuts and bolts

spare *verb* to be able to give or lend something; **spare** *adjective*

spark *noun* **1** a small bit of burning material thrown out by a fire or by the striking together of two hard objects; **2** a passage of electricity across a space that produces light; **spark** *verb*

sparkle *verb* to shine in small flashes

sparrow *noun* a small brownish bird, very common in many parts of the world

spat *see* SPIT

speak *verb* (**speaks, speaking, spoke, spoken**) to say things; to use the voice; to talk

speaker *noun* **1** a person making a speech; **2** a loudspeaker

spear *noun* a pole with a sharp point at one end used for throwing as a weapon

special *adjective* of a particular kind; not ordinary or usual; **specially** *adverb*

specialise *verb* to study one special thing

specialist *noun* a person who specialises in something

speech *noun* **1** the act or power of speaking; **2** a long set of words spoken for people to listen to

speed *noun* how fast something moves

speed *verb* (**speeds, speeding, sped**) to go fast

speedometer *noun* an instrument in a vehicle for telling its speed

¹spell *noun* a condition caused by magical power; the magic words producing this condition

²spell *verb* (**spells, spelling, spelt** *or* **spelled**) to name the letters of a word in order; **spelling** *noun*

S

spend *verb* (**spends, spending, spent**) **1** to give out money in payment; **2** to pass or use time

spice *noun* a seed, root, or other part of a plant used to give flavour to food; **spicy** *adjective*

a garden spider

spider *noun* a small eight-legged creature which makes silk threads, that it sometimes makes into nets or webs for catching insects to eat

spill *verb* (**spills, spilling, spilt** or **spilled**) to pour out accidentally, as over the edge of a container

spin *verb* (**spins, spinning, spun**) **1** to make thread by twisting cotton, wool, etc; **2** to produce thread, especially in a mass or net; **3** to turn round and round quickly

spinach *noun* a vegetable whose broad green leaves are usually eaten cooked

spine *noun* **1** also **spinal column** the row of bones in the centre of your back; **2** a stiff pointed part of a plant or animal; a prickle

spiral *noun* a curve that winds round and round, such as a spring or the thread of a screw; **spiral** *adjective*

spirit *noun* **1** the part of you that is not body, and that some people think does not die with your body; **2** a being without a body, such as a ghost; **3** a state of mind: *in high spirits;* **4** a strong alcoholic drink, such as **gin**, **brandy**, or **whisky**

spit *verb* (**spits, spitting, spat** or **spit**) to force liquid from the mouth

spite *noun* **1** not liking and wanting to annoy another person, especially in some small way; **2 in spite of** even though something else happens; **spiteful** *adjective;* **spitefully** *adverb*

¹splash *verb* to cause a liquid to fall, strike, or move noisily, in drops, waves, etc

²splash *noun* a splashing act, movement, or noise

splendid *adjective* very fine; excellent; **splendidly** *adverb*

splint *noun* a flat piece of wood, metal, etc, used for protecting and keeping a damaged part of the body, especially a bone, in position

splinter *noun* a small needle-like piece broken off something

¹split *verb* (**splits, splitting, split**) **1** to break from one end to another, especially with force or by a blow or tear; **2** to divide into separate parts; to share

²split *noun* a cut or break made by splitting

spoil *verb* (**spoils, spoiling, spoiled** *or* **spoilt**) **1** to make or become of no use; to ruin; **2** to make a child selfish from having too much attention or praise

¹spoke *noun* a bar which connects the outer ring of a wheel to the centre, as on a bicycle

²spoke *see* SPEAK

spoken *see* SPEAK

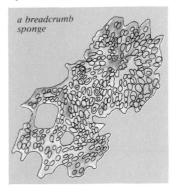

a breadcrumb sponge

sponge *noun* **1** a sea creature which lives in colonies and grows a spreading rubber-like skeleton full of small holes; a piece of this or a substance like it, which is used for washing; **2** *also* **sponge cake** a soft light sweet cake

spoon *noun* a tool for mixing, serving, and eating food, consisting of a small bowl with a handle: **spoonful, spoonfuls**

sport *noun* games, competitions, or activities done for pleasure

sportsman feminine **sportswoman** *noun* a person who plays or enjoys sports

¹spot *noun* **1** a part or area different from the main surface, as in colour; a small mark; **2** a particular place; **3** a pimple

²spot *verb* (**spotted**) **1** to see; to recognise; **2** to mark with coloured or dirty spots

spout *noun* an opening through which liquid can be poured from a container

sprang *see* SPRING

spray *verb* to scatter liquid in small drops; **spray** *noun*

spread *verb* (**spreads, spreading, spread**) **1** to put a thin covering on; **2** to open, reach, or stretch out; to be or make longer, broader, wider, etc; **3** to share or divide over an area, period of time, etc

¹spring *verb* (**springs, springing, sprang, sprung**) **1** to move quickly as if by jumping; **2** **spring a leak** to begin to let liquid through a crack, hole, etc

²spring *noun* **1** a place where water comes up naturally from the ground; **2** the season between winter and summer; **3** a coil of wire, which goes back to its original shape if you pull it

sprinkle *verb* to scatter in drops or small grains

sprout *verb* **1** to start to grow; **2** to send up new growth, as from a seed or bud

sprung *see* SPRING

spun *see* SPIN

¹spy *verb* **1** to watch secretly; **2** to try to get information secretly

²spy *noun* a person whose job is to find out secret information, usually from an enemy

S

151

square *noun* **1** a shape with four straight equal sides; **2** a piece of material in this shape; **3** an open space surrounded by buildings; **square** *adjective*

¹squash *verb* **1** to force or be forced into a flat shape; to press; **2** to push or fit into a small space; to squeeze

²squash *noun* **1** an act or sound of squashing; **2** a crowd of people in a small space; **3** a sweet fruit drink; **4** a game played by two or four players, with rackets and a small rubber ball

squeak *verb* to make a high but not loud sound; **squeak** *noun*; **squeaker** *noun*

squeal *verb* to make a long very high sound or cry; **squeal** *noun*

squeeze *verb* to press together from opposite sides; **squeeze** *noun*

squirrel *noun* a small four-legged animal with a long furry tail that climbs trees and eats nuts

stable *noun* a building where animals, especially horses, are kept and fed

stadium *noun* (plural **stadiums** *or* **stadia**) a large open building with rows of seats surrounding a sports field

stag *noun* a fully grown male deer

stage *noun* **1** a time or step in a course of events; **2** the raised floor on which plays are performed in a theatre

stain *verb* to make a mark that cannot be taken away; **stain** *noun*; **stainless** *adjective*

stair *noun* any of the steps in a set of stairs; ■ **stare**

stairs *noun* a fixed length of steps connecting floors in a building

stake *noun* a pointed piece of wood, metal, etc, for driving into the ground; ■ **steak**

stale *adjective* no longer fresh

stalk *noun* **1** the main upright part of a plant; **2** a long narrow part of a plant supporting one or more leaves, fruits, or flowers; a stem

stall *noun* a table or open-fronted shop, especially one in a market

¹stamp *verb* **1** to strike downwards with the foot; **2** to stick on a stamp

a sports stadium – Los Angeles Coliseum

²stamp *noun* **1** also **postage stamp** a small piece of paper for sticking on a piece of mail to be sent to show that payment has been made; **2** an instrument or tool for pressing or printing onto a surface

¹stand *verb* (**stands, standing, stood**) **1** to support yourself on the feet upright; **2** to rise or raise to a position of doing this; **3** to be in or take a particular position; **4 stand for** to mean; **5 stand a chance** to have a chance; **6 stand on your own (two) feet** to be able to do without help from others

²stand *noun* **1** a place or act of standing; **2** a frame, desk, or other piece of furniture for putting something on: **hat stand**; **3** an open building at a sports ground with rows of seats or standing space rising one behind another

¹standard *noun* a fixed weight, length, cost, or quality, by which things are measured or judged

²standard *adjective* ordinary; of the usual kind

¹star *noun* **1** a body, such as the sun or a planet, that appears as a bright point in the sky; **2** a shape with five or more points; **3** a famous or very skilful performer; **starry** *adjective*

²star *verb* (**starred**) **1** to mark with one or more stars; **2** to have or appear as a main performer

starboard *noun* the right side of a ship or aircraft as you face forward

starch *noun* **1** a white tasteless substance forming an important part of foods such as grain, rice, beans, and potatoes; **2** a powder made from this and used for stiffening clothes; **starchy** *adjective*

stare *verb* to look at something with wide-open eyes, for a long time; **stare** *noun;* ■ **stair**

starfish *noun* a flat sea animal with five arms forming a star shape

starling *noun* a common greenish black bird

start *verb* to begin; **start** *noun*

starve *verb* **1** to die because you do not have enough food to eat; **2** to be very hungry; **starvation** *noun*

¹state *noun* **1** a condition in which a person or thing is; **2** the government of a country; **3** a small part of a country: **United States of America**

²state *verb* to say or put into words

statement *noun* something that is said

station *noun* **1** a building on a railway or bus line where passengers or goods arrive or leave; **2** a building that is a centre for a particular kind of service: **police station**; **3** a company or apparatus that broadcasts on television or radio

stationary *adjective* standing still; not moving; ■ **stationery**

stationery *noun* materials for writing; paper, ink, pencils, etc; **stationer** *noun;* ■ **stationary**

S

statue *noun* a human or animal figure, made in some solid material, such as stone, metal, or plastic

stay *verb* **1** to stop and remain; **2** to continue to be; **3** to live in a place for a while; to be a visitor or guest; **stay** *noun*

steady *adjective* **1** firm; not shaking or moving; **2** not changing; regular; **steadily** *adverb*; **steadiness** *noun*

steak *noun* a flat piece of meat or fish; ▩ **stake**

steal *verb* (**steals, stealing, stole, stolen**) **1** to take something that belongs to another without asking for it; **2** to move secretly or quietly; ▩ **steel**

¹steam *noun* the whitish cloudy gas produced by boiling water

²steam *adjective* using steam under pressure to produce power or heat: **steamroller, steamship**

steel *noun* a hard strong metal made from iron and used for knives, machines, etc; ▩ **steal**

steel band *noun* a band playing instruments cut from metal drums and tuned to make particular notes

steep *adjective* rising or falling quickly; **steeply** *adverb*

steeple *noun* a church tower with a top part rising to a high sharp point

steer *verb* to direct or guide a ship, car, bicycle, etc

stellar *adjective* of or concerning the stars

stem *noun* the central part of a plant above the ground, or the smaller part which supports a leaf or flower

¹step *noun* **1** the act of putting one foot in front of the other in order to move along; the sound this makes; **2** a flat surface, especially in a set of surfaces each higher than the other, on which the foot is placed for climbing up and down; a stair, rung of a ladder, etc; **3** an act in a set of actions in making or doing something; **4** a type of movement of the feet in dancing; **5 in step** stepping with the left and right leg at the same time as one or

a type of steamship

more other people; **6 watch your step** to behave or act carefully

²step *verb* (**stepped**) to put one foot down usually in front of the other, in order to move along; to walk

stepchild *noun* (*plural* **stepchildren**) the child of somebody's husband or wife by another marriage: **stepbrother, stepdaughter, stepsister, stepson**

stepparent *noun* the person to whom your mother or father has been remarried: **stepfather, stepmother**

stereo *noun* a record player or radio which gives out sound by means of two loudspeakers; **stereo** *adjective*

stew *noun* a meal with meat, vegetables, etc, cooked together in liquid; **stew** *verb*

steward feminine **stewardess** *noun* a person who serves passengers on a ship or plane

¹**stick** *noun* 1 a long thin piece of wood; 2 a long thin piece of any material: *a **stick** of rock*

²**stick** *verb* (**sticks, sticking, stuck**) 1 to fix or be fixed with a sticky substance such as glue; 2 to push a pointed object into something

sticky *adjective* made of or containing material which can stick to or round anything else

stiff *adjective* 1 not easily bent; 2 painful when moving or moved; **stiffen** *verb;* **stiffly** *adverb*

stile *noun* an arrangement of steps for climbing easily over a fence or wall; ■ **style**

¹**still** *adjective* 1 not moving; 2 quiet or silent; **stillness** *noun*

²**still** *adverb* 1 up to and at this or that time: *Does this dress **still** fit you?*; 2 even so

¹**sting** *verb* (**stings, stinging, stung**) 1 to cause sharp pain to, or to feel such a pain; 2 to prick with a sting

²**sting** *noun* 1 a sharp organ used as a weapon by some animals; 2 a substance contained in hairs on a plant's surface, which produces pain; 3 a sharp pain, wound, or mark caused by a plant or animal; 4 a strong burning pain

stir *verb* (**stirred**) 1 to move round and mix by means of an object such as a spoon; 2 to move a little: *She **stirred** in her sleep;* **stir** *noun*

¹**stitch** *noun* 1 a movement of a needle and thread into cloth at one point and out at another in sewing; 2 the result of this movement; 3 a turn of the wool round the needle in knitting; 4 a sharp pain in the side, caused by running

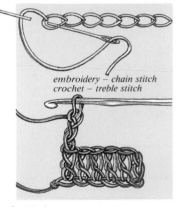

embroidery – chain stitch
crochet – treble stitch

²**stitch** *verb* to sew; to put stitches in to fasten together or for decoration

stoat *noun* a small brown furry animal

stocking *noun* one of a pair of coverings for the feet and legs

stole *see* STEAL

stolen *see* STEAL

stomach *noun* a baglike organ in the body into which food goes after it has been swallowed

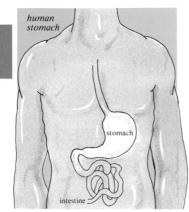

human stomach

stomach

intestine

¹stone *noun* **1** a piece of rock; **2** a hard substance; rock; **3** a single hard seed inside some fruits, such as the cherry, plum, and peach

²stone *noun* a measure of weight equal to 14 pounds or about 6.35 kilograms *(see last page)*

stood *see* STAND

stool *noun* a seat without a supporting part for the back or arms

¹stop *verb* **(stopped) 1** to finish moving; **2** to prevent something happening, moving, etc; **3** to end; to make an end to; **stopper** *noun*

²stop *noun* **1** the act of stopping or state of being stopped; **2** a place on a road where buses or other public vehicles stop for passengers

¹store *verb* to put away or keep for future use

²store *noun* **1** things kept for future use; **2** a place for keeping things; **3** a large shop

storey *noun* a floor or level in a building

storm *noun* very bad weather, with wind, rain, and often lightning; **stormy** *adjective*

story *noun* **1** a tale about something imaginary that happened; **2** a telling of events

stove *noun* an apparatus for cooking or heating which works by burning coal, oil, gas, etc, or by electricity

¹straight *adjective* **1** not bent or curved; **2** level or upright; **3** tidy; neat; in order; **straighten** *verb*; ▪ strait

²straight *adverb* **1** in a straight line; **2** directly: *go straight home;* **3** without waiting: **straightaway**; ▪ strait

strait *noun* a narrow water channel connecting two seas; ▪ straight

strange *adjective* **1** odd or unusual; surprising; **2** not what you are used to; **strangely** *adverb*

stranger *noun* a person you do not know

¹strap *noun* **1** a strong narrow band of material, such as leather, used for fastening, holding together, or wrapping; **2** also **shoulder strap** a strap that passes across the shoulder and holds up a piece of clothing, a bag, etc

S

²**strap** *verb* (**strapped**) to fasten in place with one or more straps

straw *noun* **1** dried stems of grain plants, such as wheat, used for animals to sleep on, for making baskets, mats, etc; **2** a thin tube of paper or plastic for drinking through

strawberry *noun* a red juicy fruit, eaten fresh and in jam; the plant on which this grows

a strawberry plant

stream *noun* a natural flow of water, smaller than a river

street *noun* a road with houses or other town buildings on one or both sides

strength *noun* the quality or power of being strong or something that provides this; **strengthen** *verb*

stretch *verb* **1** to make or become wider or longer by pulling; **2** to make as long as possible; **3** to try to reach; **4** to straighten the legs, arms, or body to full length; **stretch** *noun*; **stretchy** *adjective*

strict *adjective* severe, especially in rules of behaviour; **strictly** *adverb*

¹**strike** *verb* (**strikes, striking, struck**) **1** to hit; **2** to light by hitting against a hard surface: ***strike** a match;* **3** to have an effect on; to seem or appear to: *An idea **struck** me;* **4** to refuse to work

²**strike** *noun* a time when no work is done because of an argument, as over pay or working conditions

string *noun* **1** a strong thread or thin rope used especially for tying things up; **2** a thin piece of material, often one of several, stretched across a musical instrument to give sound; **stringed** *adjective*

¹**strip** *noun* a long narrow piece of something

²**strip** *verb* (**stripped**) **1** to remove the covering or parts of; **2** to undress or be undressed

stripe *noun* a band of colour, among one or more other colours; **striped** *adjective*

¹**stroke** *verb* to pass the hand gently over something

²**stroke** *noun* **1** a blow; a hit; a movement; **2** a sudden illness in part of the brain

strong *adjective* **1** having power or force; **2** powerful against harm; not easily broken, spoilt, moved, or changed; **strongly** *adverb*

struck *see* STRIKE

struggle *verb* to try very hard to do something; to fight; **struggle** *noun*

stubborn *adjective* not changing your mind or doing what others want; **stubbornly** *adverb*

S

stuck *see* STICK

student *noun* a person who is studying at a school, college, etc

studio *noun* **1** a room where a painter, photographer, etc, works; **2** a room in which films or radio or television programmes are made

stylus *noun* the needle-like instrument on a record player that picks up the sound signals from a record

subject *noun* **1** something studied, as at school, college, etc; **2** something talked or written about; **3** a person who belongs to a country

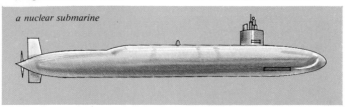

a nuclear submarine

¹study *noun* **1** the act of studying one or more subjects; learning; **2** a room used for studying and work

²study *verb* to spend time in learning about one or more subjects

¹stuff *noun* material of any sort, of which something is made

²stuff *verb* to fill

stump *noun* **1** the base of a tree left after the rest has been cut down; **2** one of the three upright pieces of wood at which the ball is thrown in cricket

stung *see* STING

stupid *adjective* silly or foolish; not clever; **stupidity** *noun*; **stupidly** *adverb*

style *noun* **1** a way of doing something; **2** fashion, especially in clothes; **3** a type or sort; **stylish** *adjective*;
  ■ **stile**

submarine also **sub** *noun* a ship that can sail under water

substance *noun* a sort of material

subtract *verb* to take a part or amount from something larger; **subtraction** *noun*

succeed *verb* to get what you wanted; to do well

success *noun* **1** the act of succeeding in something; **2** a good result; **3** a person or thing that succeeds or has succeeded; **successful** *adjective*; **successfully** *adverb*

such *adjective, pronoun* **1** so large; so much; so good: *Don't be such a fool!* **2** of the same kind; like: *flowers such as roses, sunflowers, etc*

suck *verb* **1** to draw liquid into the mouth by using the tongue, lips, and muscles at the side of the mouth, with the lips tightened into a small hole; **2** to eat something by holding in the mouth and melting by movements of the tongue; **suck** *noun*

sudden *adjective* happening, done, etc, quickly and unexpectedly; **suddenly** *adverb*

suffer *verb* to experience pain or difficulty

sugar *noun* a sweet substance used in food

suggest *verb* to say or write to somebody that something is a good idea; **suggestion** *noun*

¹**suit** *noun* **1** a set of clothes which match, usually including a jacket with trousers or skirt: **suitcase**; **2** one of the four sets of cards used in games

²**suit** *verb* **1** to satisfy or please; to be right for; **2** to match or look right with; **suitable** *adjective*

suite (*say* **sweet**) *noun* a set of furniture for a room, especially a settee and two chairs: **three-piece suite**; ◼ **sweet**

sulk *verb* to be quiet and badtempered; **sulky** *adjective*

sultana *noun* a small seedless kind of raisin used in baking

sun *noun* the very hot bright body in the sky, which the Earth goes round and from which it receives light and heat: **sunlight**, **sunshine**; **sunny** *adjective*; ◼ **son**

sunbathe *verb* to spend time in strong sunlight, usually sitting or lying; **sunbather** *noun*

Sunday *noun* the first day of the week; the day before Monday

sung *see* SING

sunk *see* SINK

sunrise also **sun-up** *noun* the time when the sun is seen to appear after the night

sunset *noun* the time when the sun is seen to disappear as night begins

super *adjective* wonderful; very nice or exciting

supermarket *noun* a large shop where you serve yourself with food and goods

S

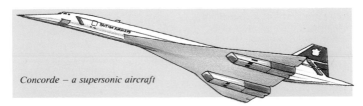

Concorde – a supersonic aircraft

sum *noun* an exercise in using numbers; ◼ **some**

summer *noun* the season between spring and autumn when the sun is hot and there are many flowers

supersonic *adjective* faster than the speed of sound

supper *noun* the last meal of the day, taken in the evening

¹**supply** *verb* to give or sell what is needed

159

²**supply** *noun* a store which can be used; an amount

¹**support** *verb* **1** to hold up; **2** to help, especially with money; **3** to be on the side of; **supporter** *noun*

²**support** *noun* something that holds up

¹**suppose** *verb* **1** to think; to guess; **2** to be expected to; ought to

²**suppose** also **supposing** *conjunction* if: *Suppose it rains, what shall we do?*

sure *adjective* having no doubt; certain; **surely** *adverb*;
⬛ shore

surface *noun* the outside, flat part, or top of something

surgery *noun* **1** a place where a doctor, dentist, or vet treats his or her patients; **2** the skill and practice of performing medical operations; **3** the performing of such operations, usually including the cutting open of the skin

surname *noun* the name you share with the other members of your family; your last name

surprise *noun* an unexpected event; a feeling caused by this event; **surprise** *verb*

surround *verb* to be or go all round something; **surrounding** *adjective*

suspect *verb* to think that something is true, though you do not know

suspend *verb* **1** to hang from above; **2** to put off, delay, or stop

suspense *noun* delay which frightens or excites people

suspicious *adjective* feeling that something is wrong; **suspicion** *noun*

¹**swallow** *noun* a small insect-eating bird which comes to the northern countries in summer

²**swallow** *verb* to move food or drink down the throat from the mouth

swam *see* SWIM

a swan and her cygnets

swan *noun* (*young* **cygnet**) a large water bird with white or black feathers and a long neck, that lives on rivers and lakes

swear *verb* (**swears, swearing, swore, sworn**) **1** to use very bad language; **2** to promise

sweat *noun* a liquid which comes out from the body through the skin to cool it; **sweat** *verb*; **sweaty** *adjective*

sweater *noun* a heavy woollen piece of clothing for the top of the body

sweep *verb* (**sweeps, sweeping, swept**) **1** to clean by brushing; **2** to move over or cover quickly

¹sweet *adjective* **1** tasting like or containing sugar; **2** pleasant or loving; **sweeten** *verb;* **sweetly** *adverb;* **sweetness** *noun;* ■ **suite**

²sweet *noun* **1** a small sweet thing, such as a toffee or chocolate, eaten for pleasure; **2** a pudding or dessert; ■ **suite**

sweet corn *noun* the yellow seeds of the **maize** plant, which are used as a vegetable

swell *verb* **(swells, swelling, swelled, swollen** *or* **swelled)** to become larger; **swelling** *noun*

swept *see* SWEEP

swerve *verb* to turn suddenly to one side, when moving; **swerve** *noun*

¹swift *adjective* fast, short, or sudden; **swiftly** *adverb*

²swift *noun* a small bird with long wings

²swing *noun* a seat on which you can swing

¹switch *noun* an apparatus for turning electricity on and off

²switch *verb* **1** to turn on or off with a switch; **2** to change: *He switched positions*

swollen *see* SWELL

sword *noun* a weapon with a long blade and a handle

swore *see* SWEAR

sworn *see* SWEAR

swum *see* SWIM

swung *see* SWING

syllable *noun* a part of a word that can be said by itself

symbol *noun* a sign, shape, or object which stands for something else; ■ **cymbals**

sympathy *noun* the feeling of sharing or understanding the pain and joy of others; **sympathetic** *adjective*

a synthesiser – used by most music groups today

swim *verb* **(swims, swimming, swam, swum)** to move through water by moving your arms and legs; **swimmer** *noun;* **swimming** *noun*

swimming pool *noun* a special pool for swimming in

¹swing *verb* **(swings, swinging, swung)** to move backwards and forwards, round and round, or in a curve from a fixed point

synthesiser *noun* an electronic musical instrument that can make many different types of sounds

syrup *noun* a thick sweet liquid, especially sugar and water

system *noun* a group of things or ideas working together in one arrangement

S

table *noun* **1** a piece of furniture with a flat top supported by legs: **tablecloth**; **2** a list of information

tadpole *noun* the young of a frog or toad

tail *noun* the movable part growing at the back of an animal's body; **tailless** *adjective;*  **tale**

Manx cats are tailless

tailor *noun* a person who makes clothes

take *verb* (**takes, taking, took, taken**) **1** to get hold of something; **2** to borrow or use without asking permission or by mistake; **3** to carry something or go with somebody to another place; **4** to eat, drink, breathe in, etc: ***take** your medicine;* **5** to travel in a vehicle: ***take** the bus;* **6** to last: *How long does the flight **take**?*

tale *noun* a story; ■ **tail**

¹talk *verb* to use words or make thoughts, ideas, etc, known by means of speech; to speak

²talk *noun* a conversation; a speech

tall *adjective* **1** higher than other people or other things; more than average height; **2** having a particular height: *4 feet **tall**;* **tallish** *adjective;* **tallness** *noun*

tambourine *noun* a small drum with metal discs round the edge that is played by shaking or striking with the hand

¹tame *adjective* gentle and not afraid; not fierce or wild; **tameness** *noun*

²tame *verb* to train an animal to be tame; **tamer** *noun*

tangerine *noun* a small loose skinned orange

tank *noun* **1** a large container for storing liquid or gas; **2** a large heavy vehicle with guns on it, that moves on two metal belts

¹tap *noun* something that you turn to control the flow of liquid or gas from a pipe, barrel, etc

²tap *verb* (**tapped**) to strike something lightly; **tap** *noun*

tape *noun* **1** a narrow strip of cloth, paper, etc; **2** a strip of plastic covered with a magnetic material, used for recording sound, pictures, or data

tape recorder *noun* an instrument that can record and play back sound using tape

target *noun* something that is aimed at

¹tart *noun* a piece of pastry with fruit or jam cooked on it

²tart *adjective* a sharp acid taste

¹taste *verb* **1** to test the taste of food or drink by taking a little into the mouth; **2** to experience the taste of; **3** to eat or drink; **4** to have a particular taste: *This soup **tastes** of chicken;* **5** to experience: *to **taste** freedom*

162

²**taste** *noun* **1** the sense by which you know one food from another by its sweetness, bitterness, etc; **2** the quality special to any food or drink that makes you able to recognise it when it is in your mouth; **3** the ability to judge whether something is good, bad, beautiful, etc; **tasteless** *adjective;* **tasty** *adjective*

taught *see* TEACH

tax *noun* money that is paid to the government

taxi *noun* a car with its driver, which will take you somewhere, if you pay

tea *noun* **1** a drink made by pouring boiling water onto the dried and cut leaves of the tea bush; these leaves: **teacup, teapot; 2** a meal eaten in the afternoon or early evening

teach *verb* (**teaches, teaching, taught**) to give knowledge or skill of something to a person; to train or give lessons; **teacher** *noun*

team *noun* a group of people who work together or who play on the same side in a game

¹**tear** (*say like* here) *noun* a drop of salty liquid from the eye

²**tear** (*say like* hair) *verb* (**tears, tearing, tore, torn**) to pull apart or into pieces

³**tear** (*say like* hair) *noun* a torn place in cloth, paper, etc

tease *verb* to make fun of playfully or unkindly

teenager *noun* a person aged between thirteen and nineteen

teeth *see* TOOTH

¹**telephone** *noun* an apparatus that receives or sends sounds over distances by electricity

²**telephone** *verb* to speak to somebody by telephone

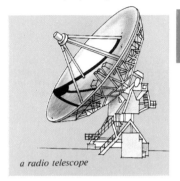

a radio telescope

telescope *noun* an instrument used for detecting distant objects

television also **TV** *noun* **1** the sending and receiving of pictures and usually sound by means of electrical waves; **2 TV set** an apparatus in a box, for receiving these pictures and sound

tell *verb* (**tells, telling, told**) **1** to make something known in words to somebody; to give information or advice; **2** to find out; to decide or know: *It's impossible to **tell** who will win*

temper *noun* **1** a particular state of mind; the way you feel; **2 lose your temper** to become angry

temperature *noun* the hotness or coldness of a place, object, etc

temple *noun* a place for worship in various religions

T

temporary *adjective* only lasting for a short time; not permanent; **temporarily** *adverb*

tempt *verb* to try to make somebody do something wrong; **temptation** *noun*

ten *adjective, noun* the number 10; **tenth** *adjective, adverb (see last page)*

tennis *noun* a game for two people **(singles)** or two pairs of people **(doubles)** who use rackets to hit a ball over a net

¹tense *adjective* 1 full of excitement; 2 tightly stretched

²tense *noun* the form of a verb that shows when the action of the verb happens: **present tense, past tense, future tense**

tent *noun* a movable shelter made of cloth supported by a framework of poles and ropes

a mountaineering tent

term *noun* 1 one of the periods of time into which the school, university, etc, year is divided; 2 a fixed period of time; 3 **terms** the conditions by which you agree to do something or pay for something

terrible *adjective* very bad or frightening

terrific *adjective* excellent; wonderful

terrify *verb* to fill with fear

terror *noun* very great fear

test *noun* a number of questions, things to do, etc, set to measure somebody's ability or knowledge; **test** *verb*

than *conjunction, preposition* used when comparing two things or people: *older **than** you*

thank *verb* to say that you are grateful to somebody

¹that *adjective, pronoun (plural **those)** 1* the one described or shown; 2 the one of two or more people or things that is further away; 3 who, whom, or which

²that *adverb* so; to such an amount: *I like him but not all **that** much!*

³that *conjunction* used for joining two parts of a sentence: *It's true **that** he's French*

thaw *verb* to warm to above freezing point and so make or become liquid or soft

the 1 used when it is clearly understood who or what is meant; 2 used with a person, thing, or group that is the only one of its kind

theatre *noun* a special building or place where plays are performed

theft *noun* stealing

their *adjective* belonging to them; ■ **there**

theirs *pronoun* that or those belonging to them

them *see* THEY

themselves *see* THEY

then *adverb* **1** at that time;
2 next; afterwards; **3** in that
case; if that has happened

there *adverb* **1** to, at, or in that
place; **2** used as the first
word in a sentence or as the
second word in a question
with a verb such as *be* or
seem: ***There** is a man at the
door; Is **there** something
wrong?* ■ **their**

therefore *adverb* as a result;
for that reason; so

thimble *noun* a cap put over
the finger that pushes the
needle during sewing

thin *adjective* **(thinned) 1** having
a small distance between
opposite surfaces; narrow;
not thick; **2** having little fat
on the body; not fat;
3 watery; flowing easily: *thin
gravy;* **4** not closely packed;
thinly *adverb;* **thinness** *noun*

thing *noun* **1** any object;
anything that can be touched
or seen; **2** an idea or
thought; **3** an act or event

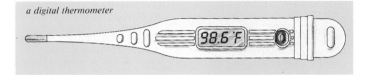
a digital thermometer

thermometer *noun* an
instrument for measuring and
showing temperature

these *see* THIS

they *pronoun* **(them,
themselves)** those people,
animals, or things; the ones
being talked about

thick *adjective* **1** having a large
distance between opposite
surfaces; wide; not thin;
2 measuring a particular
amount from side to side or
from top to bottom: *ice
5 centimetres **thick;*** **3** not
watery; flowing easily:
***thick** soup;* **4** difficult to see
through: ***thick** mist;* **5** having
many objects set close
together; **thicken** *verb;* **thickly**
adverb; **thickness** *noun*

thief *noun (plural* **thieves***)* a
person who steals

think *verb* **(thinks, thinking,
thought) 1** to use your mind
to imagine, understand,
believe, or consider
something; **2** to form an
opinion or have an idea

third *adjective, adverb, noun,
pronoun;* **1** the one after the
second; 3rd; **2** one of three
equal parts into which
something is divided *(see last
page)*

thirst *noun* a feeling of dryness
in the mouth caused by
wanting or needing to drink;
thirstily *adverb;* **thirsty**
adjective

thirteen *adjective, noun* the
number 13; **thirteenth**
*adjective, adverb (see last
page)*

thirty *adjective, noun* the
number 30; **thirtieth** *adjective,
adverb (see last page)*

this *pronoun, adjective (plural* **these***)* **1** the one being talked about or considered; **2** the one of two or more people or things that is nearer

a spear thistle

thistle *noun* a wild plant with prickly leaves and yellow, white, or purple flowers

thorn *noun* a prickle growing on a plant

those *see* THAT

though *adverb, conjunction* in spite of the fact

¹thought *noun* **1** the act of thinking; **2** a result of thinking; an idea, opinion, etc; **thoughtful** *adjective;* **thoughtless** *adjective*

²thought *see* THINK

thousand *adjective, noun* the number 1,000; **thousandth** *adjective, adverb (see last page)*

¹thread *noun* **1** a long thin piece of cotton, nylon, etc, used for sewing or making cloth; **2** a raised line that winds round the outside of a screw or the inside of a nut

²thread *verb* to pass one end of a thread through the eye of a needle

three *adjective, noun* the number 3 *(see last page)*

threw *see* THROW; ■ **through**

throat *noun* **1** the tube inside the neck that divides into two, one part taking air to the lungs and the other taking food to the stomach; **2** the front of the neck

through *preposition, adverb* **1** from one side, surface, or end of something to the other; **2** by means of; **3** as a result of; because of; **4** among or between; ■ **threw**

¹throw *verb* (**throws, throwing, threw, thrown**) **1** to send something through the air by a sudden movement of the arm; **2** to move yourself or part of your body suddenly and with force; **3 throw away** to get rid of something

²throw *noun* an act of throwing

thrush *noun* a brownish bird that sings well

thumb *noun* the short movable part of the hand that is set apart from the fingers

thunder *noun* the usually loud noise that follows a flash of lightning; **thunder** *verb*

Thursday *noun* the fifth day of the week

thus *adverb* **1** in this way; **2** with this result; so

¹tick *noun* a small animal that feeds on the blood of sheep, cows, etc

²tick *noun* **1** the short regularly repeated sound made by a clock or watch; **2** a mark (✓) put against something to show that it is correct

³**tick** verb **1** to make a regularly repeated tick; **2** to show that something is correct by marking with a tick

ticket noun a piece of paper or card that shows that a person has paid for something, such as a journey on a bus or entrance into a cinema

tickle verb to touch a person's skin lightly to produce laughter; **tickle** noun

tide noun the regular rise and fall of the seas

tidy adjective neat; neatly arranged; **tidily** adverb; **tidiness** noun; **tidy** verb

¹**tie** noun **1** a band of cloth worn round the neck and tied in a knot; **2** an equal result or score in a game, competition, etc

²**tie** verb (**ties, tying, tied**) **1** to fasten with string, rope, etc; **2** to finish a match or competition with equal points

tiger noun (female **tigress**, young **cub**) a large fierce cat that is yellowish with black stripes

tight adjective **1** closely fastened, held, knotted, etc; **2** fitting too closely; not loose; **tighten** verb; **tightly** adverb; **tightness** noun

tights noun a very close fitting piece of clothing that covers the legs and lower part of the body

tile noun a thin shaped piece of baked clay, plastic, etc, used for covering roofs, floors, etc

¹**till** noun a machine in a shop, pub, etc, that adds up the prices of the goods bought and usually has a drawer in it for keeping money

²**till** preposition, conjunction until

¹**time** noun **1** the passing of the minutes, hours, days, months, or years; **2** a particular point in the day: **bedtime, playtime, teatime**; **3** a period or occasion: a good **time**; **4** a number of minutes, hours, etc, needed or available for something; **5** the speed or rhythm or beat of a piece of music

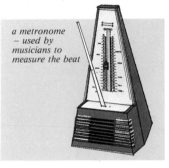

a metronome – used by musicians to measure the beat

²**time** verb to measure the time taken to do something

times preposition multiplied by

timetable noun a table of the times at which something happens, such as when buses, trains, etc, arrive and leave or when different lessons begin

tin noun **1** a soft metal; **2** a small metal box or container

tiny adjective very small

¹**tip** noun the end of something

²**tip** verb (**tipped**) to lean or cause to lean at an angle; to turn over or cause something to turn over

common toad

T

³**tip** *noun* a place where rubbish is left

⁴**tip** *noun* **1** a small amount of money given for a service; **2** a helpful piece of advice

⁵**tip** *verb* (**tipped**) to give a small amount of money to a waiter, waitress, etc

tire *verb* to make somebody feel tired; ■ **tyre**

tired *adjective* **1** needing rest or sleep; **2** no longer interested: *I'm **tired** of your conversation;* **tiredness** *noun*

title *noun* **1** the name of a book, film, etc; **2** a word, such as *Sir* or *Dr*, used in front of a person's name to show his or her position

to *preposition* **1** in the direction of; towards; **2** as far as; **3** reaching or in the state of: *until the lights change **to** green;* **4** in a touching position with; against; **5** until: *from midday **to** midnight;* **6** compared with: *5 goals **to** 3;* ■ **too, two**

toad *noun* an animal like a large frog that creeps rather than jumps. It usually lives on land, but goes into water for breeding

to and fro *adverb* backwards and forwards; from side to side

¹**toast** *verb* to make bread, cheese, etc, brown by holding close to heat

²**toast** *noun* bread made brown by being held in front of heat

tobacco *noun* the dried leaves of a plant, used in cigarettes, pipes, etc

toboggan *noun* a long light sledge

today *noun, adverb* **1** this day; **2** the present time

toddler *noun* a child who has just learnt to walk

toe *noun* **1** one of the five movable parts at the end of each foot: **toenail;** **2** the part of a sock, shoe, etc, that fits over the toes; ■ **tow**

toffee *noun* a hard sticky sweet brown substance made by boiling sugar and butter with water

together *adverb* **1** in or into one group, body, or place; **2** at the same time

toilet *noun* a lavatory

told *see* TELL

tomato *noun* (*plural* **tomatoes**) a red juicy fruit eaten raw or cooked

tomorrow *noun, adverb* **1** the day following today; **2** the future

ton *noun* a measure of weight equal to 2,240 pounds or 1.016 tonnes (*see last page*)

barbecue tongs

tongs *noun* a tool consisting of two movable pieces joined at one end, used for holding or lifting things

tongue *noun* the large movable fleshy part in the mouth

tonight *noun, adverb* the night of today

tonne also **metric ton** *noun* a measure of weight equal to 1,000 kilograms or 0.984 tons *(see last page)*

too *adverb* **1** also; as well; **2** more than enough or is needed or wanted; ▪ **to, two**

took *see* TAKE

tool *noun* any instrument or apparatus for doing a special job

tooth *noun (plural **teeth**)* **1** one of the small hard white bony objects growing in the upper and lower mouth of most animals: **toothache, toothbrush, toothpaste; 2** one of the narrow pointed parts that stand out from a comb, saw, etc; **toothed** *adjective;* **toothless** *adjective*

¹**top** *noun* **1** the highest part or point; **2** the upper surface; **3** the most important part of anything; **4** a lid; **5** a piece of clothing worn on the upper part of the body; **top** *adjective*

²**top** *noun* a toy that balances on its point and spins

torch *noun* a small electric light carried in the hand

tore *see* TEAR

torn *see* TEAR

tortoise *noun* a slow-moving reptile that has a body covered by a hard shell into which the legs, tail, and head can be pulled for protection

¹**total** *adjective* complete; whole; **totally** *adverb*

²**total** *noun* the complete amount; everything added together

¹**touch** *verb* **1** to feel with the hands or fingers or another part of the body; **2** to be on or against something; **3** to have no space separating two things

²**touch** *noun* the sense by which an object is felt and by which it is known to be hard, smooth, rough, etc

tour *noun* **1** a journey during which several places of interest are visited; **2** a short trip to or through a place in order to see it; **tour** *verb;* **tourist** *noun*

tow *verb* to pull a vehicle along by a rope or chain; ▪ **toe**

towards also **toward** *preposition* **1** in the direction of something or somebody; **2** in a position facing something or somebody; **3** for part payment of: *He gave her £5 **towards** her holiday*

towel *noun* a piece of cloth or paper used for rubbing or drying wet skin, dishes, etc

T

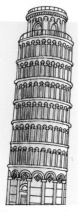

the Leaning Tower of Pisa, Italy

tower *noun* a tall building standing alone or forming part of a castle, church, etc

town *noun* a large group of houses and other buildings where people live and work

toy *noun* an object for children to play with

¹trace *verb* 1 to copy a picture, map, etc, by drawing on thin paper over it: **tracing paper; 2** to find or discover something or somebody, especially by following up clues or signs

²trace *noun* a mark or sign left behind by somebody or something

track *noun* 1 marks left by a moving person, animal, or vehicle; 2 a rough path; 3 a special path or road for racing; 4 a railway line; 5 one of the pieces of music on a record or tape

tracksuit *noun* a loose fitting suit of warm material that is usually worn when exercising

tractor *noun* a powerful motor vehicle used for pulling farm machinery or other heavy objects

¹trade *verb* to do business with; to buy or sell goods

²trade *noun* 1 the buying and selling of goods; 2 a job or particular kind of business

traffic *noun* the cars and other vehicles moving along roads or streets

traffic lights *noun* a set of coloured lights used for controlling and directing traffic

¹train *noun* 1 a line of connected railway carriages drawn by an engine; 2 a part of a long dress that spreads on the ground behind the person wearing it

²train *verb* to make yourself, or somebody or something else ready to do something difficult; **trainer** *noun;* **training** *noun*

trainers *noun* sports shoes for running, jogging, etc

transistor *noun* a small part of an electronic circuit for controlling an electric current: **transistor radio**

transparent *adjective* allowing light to pass through so that objects behind can be clearly seen

¹transport (*say* trans**port**) *verb* to carry goods, people, etc, from one place to another; **transportable** *adjective*

²transport (*say* **trans**port) *noun* 1 the act of transporting goods or people; 2 vehicles, such as cars, lorries, ships, or aircraft, used for transporting goods or people

¹trap *noun* 1 an apparatus for catching and holding an animal; 2 a position in which somebody is caught; a plan for catching a person; 3 a light two-wheeled vehicle pulled by a horse

²**trap** *verb* (trapped) to catch in a trap or by a trick

travel *verb* (travelled) to go from place to place; to make a journey; **travel** *noun;* **traveller** *noun*

tray *noun* a flat piece of material with raised edges, used for carrying things

treacle *noun* a thick dark sticky liquid made from sugar

treasure *noun* a collection or store of valuable things, such as gold and silver coins

¹**treat** *verb* **1** to act or behave in a particular way towards a person or an animal; **2** to deal with; to handle; **3** to try to cure by giving medicine; **4** to buy or give somebody something special; **treatment** *noun*

²**treat** *noun* something that gives pleasure

¹**treble** *noun* the highest part sung or played in music

²**treble** *adjective, adverb* high in sound

³**treble** *adjective* three times as big, as much, or as many as

tree *noun* a tall plant with a wooden trunk and branches

tremble *verb* to shake without being able to stop, perhaps with fear

triangle *noun* **1** a flat shape with three straight sides and three angles; **2** an instrument made of a piece of metal bent into the shape of a triangle, that is played by being struck with a metal rod; **triangular** *adjective*

tribe *noun* a group of people of the same race, language, habits, etc; **tribal** *adjective*

¹**trick** *noun* **1** an act needing special skill that is done especially to confuse or amuse people; **2** something done to deceive or cheat somebody

²**trick** *verb* to deceive or cheat somebody

trifle *noun* a dish of cake, fruit, and jelly covered with custard and cream

¹**trip** *verb* (tripped) to catch your foot and lose your balance

²**trip** *noun* a journey

trombone

trombone *noun* a brass musical instrument with a sliding tube which is pushed out or in to change the note; **trombonist** *noun*

tropical *adjective* to do with or coming from the very hot parts of the world (the **Tropics**) near the Equator

trot *verb* (trotted) to move or cause a horse to move at a speed between a walk and a gallop; **trot** *noun*

¹**trouble** *noun* **1** difficulty, worry, or anxiety; **2** **in trouble** in the position where you are blamed for doing something wrong or are thought to have done something wrong

²trouble verb to cause worry, anxiety, pain, etc, to somebody

trousers noun a piece of clothing which covers the body from the waist down and divides into two parts each fitting a leg

truck noun 1 a lorry or other motor vehicle for carrying goods; 2 an open cart used on a railway

true adjective real; actual; not false; **truly** adverb

trumpet noun a brass instrument that is played by blowing; **trumpeter** noun

trunk noun 1 the main stem of a tree; 2 the human body without the head, arms, and legs; 3 a large case or box used for carrying clothes when travelling; 4 the long nose of an elephant

trust verb to believe in the honesty and goodness of somebody; to have faith in or depend on somebody or something; **trust** noun

truth noun the true facts; what is true; **truthful** adjective; **truthfully** adverb; **truthfulness** noun

try verb 1 to make an effort to do something; 2 to test something; to use, taste, etc, something in order to find out what it is like; 3 to examine a person in a court of law; **try** noun

T-shirt noun a piece of clothing for the upper part of the body that is made of light material

tub noun a large round container

tuba noun a large brass instrument that makes a deep sound when blown

tube noun 1 a hollow round pipe of metal, glass, plastic, etc; 2 a small soft container for holding toothpaste, paint, etc; **tubular** adjective

Tuesday noun the third day of the week

¹tug verb (**tugged**) to pull hard with force or much effort

²tug noun a sudden strong pull

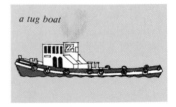
a tug boat

³tug noun a small powerful boat used for guiding large ships in and out of a port

tulip noun a garden plant that grows from a bulb

tumble verb to fall suddenly

tumble dryer noun a machine in which wet clothes, sheets, etc, are dried

tummy noun the stomach

¹tune noun a series of musical notes that produces a pleasing pattern of sound; **tuneful** adjective; **tunefully** adverb; **tunefulness** noun

²tune verb to set the strings of a musical instrument so that it produces the correct notes

tunnel *noun* a passage for a road, railway, etc, through or under a hill, river, etc

turkey *noun* a large farm bird kept for its meat

¹turn *verb* **1** to move round; **2** to change direction or position; **3** to become or make something become different: *to **turn** brown*

²turn *noun* **1** a single movement completely round a fixed point; **2** a change of direction; **3** a place or time in a particular order: *You've missed your **turn***

turnip *noun* a plant that has a large round root which is eaten as a vegetable

turntable *noun* the round part of a record player on which a record is placed

turtle

turtle *noun* an animal that lives mainly in water and has a hard shell into which its soft head, legs, and tail can be pulled

tusk *noun* a long pointed tooth that grows beyond the mouth in some animals, such as the elephant

TV *noun* television

twelve *adjective, noun* the number 12; **twelfth** *adjective, adverb (see last page)*

twenty *adjective, noun* the number 20; **twentieth** *adjective, adverb (see last page)*

twice *adjective, adverb* two times

twig *noun* a thin stem going off from a branch

¹twin *noun* **1** either of two children born of the same mother at the same time; **2** either of two things very like each other

²twin *verb* (**twinned**) to join a town closely with another town in another country

twist *verb* **1** to wind threads together or round something else; **2** to turn; **3** to hurt a joint or limb by pulling and turning sharply; **twist** *noun;* **twisty** *adjective*

two *adjective, noun* the number 2; *(see last page)* ■ **to, too**

¹type *noun* **1** a particular kind, class, or group; **2** a person or thing that is an example of such a group or class

²type *verb* to write something with a typewriter

typewriter *noun* a machine with a keyboard for printing letters on paper

typical *adjective* having the main signs of a particular kind, group, or class; the same as others of a particular kind; **typically** *adverb*

typist *noun* a person whose job is to use a typewriter

tyre *noun* a thick rubber tube that fits round the outside edge of a wheel; ■ **tire**

U *noun, adjective* a film that anyone of any age may see in a cinema

ugly *adjective* unpleasant to see; not beautiful; **ugliness** *noun*

umbrella *noun* a piece of cloth or plastic stretched over a frame, used for keeping rain off your head

unable *adjective* not able to do something

uncle *noun* the brother of your father or mother or the husband of your aunt

unclean *adjective* not clean

uncomfortable *adjective* not comfortable; **uncomfortably** *adverb*

unconscious *adjective* not conscious; not knowing what is going on around you and not feeling anything; **unconsciousness** *noun*

under *preposition, adverb* 1 in or to a lower place than; directly below; 2 less than; 3 lower in position than; serving or obeying; 4 beneath the surface of: **underground**; 5 during; in

underneath *preposition, adverb* so as to go under something

understand *verb* (**understands, understanding, understood**) 1 to know or get the meaning of something; 2 to know or feel closely the nature of a person, feelings, etc; **understandable** *adjective*; **understandably** *adverb*

underwear also **underclothes, underclothing** *noun* the clothes worn next to the body under other clothes: **underpants**

undo *verb* (**undoes, undoing, undid, undone**) to unfasten or untie

undress *verb* to take your clothes off

unexpected *adjective* not expected; **unexpectedly** *adverb*

unfasten *verb* to stop being fastened; to undo

unhappy *adjective* not happy; **unhappily** *adverb*; **unhappiness** *noun*

unicorn *noun* an imaginary creature like a horse, with one horn

a unicorn

uniform *noun* clothing which all members of a group wear

uninteresting *adjective* not interesting

unite *verb* to join together

universal *adjective* for all people or every purpose

universe *noun* all space and all the stars, planets, etc, that are in it

university *noun* a place of education at the highest level

unkind *adjective* not kind; cruel or thoughtless; **unkindly** *adverb*

unless *conjunction* if ... not; except in the case that: *I will leave at 9, **unless** you want to go earlier*

unlikely *adjective* not likely to happen or be true; not expected

unlock *verb* to unfasten the lock of

unlucky *adjective* not having or giving good luck

unnecessary *adjective* not necessary; **unnecessarily** *adverb*

unpack *verb* to remove things from boxes, suitcases, etc, where they have been stored

unpleasant *adjective* not nice or pleasant; **unpleasantly** *adverb*

unsteady *adjective* not safe or sure; **unsteadily** *adverb*

untidy *adjective* not tidy; **untidily** *adverb*

untie *verb* to undo string, a knot, etc

until also **till** *preposition, conjunction* up to the time that

unusual *adjective* **1** not usual; strange; **2** interesting because different from others; **unusually** *adverb*

up *adverb, adjective, preposition* **1** to, at, or in a higher place or position; above; **2** at an end; so as to be completely finished; **upwards** *adverb*

upon *preposition* on

upper *adjective* in a higher position; further up

upright *adjective* straight up and down

upset *verb* (**upsets, upsetting, upset**) **1** to knock over; **2** to cause to worry, be unhappy, etc; **3** to make ill, usually in the stomach; **upset** *noun, adjective*

upside down *adverb* in a position with the top turned to the bottom

upstairs *adverb, adjective* at, on, or to the upper floor or floors of a building; **upstairs** *noun*

Uranus *noun* the planet seventh in order from the sun

urgent *adjective* needing immediate attention; showing that something important must be done quickly; **urgently** *adverb*

urn *noun* **1** a large metal container in which large quantities of tea or coffee may be made; **2** a large vase in which the ashes of a dead body are kept; ■ **earn**

us *see* WE

¹use (*say* yuze) *verb* **1** to do something with; **2** to have a purpose for; **3 use up** to finish: *All the paper has been used up;* **4 used to** to have done regularly or often: *We used to go there every year*

²use (*say* yuse) *noun* **1** using; being used; **2** the purpose or reason for using something; **useful** *adjective;* **usefully** *adverb;* **useless** *adjective;* **uselessly** *adverb*

usual *adjective* done or happening regularly; normal; **usually** *adverb*

U

vacuum *noun* a space that is completely empty of all air or gas

vacuum cleaner *noun* an apparatus that cleans floors and floor coverings by sucking up the dirt

vain *adjective* too proud of yourself, especially of what you look like; ■ **vane, vein**

valley *noun* **1** the land lying between two lines of hills or mountains; **2** the land through which a river flows

value *noun* what something is worth; **valuable** *adjective*

van *noun* a covered vehicle for carrying goods and sometimes people

vane *noun* **1** one of the blades of a windmill, propeller, etc; **2** also **weather vane** a movable metal apparatus which shows wind direction; ■ **vain, vein**

vanish *verb* to go out of sight; to disappear

variety *noun* a lot of different things; **various** *adjective*

vase *noun* a container used either for flowers or as an ornament

VDU also **visual display unit** *noun* an instrument like a television set, on which the results of computer programs can be shown

vegetable *noun* a plant that is grown for food

vehicle *noun* something in or on which people or goods can be carried from one place to another

vein *noun* a tube that carries blood from any part of the body to the heart; ■ **vain, vane**

velvet *noun* a fine silky cloth having a short soft thick raised surface of cut threads on one side only; **velvety** *adjective*

Venus *noun* the planet second in order from the sun, and next to the Earth

verb *noun* a word (or words) which tells you what somebody or something does or is

verse *noun* a set of lines that forms one part of a poem or song, and usually has a pattern that is repeated in the other parts

very *adverb* especially; most

vest *noun* a short piece of underwear for the upper part of the body

vet also **veterinary surgeon** *noun* an animal doctor

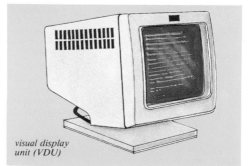

visual display unit (VDU)

video *noun* **1** film for showing on a television set; **2** also **video recorder** a machine for recording television programmes, etc

view *noun* **1** something you see, especially pleasant countryside; **2** a picture or photograph of a piece of scenery, a building, etc; **3** an opinion, idea, etc, about something

village *noun* a small collection of houses and other buildings, smaller than a town

vine also **grapevine** *noun* a type of climbing plant that produces grapes

vinegar *noun* a very sour liquid used for flavouring food

viola *noun* a stringed musical instrument like a violin, but a little larger

violent *adjective* having great force or strength; **violence** *noun*; **violently** *adverb*

violet *noun* **1** a small plant with purplish-blue flowers; **2** a purplish-blue colour; **violet** *adjective*

violin *noun* a four-stringed wooden musical instrument, supported between the left shoulder and the chin and played by drawing a bow across the strings; **violinist** *noun*

visit *verb* to go and spend some time in a place or somebody's house; **visit** *noun*; **visitor** *noun*

visual display unit *noun* a VDU

vixen *noun* a female fox

voice *noun* the sound or sounds you produce when speaking and singing

volcano *noun* (*plural* **volcanoes** *or* **volcanos**) a mountain with a large opening (**crater**) at the top through which lava, steam, etc, escape from time to time

how a volcano works

ash and lava flow out

layers of ash and lava

rock

hot molten rock

volt *noun* a measurement of electricity

volume *noun* **1** a large book; one of a set of books of the same kind; **2** the space inside or filled by something; **3** the amount of sound something makes

vowel *noun* any of the five letters a, e, i, o, u, or their sounds – *compare* CONSONANT

vulture *noun* a large bird with almost no feathers on its head and neck, which feeds on dead animals

177

wag *verb* (**wagged**) to shake to and fro; **wag** *noun*

wage *noun* money given to us for the work we do

waggon or **wagon** *noun* a four-wheeled vehicle, mainly for heavy loads, drawn by horses, railway engines, etc

wail *verb* to make a long cry showing sadness or pain; **wail** *noun*; **whale**

waist *noun* the narrow part of the human body just above the hips; **waste**

wait *verb* to stay somewhere without doing anything until somebody comes or something happens; **wait** *noun*; **weight**

waiter feminine **waitress** *noun* a person who serves food at the tables in a restaurant

wake *verb* (**wakes, waking, woke** *or* **waked, woken**) to stop or make somebody stop sleeping

¹**walk** *verb* **1** to move along on your feet at a normal speed without running; **2** to take for a walk: *walking the dog*; **walker** *noun*

²**walk** *noun* a journey on foot

wall *noun* **1** an upright dividing surface, especially of stone or brick, that goes round a house, town, field, etc; **2** the side of a room

walrus *noun* a large animal like a seal, with two long tusks

wander *verb* to move about in no particular direction; **wander** *noun*

want *verb* **1** to wish to have something; **2** to need

war *noun* fighting between people, countries, etc

ward *noun* a room of a hospital with beds for patients

warden *noun* a person who looks after a place and people

wardrobe *noun* a room or cupboard in which you hang up clothes

warlock *noun* a male witch

warm *adjective* **1** fairly hot; **2** able to keep in heat: *warm clothes*; **warm** *verb*; **warmly** *adverb*; **warmth** *noun*

warn *verb* to tell of something bad that may happen, or of how to prevent something bad; **worn**

was *see* BE

¹**wash** *verb* **1** to make clean with water; **2** to flow over or against continually; **washing** *noun*

the Great Wall of China

178

²**wash** *noun* **1** washing or being washed; **2** things to be washed

washing machine *noun* a machine for washing clothes

wasn't *see* BE

wasp *noun* a flying stinging insect related to the bee, usually yellow and black

¹**waste** *verb* to use wrongly, not use, or use too much of; ▪ **waist**

²**waste** *noun* **1** an act of wasting; **2** things that are used, damaged, or not wanted; ▪ **waist**

¹**watch** *verb* **1** to look at; **2** to take care of

²**watch** *noun* **1** a small clock worn on the wrist or carried in a pocket; **2** one or more people ordered to watch

a pocket watch

¹**water** *noun* the most common liquid, without colour, taste, or smell, which falls from the sky as rain, forms rivers, lakes, and seas, and is drunk by people and animals; **watery** *adjective*

²**water** *verb* **1** to pour water on, especially onto land or plants: **watering can**; **2** to supply with water

waterfall *noun* water falling straight down over rocks

waterproof *adjective* not allowing water to go through

watt *noun* a measurement of electrical power

¹**wave** *noun* **1** a raised curving line of water on the surface, especially of the sea; **2** an evenly curved part of the hair; **3** a form in which some forms of energy move: **radio waves**; **wavy** *adjective*

²**wave** *verb* to move in the air, backwards and forwards, up and down, or from side to side; **wave** *noun*

wave band *noun* a set of waves, especially radio waves

wavelength *noun* **1** a radio signal sent out on radio waves a particular distance apart; **2** the distance between one energy wave and another

wax *noun* a solid material of fats or oils that melts when heated and is used for making candles, polish, crayons, etc

way *noun* **1** a road or path; **2** the right direction to follow; **3** the distance to be travelled to reach a place; **4** how a thing is done or works; ▪ **weigh**

we *pronoun* **(us, ourselves)** the people speaking or doing

weak *adjective* **1** not strong in body or character; **2** containing a lot of water: *weak soup*; **weaken** *verb*; **weakly** *adverb*; **weakness** *noun*; ▪ **week**

wealthy *adjective* rich

weapon *noun* a tool for injuring or killing

wear *verb* **(wears, wearing, wore, worn) 1** to have or carry on the body; **2** to change by continued use; **3** to last; where

weasel *noun* a small thin furry animal with a pointed face

weather *noun* the condition of wind, rain, sunshine, snow, etc, at a certain time; ■whether

weather vane *see* VANE

weave *verb* **(weaves, weaving, wove, woven) 1** to form threads into material by drawing one thread at a time under and over a set of longer threads on a special machine **(loom)**; **2** to make something by doing this

web *noun* **1** a net of threads spun by spiders and some insects; **2** the skin between the toes of swimming birds and animals; **webbed** *adjective*

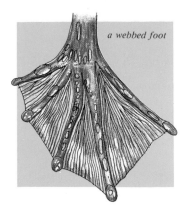

a webbed foot

wedding *noun* a marriage ceremony, especially with a party afterwards

Wednesday *noun* the fourth day of the week

weed *noun* a wild plant that grows where it is not wanted

week *noun* **1** a period of seven days and nights, especially from Sunday to Saturday; **2** the period of time during which you work, go to school, etc; **weekly** *adverb*; ■weak

weekday *noun* any day except Saturday or Sunday

weekend *noun* Saturday and Sunday

weep *verb* **(weeps, weeping, wept)** to let tears fall from the eyes; to cry

weigh *verb* **1** to find the weight of something, especially by a machine; **2** to have a certain weight; ■way

weight *noun* **1** the heaviness of anything; **2** a heavy object for holding something down: **paperweight**; ■wait

¹welcome *verb* to greet somebody with pleasure

²welcome *adjective* wanted; happily accepted

³welcome *noun* a greeting when somebody arrives

¹well *adjective* in good health; not ill

²well *adverb* **(better, best) 1** in a good or satisfactory way; **2** completely; **3** much; quite; **4 as well** also

oil wells

³**well** *noun* a place where water or oil comes from underground

went *see* GO

wept *see* WEEP

were *see* BE

weren't *see* BE

west *noun* one of the four main points of the compass; the direction in which the sun sets; **west** *adjective, adverb;* **westerly** *adverb;* **western** *adjective*

wet *adjective* (**wetter**) **1** covered in liquid or not dry; **2** rainy; **wet** *verb;* **wetness** *noun*

whale *noun* a very large animal that lives in the sea. Whales look like fish, but are mammals, and feed their young with milk; ■ **wail**

¹**what** *adjective, pronoun* **1** which thing or person? **2** which? **3** that which; a/the thing that: *I believed **what** he told me*

²**what** *adverb* to what degree?

whatever *adjective, pronoun* **1** anything at all that; no matter what; **2** what?

wheat *noun* a grass plant with grain seeds that are made into flour

wheel *noun* **1** a circular object with an outer frame which turns round an inner part (**hub**) to which it is joined, used for turning machines, making vehicles move, etc; **2** the steering wheel of a car or ship; **wheeled** *adjective*

when *adverb, conjunction* **1** at what time? **2** at the time at which

whenever *adverb, conjunction* **1** at any time at all that; every time; **2** when?

where *adverb, conjunction* **1** at or to what place? **2** at, in, or to which; ■ **wear**

wherever *adverb, conjunction* **1** at or to any place at all that; **2** where?

whether *conjunction* **1** if...or not; **2** no matter if...; ■ **weather**

which *adjective, pronoun* **1** what thing or person? **2** being the one or ones that; **3 which is which?** what is the difference between the two? ■ **witch**

whichever *adjective, pronoun* **1** any one that; **2** no matter which; **3** which?

while *also* **whilst** *conjunction* during the time that; all the time that

whine *verb* **1** to make a high sad sound; **2** to complain unnecessarily; **whine** *noun;* ■ **wine**

W

¹whip *noun* **1** a long piece of rope or leather fastened to a handle used for punishing somebody, driving an animal, or spinning a top; **2** a sweet food made of beaten eggs and other foods whipped together

²whip *verb* **(whipped) 1** to beat with a whip; **2** to beat eggs, cream, etc, until stiff

whirl *verb* to move or make something move round and round very fast; **whirl** *noun*

cat's whiskers

whisker *noun* **1** one of the long stiff hairs near the mouth of a cat, rat, etc; **2 side whiskers** hair allowed to grow on the sides of a man's face, not meeting at the chin

¹whisper *verb* to speak quietly with noisy breath

²whisper *noun* **1** whispered words; **2** a soft windy sound

whistle *noun* **1** a simple musical instrument that makes a high sound when you blow through it; **2** the high sound made by passing air or steam through an instrument, your lips, etc; **whistle** *verb*

white *noun* **1** the colour of snow or milk; the lightest colour; **2** the white part of the eye; **3** the part of an egg that is white after cooking; **white** *adjective;* **whiteness** *noun;* **whitish** *adjective*

who *pronoun* **1** what person or people? **2** that one person; those ones

whoever *pronoun* **1** any person that; **2** no matter who; **3** who?

¹whole *adjective* complete; total; not spoilt or divided; ■hole

²whole *noun* the complete amount, thing, etc; ■hole

whom *pronoun* used instead of *who* after words such as *to, with,* or *from: the man with **whom** he talked*

whose *adjective, pronoun* **1** of who or whom? **2** belonging to who or whom

why *adverb, conjunction* for what reason?; the reason for which

wicked *adjective* very bad; evil; **wickedly** *adverb*

¹wide *adjective* **1** large from side to side; **2** fully or completely open; **widely** *adverb*

²wide *adverb* completely

width *noun* the distance from one side of something to the other; how wide something is

wife *noun (plural* **wives***)* the woman to whom a man is married

wild *adjective* **1** living in natural conditions and having natural qualities not produced by human beings; not tame; **2** having strong feelings; **wildly** *adverb*

a windmill

will *noun* **1** the power in the mind to choose what you do; **2** what we want to do; **3** a piece of paper on which a person says who will have his or her property after his or her death

willing *adjective* eager; ready; **willingly** *adverb*

willow *noun* a tree which often grows near water; the wood of this tree

win *verb* (**wins, winning, won**) **1** to be the best or first in a fight, competition, race, etc; **2** to get as the result of success in a competition, race, or game of chance: *He won a prize;* **winner** *noun*

¹wind (**say** wind) *noun* air moving quickly; **windy** *adjective*

²wind (**say** wynd) *verb* (**winds, winding, wound**) **1** to turn round and round; **2** to bend and turn; **3** to make into a ball or twist round something; **4** to tighten the working parts of by turning: *to wind a clock*

windmill *noun* **1** a building containing a machine that crushes grain into flour, pumps water, etc, and is driven by large sails turned round by the wind; **2** a toy consisting of a stick with usually four small curved pieces at the end that turn round when blown

window *noun* an opening in the wall of a building to let in light and air, usually with glass in it

wine *noun* drink made from grapes or other fruit, plants, etc; ■ **whine**

wing *noun* **1** one of the two limbs of a bird or insect with which it flies; **2** one of the parts of a plane which support it in flight; **3** any part which stands out from the side: *the west wing of the house*

wink *verb* to close and open one eye quickly; **wink** *noun*

winter *noun* the cold season between autumn and spring; **wintery, wintry** *adjective*

wipe *verb* to pass a cloth over something to remove dirt, liquid, etc; **wipe** *noun*

wire *noun* a thin metal thread

wise *adjective* sensible, clever, and able to understand; **wisdom** *noun*; **wisely** *adverb*

¹wish *verb* **1** to want what is not possible; **2** to try to cause a particular thing by magic; **3** to want something or somebody to be or to have: *We wish you a merry Christmas;* **4** to want: *Do you wish to eat alone?*

²wish *noun* **1** a feeling of wanting; **2** an attempt to make a particular thing happen by magic; **3** what is wished for

W

witch *noun* a woman who has magic powers; 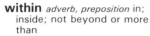 **which**

with *preposition* **1** in the company of; beside, near, among, or including; **2** having; **3** using; **4** because of

within *adverb, preposition* in; inside; not beyond or more than

without *adverb, preposition* not having

wives *see* WIFE

wizard *noun* a man who has magic powers

wobble *verb* to move or make something move unsteadily; **wobble** *noun;* **wobbly** *adjective*

woke *see* WAKE

woken *see* WAKE

wolf *noun (plural* **wolves***) (young* **cub***)* a wild animal of the dog family, that hunts in a pack

common wolf

woman *noun (plural* **women***)* a fully grown human female

won *see* WIN; 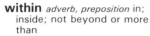 **one**

¹**wonder** *noun* **1** a feeling of surprise and admiration; **2** somebody or something causing this feeling: *The Seven* **Wonders** *of the World*

²**wonder** *verb* **1** to be surprised; **2** to wish to know

wonderful *adjective* unusually good; **wonderfully** *adverb*

won't *see* WILL

wood *noun* **1** the material of which trunks and branches of trees are made; **2** a place where trees grow, smaller than a forest;  **would**

a carved wooden chair from Tutankhamen's tomb in Egypt

wooden *adjective* made of wood

wool *noun* **1** the soft thick hair of sheep and some goats and rabbits; **2** thread or cloth made from this; **woollen** *adjective;* **woolly** *adjective*

word *noun* **1** a letter or letters, a sound or sounds that together make something we can understand; **2** news; a message; **3** a promise

wore *see* WEAR

¹**work** *noun* **1** activity which uses effort, especially with a special purpose, not for amusement; **2** a job or business; **3** what is produced by work

184

²work *verb* **1** to do an activity that uses effort, especially as employment; **2** to be active; to move or go properly; **3** to make somebody or something work; **worker** *noun*

workman *noun (plural* **workmen)** a man who works with his hands

world *noun* **1** the Earth; **2** a planet or star system; **3** all human beings thought of together

worm *noun* a small thin creature with a soft body without bones or legs: **earthworm**

worn *see* WEAR; ■ **warn**

¹worry *verb* to make or be anxious

²worry *noun* **1** a feeling of anxiety; **2** a person or thing that makes you worried; **worried** *adjective*

worse *see* BAD, ILL

worship *verb* **(worshipped)** to pray and show great respect, admiration, etc; **worship** *noun*

¹worst *see* BAD, ILL

²worst *noun* the most bad thing or part

¹worth *preposition* of the value of

²worth *noun* value; **worthless** *adjective;* **worthy** *adjective*

would *see* WILL; ■ **wood**

wouldn't *see* WILL

¹wound *(say* woond) *noun* an injury to the body caused by violent means, or an injury to your feelings; **wound** *verb*

²wound *(say* wownd) *see* ²WIND

wove *see* WEAVE

woven *see* WEAVE

wrap *verb* **(wrapped)** to cover; to fold round

¹wreck *noun* a ship, car, building, etc, that has been partly destroyed; **wreckage** *noun*

²wreck *verb* to destroy or cause to destroy

wren *noun* a very small song bird

wrestle *verb* to fight by holding and throwing a person to the ground; **wrestler** *noun;* **wrestling** *noun*

wriggle *verb* to twist from side to side; **wriggle** *noun*

wring *verb* **(wrings, wringing, wrung)** to twist; to remove water by twisting and pressing; **wring** *noun;* ■ **ring**

wrinkle *noun* a line in something which is folded or squashed, especially on the skin; **wrinkle** *verb;* **wrinkly** *adjective*

wrist *noun* the joint between the hand and the lower arm

write *verb* **(writes, writing, wrote, written) 1** to make letters or words, especially with a pen or pencil on paper; **2** to produce and send a letter; **writer** *noun;* ■ **right, rite**

¹wrong *adjective* **1** not correct; **2** evil; not good; **3** not suitable; **wrongly** *adverb*

²wrong *noun* what is bad: *to know right from* **wrong**

wrote *see* WRITE

wrung *see* WRING; ■ **rung**

W

X

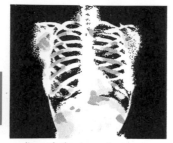

radiograph showing a chest x-ray

x-ray *verb* (x-rays, x-raying, x-rayed) to photograph, examine, or treat by X-rays

X-ray *noun (plural X-rays)* 1 a powerful invisible beam of light which can pass through substances that are not transparent, and which is used for photographing conditions inside the body, for treating certain diseases, and for various purposes in industry; 2 a photograph taken using this

xylophone *noun* a musical instrument made of flat bars that produce musical notes when struck with small hammers

xylophone

Y

yacht (*say* yot) *noun* a sailing boat; **yachting** *noun*

¹yard *noun* a measure of length equal to 3 feet or about 0.914 metres *(see last page)*

²yard *noun* 1 a piece of ground next to a building, with a wall or fence round it; 2 a piece of ground used for a special purpose: **coalyard, shipyard**

yawn *verb* to open the mouth wide and breathe deeply as when tired or bored; **yawn** *noun*

year *noun* a measure of time equal to 365¼ days, 52 weeks, or 12 months; the time it takes the Earth to travel round the sun; **yearly** *adverb*

yell *verb* to shout loudly; to cry out; **yell** *noun*

yellow *noun* the colour of butter, gold, or the yolk of an egg; **yellow** *adjective;* **yellowish** *adjective*

yes *adverb* a word used to answer a question, to show that something is true or that you agree with something

yesterday *adverb, noun* the day before this one

yet *adverb* at this moment; then; so far; up to now

yogurt or **yoghourt, yoghurt** *noun* a dessert made from milk treated in a special way to make it thick and a bit sour

yolk (*say* yoke) *noun* the yellow central part of an egg

you *pronoun* (**yourself, yourselves**) **1** the person or people being spoken to; **2** one; anyone

¹young *adjective* not having lived very long; not old; **youngish** *adjective;* **youngster** *noun*

²young *noun* young people or animals

your *adjective* belonging to you; ■ **you're**

you're shortened form of you are; ■ **your**

yours *pronoun* **1** that or those belonging to you; **2** written at the end of a letter: *yours sincerely*

yourself *see* YOU

yourselves *see* YOU

youth *noun* **1** the time when you are young; **2** a young man; **3** young people as a group; **youthful** *adjective*

yo-yo *noun* a toy made of a round piece of wood, plastic, etc, that can be made to run up and down a string tied to it

zebra *noun* a wild animal like a horse, that has dark brown and white stripes

zebra crossing *noun* a street crossing marked by black and white lines

zero *noun* (*plural* **zeros** *or* **zeroes***)* the figure 0; a nought; nothing *(see last page)*

zigzag *noun* a line shaped like a row of Zs

¹zip *noun* **1** also **zip fastener** a fastener that is often used on clothes, and has two sets of teeth which can be joined together; **2** a zipping sound

²zip *verb* (**zipped**) **1** to open or fasten with a zip; **2** to make the sound of something moving quickly through the air

zebra

zodiac *noun* an imaginary area in space along which the sun and planets appear to travel, divided into twelve signs each named after a special group of stars *(see page 142)*

zoo *noun* a collection of wild animals kept in a garden or park for people to look at or for conservation purposes

zoom *verb* to go or rise quickly

MEASUREMENTS

WEIGHT

Metric

mg	1000 milligrams = 1 gram
g	1000 grams = 1 kilogram
kg	1000 kilograms = 1 tonne

Imperial (equivalents)

1g = 0.035 ounces
1kg = 2.21 pounds
1 tonne = 0.98 tons

Imperial

oz	16 drams = 1 ounce
lb	16 ounces = 1 pound
st	14 pounds = 1 stone
qtr	2 stones = 1 quarter
cwt	4 quarters = 1 hundredweight 112 pounds = 1 cwt 20 cwt = 1 ton

Metric (equivalents)

1 ounce = 28.35 g
1 pound = 0.45 kg
1 stone = 6.35 kg
1 hundredweight
  = 50.8 kg
1 ton = 1.016 tonnes

LENGTH

Metric

mm	10 millimetres = 1 centimetre
cm	10 centimetres = 1 decimetre
dm	10 decimetres = 1 metre

m	1000 metres = 1 kilometre
	1 metre = 1000 mm
	            100 cm
	            10 dm

Imperial

in	12 inches = 1 foot
ft	3 feet = 1 yard
yd	22 yards = 1 chain 10 chains = 1 furlong 8 furlongs = 1 mile 1760 yards = 1 mile 5280 feet = 1 mile

Imperial (equivalents)

1 in = 2.54 cm
1 ft = 30.48 cm
1 yd = 0.91 m
1 mile = 1.609 km

Metric (equivalents)

1 mm = 0.04 in
1 cm = 0.394 in
1 m = 1.09 yd or 3.28 ft
1km = 0.62 miles
  or approx $^5/_8$ mile